RUDOLF
HESS

About the Authors

John Harris and Richard Wilbourn have been collaborating on their investigation of the Hess story since the early 1990s. Their research has taken them throughout Europe and they claim credit for discovering the roles of Mary Violet Roberts, Tancred Borenius and Wladyslaw Sikorski in the affair. John has produced three previous titles on Hess and has written articles for *History Today*, *Eye Spy* and for national newspapers. When not pursuing their obsession, John is a chartered accountant and farmer in Northamptonshire and Richard is a farm manager in Norfolk.

RUDOLF HESS

A NEW TECHNICAL ANALYSIS OF THE HESS FLIGHT, MAY 1941

John Harris and Richard Wilbourn

First published 2014
This paperback edition first published 2022

The History Press
97 St George's Place, Cheltenham,
Gloucestershire, GL50 3QB
www.thehistorypress.co.uk

British Library Cataloguing in Publication Data.
A catalogue record for this book is available from the British Library.

ISBN 978 1 80399 023 1

Typesetting and origination by The History Press
Printed and bound in Great Britain by TJ Books Limited, Padstow, Cornwall.

CONTENTS

ACKNOWLEDGEMENTS

Arthur Bauer – for his permission to reproduce his 2004 treatise on radio direction finding.

Ian Alder, RAF Museum, Stafford – for access to the other parts of the Bf 110.

Aurelia Borenius and her late father, Lars – for insight as to Tancred Borenius.

Chris Higley, John Cruickshank and The Charles Close Society – for permission to reproduce fourth edition ordnance survey quarter-inch map index and very helpful information concerning the Lennoxlove map.

Helen Cara – for diagrams, correspondence and file management.

Mr G. Day, Air Historical Branch – for trying to locate Elektra charts.

Peter Devitt, RAF Museum, Hendon – for encouragement and introduction to RAF Stafford.

Thomas Dunskus, Germany – for encouragement and support.

Gudmundur Helgason, U-boat Museum, Germany.

Matthew Hogan Research Services, Washington, USA – reference the Mercury article, 1943.

Dominic Hunger, University of Basle Library – reference Burckhardt.

Phil Judkins – for encouragement and help with Elektra stations.

Les Taylor and Whittles Publishing – for permission to reproduce the plans of the 1941 raids on Glasgow from the excellent book, *Luftwaffe over Scotland*.

Luftfahrt Archiv Hafner, Ludwigsburg – for supplying various technical manuals, relating to the Bf 110 and FuG 10EL.

Tony Maasz, the Royal Observer Corps (ROC) Museum Trust, Winchester.

Emily Oldfield, the British Red Cross Museum, London.

Peter Padfield – for giving us the opportunity to explain the pilot's notes and the Cuddie vector.

David Priest, The National Archives, Kew – for reference to Scottish Artillery records.

Michael (SES) Svejgaard, Denmark – for help with Elektra and Husum.

The Radar Museum, RAF Neatishead – for attempting to track down the elusive Elektra charts.

Dr A. Suchitz, The Polish Institute and Sikorski Museum, London – reference Roman Battaglia.

Werner Schmittner (DJ4WG – Duxford Radio Society), Ochsenfurt, Germany – for help with Elektra and Sonne.

Wasyl Sydorenko, University of Toronto Library.

The staff of:
- The National Archives, Kew, London
- Bundesarchiv, Freiburg and Koblenz, Germany
- Cambridge City Library
- Cambridge Crematorium
- Northampton Central Library
- The Indian and Oriental Collection, London
- The Imperial War Museum, Duxford and London
- Trinity House, London
- East Kilbride Library, Scotland
- The Carnegie Library, Ayr, Scotland

And finally to our wives, Ann and Anne – 'only seven years'?

PREFACE

In July 2011, the BBC reported that the Lutheran Church in Wunsiedel, Bavaria had decided to terminate the graveyard lease of the burial plot of Rudolf Hess and members of his close family. Since 1987, the grave had increasingly become a site of pilgrimage for the German Far Right. The remains were disinterred and, according to the report, subsequently cremated and scattered at sea. As part of the above process, the gravestone bearing the names of Rudolf and Ilse Hess was also taken away, leaving no physical record of the original burials.

In addition to the names and dates of the deceased being engraved, the original gravestone had also carried a quotation, recorded as being from an Ulrich von Hutten who, rather like Rudolf Hess, had performed one life-defining act. In his case he had chosen to attack the Archbishop of Trier in 1522 in order to advance the cause of the Lutherans. He failed and spent the rest of his life in exile on an island on Lake Zurich. Nearly 500 years later, the apparent comparison is obvious. Ulrich von Hutten had marked his endeavour with a motto, which started with the sentence, '*Ich hab's gewagt*'. It was precisely these words that the Hess family had used on the Wunsiedel gravestone: 'I have dared'.

The Hess family gravestone.

There is no doubt that Rudolf Hess had dared to fly solo one of the fastest aircraft in the world from Germany to Scotland in 1941. The type was normally flown by a pilot and navigator. No mean feat. There is also no doubt that Hess dared to leave his Führer, his family, his position and all he held dear. No mean sacrifice.

However, this book seeks to analyse the flight in further detail so as to ascertain the precise method by which it was achieved, its true motives and its methodology. We look to establish the nature of the flight and its character. Was it really the act of a madman, a 'lone flyer' or was it actually part of a predetermined, negotiated peace plan with a chance of success? Just exactly how much was 'dared'? It is an analysis which then seeks to establish whether the comparison with von Hutten is really justified. Was Hess actually making a 'flight for peace' in 1941? Perhaps even a 'von Hutten-like' act of martyrdom? Or was it simply yet another cynical Nazi act of war?

INTRODUCTION

The ghost of Rudolf Hess continues to attract many people, for almost the same number of reasons. As mentioned in the preface, Neo Nazis are apparently attracted to Rudolf Hess because of what they believe he continues to stand for. Those interested in legal history cite his treatment at Nuremberg; those studying psychiatry will have read with interest the records of his behaviour after his capture; and aviation enthusiasts will study the finer detail of his Messerschmitt Bf 110. His death in 1987 and the consequences thereof could be seen as the stuff of a murder mystery. His role and duties within the Nazi Party are fundamental to the history of that organisation and all that it meant to German history.

It is perhaps because of the many aspects of the affair that sensible academics have chosen to leave it well alone. It is far from a simple story. The publishing fiasco over *The Hitler Diaries* in 1983 has amply demonstrated what can happen to academics when they make mistakes. Furthermore, those authors seeking sensationalist material have made unearthing the truth much less simple. Any researcher has to discriminate between fact and speculation; the Hess affair now has masses of both. In the early post-war days, much of the work came from the families of the main protagonists, as each told their side of the story, largely to justify their relative's actions, or, in the Hess family's case, to try and influence a release.

We very much doubt that the family members then writing their side of the story knew all the details concerning the affair. Indeed, Ilse Hess even writes of the 'Chinese Wall' that was established within the Hess household, dividing work and family matters.[1] While we doubt the veracity of this statement, it was however a start in explaining the sequence of events and we do not doubt their intentions or motives. Clearly the Hess family was working towards a release, whilst the Hamilton family was seeking to distance the 14th Duke of Hamilton and his brothers from the affair.

The basic historiographical timeline of the Hess affair can be summarised as follows:

10 May 1941 – Rudolf Hess parachutes from his Messerschmitt Bf 110 over Eaglesham, Scotland. He enters lifelong captivity.

12 July 1941 – An article is published in *Liberty*, a US magazine, claiming that Hess was lured to Britain by British Intelligence. The author is Johannes Steel, a German émigré with links to Russian Intelligence.

1943 – An article is published in *American Mercury*, a US magazine, claiming that Hess was lured to Britain by British Intelligence.[2] The source remains anonymous to this day.

1947 – J.R. Rees writes *The Case of Rudolf Hess*.[3] Whilst principally dealing with Hess' post-1941 mental state, it somewhat oddly includes the first flight plan, supposedly drawn by Hess in 1941. It is this plan that most authors refer to and try to justify.

1954 – Ilse Hess writes *Prisoner of Peace*,[4] translated into English by Meyrick Booth. This book uses extracts of letters from Rudolf Hess to his wife in order to give the reader an explanation of events. It certainly gives no answers to the major issues surrounding the flight, but does give some clues that will be explored in further detail later.

1962 – James Leasor writes *Rudolf Hess: The Uninvited Envoy*.[5] Whilst the pretext for the title is still worthy of debate, the work is very useful as it draws on the experiences of many actually involved in the flight who were still alive at the time the book was being researched. We understand that James Leasor was a *Daily Express* journalist and, as such, Lord Beaverbrook, his employer, encouraged the book to be published. It introduces the connection between the Haushofer family and Rudolf Hess. While we challenge the conclusion, it is one of the first books to be written independently of the families involved.

1971 – James Douglas-Hamilton writes *Motive for a Mission*.[6] This book deals in detail with the pre-war relationship between the Hamilton family and Albrecht Haushofer.

1973 – The 14th Duke of Hamilton dies on 30 March.

1976 – Derek Wood writes *Attack Warning Red*. This history of the Royal Observer Corps (ROC) includes a detailed plan of the Hess flight over Scotland.[7] Subsequent to the disbandment of the ROC in 1995, much of the archive material on which this book drew has either been lost or destroyed.

1986 – Wolf Rüdiger Hess, then 48 years old, writes *My Father, Rudolf Hess*.[8] This book seeks to justify the action of his father, then still alive in Spandau, Berlin. He questions the role of the British Secret Service and understandably asks that his 93-year-old father be released.

1987 – Rudolf Hess is found dead in Spandau prison on 17 August.

1992 – Douglas Hurd, the then foreign secretary, announces the release of two batches of Hess documents. In the main from the Foreign Office, they also included WO199/3288B from the War Office and DEFE 1/134 from the Ministry of Defence. Many of these papers deal with the treatment of Hess on arrival in Britain. Douglas Hurd also commented that he had kept at least one file back because it contained certain records which 'still pose a risk to national security'.[9] Interestingly, James Douglas-Hamilton writes that the files not released were withheld 'for reasons which have nothing to do with the substance of the Hess case.' How would James Douglas-Hamilton know this?

1994 – John McBlain produces *Rudolf Hess: The British Conspiracy*, which details the role of Mrs Roberts, the wartime intermediary between Albrecht Haushofer and the Duke of Hamilton. Mrs Roberts' nephew was an important member of SO1, the wartime black propaganda department. This is further expanded upon in 1999 with Mei Trow in *Hess: The British Conspiracy*. This book also reveals the fact that Sikorski, the prime minister of the Polish government in exile, had landed at Prestwick on 11 May 1941.[10]

2001 – The book *Double Standards* is released.[11] Whilst sensationalist in part, there was some good original research that once again brought the Hess affair to prominence, this time suggesting that Hess was to be met by the Duke of Kent at Dungavel.

On 24 October, Wolf Hess dies in Munich.

2010 – John Harris writes *Rudolf Hess: The British Illusion of Peace*,[12] which details the role of Tancred Borenius, the Finnish art historian, in the affair. It also questions the role of the Duke of Hamilton and points out that the Hamilton family owned the site of RAF Prestwick. It also states that if Churchill were to be removed as part of any Anglo-German peace plan, constitutionally King George VI would have to be involved.

So, the debate has certainly moved on, albeit slowly. On 12 May 1941, the German government issued a press release explaining the fact that the Deputy Führer had flown to the enemy: 'Party Member Hess had got hold of an aircraft and taken off against orders. As yet he had not returned. A letter that was left behind unfortunately showed signs of mental derangement which gives rise to fears that Party Member Hess was the victim of delusions.'[13]

In other words, Hess was insane. Hess had put this idea in his Führer's mind in a letter hand delivered to Hitler by his adjutant, Karl-Heinz Pintsch, on 11 May 1941. This communiqué gave rise to the 'lone flyer' theory that seems to have lasted, unchallenged, until 1994, when the role of the British Secret Service was perhaps questioned for the first time, supported by some evidence, albeit far from definitive.

The British initially said nothing officially, but after the news had been broken in Scotland, Churchill finally authorised a response at 2300hrs on 13 May 1941. It said nothing apart from confirming it was Hess that had landed by parachute near Glasgow. The British government was petrified. All Churchill's efforts at that time were focused on the prospect of US support, nothing else. If the isolationists in the US suspected that Britain was secretly attempting to entreat with Germany, his central foreign policy tenet lay in ruins. Churchill was unsure quite what to say – so he said nothing.

Apart from the article in *Liberty* and the unattributed article in *American Mercury*, the German explanation of 1941 seemed to be accepted. Hess was mad. He was losing favour with Hitler and flew to restore his prestige. Indeed, some still believe this to be the case.

However, in 1942 Winston Churchill, with US support now crystallised into an alliance, felt confident enough to answer a question on Hess in the House of Commons. The exchange is reproduced from Hansard below:

> The Prime Minister: Surely the hon. Gentleman is not the man to be frightened of a Whip? The House of Commons, which is at present the most powerful representative Assembly in the world, must also—I am sure, will also—bear in mind the effect produced abroad by all its proceeding. We have also to remember how oddly foreigners view our country and its way of doing things. When Rudolf Hess flew over here some months ago he firmly believed that he had only to gain access to certain circles in this country for what he described as 'the Churchill clique'.
>
> Mr. Thorne (Plaistow): Where is he now?
>
> The Prime Minister: Where he ought to be – to be thrown out of power and for a Government to be set up with which Hitler could negotiate a magnanimous peace. The only importance attaching to the opinions of Hess is the fact that he was fresh from the atmosphere of Hitler's intimate table. But, sir, I can assure you that since I have been back in this country I have had anxious inquiries from a dozen countries, and reports of enemy propaganda in a score of countries, all turning upon the point whether His Majesty's present Government is to be dismissed from power or not.

This, we believe, is the beginning of the conundrum. Who or what was going to remove the Churchill clique? It seems obvious to the authors that the reason Hess chose Scotland was because he intended to meet persons sympathetic to his cause (or so he may have thought). If he wished simply to broker a peace with the British government, then why fly at all? There were plenty of diplomatic channels through which this was possible; channels that had been used to near exhaustion both before and after September 1939.

No, Churchill has clearly stated why Hess flew – to gain access to the certain circles that could remove Churchill and his government from power. We shall examine how closely Hess came to achieving that goal, both physically and politically.

Churchill was not alone in his suspicions. Albert Speer, in his book *Inside the Third Reich*,[14] said that Hess had flown with a peace plan: 'That was the message he took to Britain – without managing to deliver it.' We know that the Hess peace plan was certainly debated with the government, so to whom was it intended to be delivered?

Lieutenant Colonel Gibson Graham of the Royal Army Medical Corps (RAMC), who looked after Hess during most of May 1941, was quite clear on the matter:

> [Hess was] … seeking the Duke of Hamilton and then the King in order to be on hand with peace proposals when a new government arose in this country. Why a new government should arise he could not say, but he seems convinced of this; nor did he know its composition. The present British Government would try and prevent peace proposals taking shape; moreover, his government would not deal with them, only their successors.
>
> Hess was seeking the chivalry of the King.[15]

J.R. Rees concurs that Hess was seeking 'the Duke of Hamilton, who would conduct him to King George VI. The British Government would be thrown out of office and a party desiring peace installed in its place.'[16] Similarly, Anthony Eden, when later instructing Sir John Simon prior to his interrogation of Hess at Mytchett, wrote: 'The man dreams of a change of government.'[17] At Nuremberg, Hess told Maj. Kelley, the chief US Army psychiatrist: 'Only he [Hess] could get the King or his representatives to meet with Hitler and make peace …'[18]

This would certainly explain why the flight was not to England. That would be flying straight into the hands of the British government. What is not so easy to decide is the motive of the receiving party. Did they really wish to make a peace, or was the whole affair an intelligence-based trick, as the articles published in the US magazines *Liberty* and *American Mercury* suggest? The two options are not necessarily mutually exclusive.

Indeed, did the reception party actually exist at all? Was the whole exercise just a ruse to buy time before Hitler invaded the Soviet Union and relieved the pressure on Britain? Given that Britain knew of Hitler's plans through Ultra, this is also quite plausible.

It is through an analysis of the position of Britain and Germany in the spring of 1941 and the details of the flight that the authors hope to demonstrate it was an officially sanctioned peace mission by a Nazi government almost desperate for a western settlement: a Nazi government for whom the Deputy Führer would certainly be prepared to dare …

PART 1

BACKGROUND

1. WAS HESS SANE?

Before attempting to describe the various factors that may have influenced Hess to fly from Nazi Germany in May 1941 and the means by which he achieved the feat, it is important to challenge, or even lay to rest, once and for all, the myth that Rudolf Hess was mad, or delusional, as the official Nazi Party communiqué subsequently declared.[1] This is important because if the Deputy Führer was insane, presumably logical, sensible decisions would prove beyond him and, consequently, it would be even more difficult to analyse and assess his true motives. If, however, Rudolf Hess was sane, we can feel confident to continue our analysis.

We have already recorded that the pre-flight myth that Hess was insane was self-instigated and, until Nuremberg, self-perpetuated. The letter he had allowed Karl-Heinz Pintsch, his adjutant, to deliver to Hitler at Obersalzburg on 11 May 1941 had supposedly included words to the effect of: 'If all else fails, simply say I had gone mad …'[2] The fact that both copies of the document are not currently in the public domain may well be significant, but, we suspect, not as evidence of his supposed insanity. Alfred Rosenberg had met with Hess just prior to his flight[3] and stated at Nuremberg: 'Hess gave no evidence of any abnormality …'[4]

There is absolutely no evidence to suggest that Rudolf Hess was insane before he made his flight. Somewhat idiosyncratic, perhaps: but insane, no. He was quite capable of rational decision making. After his arrival, his demeanour may well have changed, but in this analysis we are attempting to ascertain if there is any evidence of insanity prior to 10 May 1941. The 'madness' alibi supposedly would cover why Hess chose to do what he did and allay any suspicions that the Russians might have that an Anglo-German peace was being jointly negotiated before an eastwards invasion was mounted.

The British have also helped perpetuate the myth that Hess was insane on arrival in May 1941. Shortly after his arrival, the Communist Party of Great Britain accused the Duke of Hamilton of assisting Hess in his mission. The duke, in order to defend his position, launched a legal action against Harry Pollitt, the party's secretary, and threatened to call Hess as a witness in the action. The Public Records Office (PRO) file AIR 19/5 deals with the matter. On 23 June 1941, David Margesson, the Secretary of State for War, wrote: 'I will see that Hess is not permitted to appear as a witness …' On 19 June 1941, the same file records a medical report: 'Hess's condition has deteriorated markedly … his mental condition has now declared itself as a true psychosis … the outlook is rather gloomy.' Is this not an example of using mental instability as a means to avoid a court appearance, though in this case not instigated by the defendant? Is it any wonder the myth has been perpetuated? Both accuser and defendant have, in turn, used the same ploy: the British in 1941, Hess in 1946.

We are obviously not qualified to comment in an expert medical sense, but during the research we have completed, we found mention of stomach cramps from time to time, but certainly no major illness.[5] A keen interest in homeopathy[6] presumably does not indicate insanity, though it may well have been deemed unusual in 1938. An avid interest in aviation would suggest intellectual acuity, particularly the pre-war level at which Hess participated.[7] In many ways, and certainly by comparison with his former colleagues, Hess could actually be seen to be reasonably well rounded. Well educated, a fluent French speaker, together with some English, he came from a comfortable (in English terms) upper middle class background. Certainly a very safe and secure background until the First World War destroyed the very foundations on which the Hess family had relied.[8] He was not alone in Germany in sharing that fate. J.R. Rees relates how he was well thought of by his staff, and one secretary commented that: 'He was so kind and noble that one felt obliged to be the same way as much as possible.'

Given their eventual collective fate, it could be argued that membership of the Nazi Party was an illogical act and therefore evidence of insanity. It is a poor argument. The German people were actively looking for a strong leadership with clear and simple principles in 1919/20. This does not make Hess and Hitler insane; political opportunists quite possibly, but insane, no. Once in power, Hess quickly became known as the 'conscience of the party'. Compared to the more radical members of the party, Hess sometimes acted as a moderator, and these were times in which it was difficult to be a moderate. Richard Evans, in 2005, quotes Hess as offering to shoot members of the Brownshirts following an uprising by Ernst Röhm and his followers in 1934. J.R. Rees makes the same allegation. (By contrast, David Irving makes a convincing case that Hess actually tried to save some of those executed.)[9] In 1935, Hess was party to and signed the Nuremberg Race Laws. He then proceeded on an individual basis to employ, protect and help Jews.[10] Certainly there seems to be two sides to Hess: one the ardent Nazi, prepared to do literally anything for his Führer; the other, when off duty, the quiet, unassuming family man.

However, above all, the one inescapable fact is that Hess was loyal to Hitler. One of the earliest Nazi Party members, imprisoned with Hitler at Landsberg in 1923, Hess was unquestionably loyal and this loyalty never faded. Even at Nuremberg, when it was quite possible he might have been executed because of his former association, he declared: 'I was permitted to work for many years of my life under the greatest son whom my people have brought forth ... I do not regret anything.'

Clearly, there was no repentance. When John Harris met Wolf Hess in 1995, it was also clear that this feeling of justification had passed down the generations.

Without trying to labour the point, we do not believe that what could be construed as making a terrible mistake is evidence of insanity.

In conclusion, it seems that his behaviour was wholly typical of the times in which he was thoroughly immersed. We see him as a spirited, adventurous individual, albeit with an intelligent, thoughtful, sensitive side, hailing from a wealthy family who had been deprived of their birthright by the British. Perhaps he was a reflection of the times in which he lived, looking to set the agenda, do something about it, perhaps even looking to avenge. We can find no mention of mental illness in the pre-war era, either in official or private documents.

In 1941, on his arrival in Scotland, Hess was medically examined by Lt Col Gibson Graham, Officer in Charge of the Medical Division at Drymen Military Hospital located in Buchanan Castle, Scotland, who concluded that: '… he did not strike me of unsound mind …'[11] At Nuremberg, the three Russian medical professors, Krashnushkin, Sepp and Kurshakov stated: 'Rudolf Hess, prior to his flight to England, did not suffer from any form of insanity …'[12] J.R. Rees telephoned his report, dated 19 November 1945, to Nuremberg from London, stating: 'At the moment he is not insane in the strict sense.' The Americans and French wrote in confirmation: 'Rudolf Hess is not insane at the present time in the strict sense of the word.' They also made the interesting point that 'the existing hysterical behaviour which the defendant reveals was initiated as a defence against the circumstances in which he found himself while in England.' When Hess did not wish to speak or answer, the stock phrase of 'I don't remember' was used to good effect.

In 1941 Hess had just completed a challenging aeronautical flight. Was the outcome really that likely if the aviator was of unsound mind?

We are not qualified to comment on the potential effect of the perception of massive personal failure, or on the use of drugs or their effects, or even the potential use of electroconvulsive therapy or a lobotomy. There have been various cases made that Rudolf Hess experienced one or even a combination of these – we will never know. What we do know is that Rudolf Hess was an extremely wily character whilst in captivity and would certainly lie when he thought it necessary or appropriate. At Nuremberg he was quite happy to cultivate the impression that he was mentally ill, until he chose to reveal to the court that his illness was a charade. This ability to 'act' was certainly used to good effect. An insanity plea was a powerful defence for when it was most needed and Hess was most vulnerable.

Hess was eventually adjudged sane to stand trial.[13] While in Spandau, Hess showed a healthy interest in various matters; astronomy and the NASA space program in particular. Yes, he was moody and irritable, which reveals nothing. We can only conclude that Hess was rational and, consequently, we will judge him and his actions on that basis.

Occam's Razor

Before going on to analyse the various issues pertinent to the decision Hess made in May 1941, the authors would like to make the following observations. These are made without any recourse to historical evidence – just plain common sense.

Hess would not have flown merely to have discussions about peace. That process could have been facilitated in a much less dangerous fashion. If Hess wished to personally participate in such meetings, rather than perhaps utilise Albrecht Haushofer, a short visit and meeting in a neutral country would have been far more safe and sensible. Indeed, there is some evidence that Hess did attend just such a meeting in Madrid during April 1941.

Why Scotland? Was it chosen and targeted simply because Hess believed that by flying there he would meet parties who would help him achieve his aim? A flight to England, for example, would have been easier aeronautically, but he would not have been able to have independently met those parties who were, perhaps, to help him in achieving his goal.

There had been many peace proposals and attempts at peace between Germany and Great Britain since 3 September 1939. We will concentrate on just one: that beginning with the 31 August 1940 meeting between Karl Haushofer and Rudolf Hess. By May 1941 there had already been negotiations, in Sweden, Switzerland and in Spain. The groundwork had been done. Hess was not flying to add to the detail – that had already been agreed. He was flying in to seal the deal and his arrival was to demonstrate his commitment – at the highest level.

Hess had to have Hitler's prior approval in a tangible form. There is no way that any British peace party would risk breaking cover if they were dealing with the second or third most important person in the Nazi Party. What if, on the return to Germany, Hitler or Göring had then dissented to the draft proposals? The choice of aircraft would also imply that a return flight was not anticipated, at least in the short term.

Hess was unsure of the outcome of Operation Barbarossa. Had he been sure of the outcome he would not have seen the need to neutralise the British. If he thought victory assured, why fly anywhere? Hitler and Hess were running out of time – Operation Barbarossa was about to be launched on 22 June 1941. They had previously stated that a war on two fronts was out of the question and that very prospect was less than a month and a half away. There was no more time to negotiate.

When discussing the Hess case, we often remind ourselves to use the principle of Occam's Razor. The razor states that one should proceed to simpler theories until simplicity can be traded for greater explanatory power.

2. THE GERMAN POSITION, SPRING 1941

Since early 1938, Adolf Hitler had been the self-appointed head of the German Armed Forces. At the same time, in the wake of the Blomberg-Fritsch affair, Wilhelm Keitel was appointed as the malleable head of the *Oberkommando der Wehrmacht* (Supreme Command of the Armed Forces – OKW), Hitler's successor to the previous Ministry of War. The appointment ensured that Hitler would get his way without effective protest; personal challenge or questions were not tolerated and Keitel rarely dissented. Albert Speer writes: 'From an honourable, solidly respectable General he [Keitel] had developed in the course of years into a servile flatterer with all the wrong instincts.'[14]

The Night of the Long Knives and the treatment of Fritsch demonstrated what happened when the '*Führerprinzip*' was questioned; one that would hardly encourage healthy debate before action. Quite possibly this is exactly how Hitler had succeeded to date, but what would happen when times became more difficult? The nominal leader of all German armed forces had no professional experience in strategy, or modern warfare, save for the bitter experiences of the trenches during the First World War. As Albert Speer belatedly stated: 'Amateurishness was one of Hitler's dominant traits.'[15]

Dangerously, in early 1941, and perhaps precisely because of his unconventional, untrained behaviour, Hitler was buoyed by success; there is no doubt that he had achieved outstanding military, political and diplomatic successes. From the Rhineland in 1936 through Austria, Czechoslovakia, Poland, Norway, the Low Countries, then to France in May 1940. In early 1941, he was as yet undefeated on the battlefield and was ready to take on his greatest challenge. He controlled a European coast from Northern Norway to the Spanish border, but had yet to face a determined enemy such as the Russians, who seemingly had scant regard for the lives of their soldiers. His tactics and success may have surprised his opponents so far, but was he becoming overconfident? We are not sure if Hess agreed with the Russian action; David Irving suggests that he did not.[16] Were doubts as to Hitler's military leadership in his mind?

Clearly, Hitler's confidence was not without justification. In 1940, the much-vaunted French Army, numerically superior to the *Wehrmacht*, had been defeated in twenty-eight days. Much of the success to date had come from the modern strategy of *Blitzkreig* (Lightning War): a co-ordinated approach combining air power and fast-moving armour with infantry support. The equipment being manufactured obviously supported this tactic, with the Junkers Ju 87 'Stuka' dive-bomber aircraft and Panzer (tank) units being all-conquering. The tactic had been very successful.

This was all very well while speed could be exploited. What Germany could not afford was to be dragged into a long, drawn-out struggle; they did not have either the resources or the appropriate equipment. In a long war, the Allies would have the time to 'out-produce' the Germans; they had overwhelming superiority in means of production and an empire of resources to draw from. Hitler knew this and he was also aware of the huge potential of the Russian arms industry and the danger of direct US involvement. It had to be a short war, which in itself created its own pressures.

Franz Halder, the German Chief of Staff, was in no doubt as to the importance of the Barbarossa decision, as it was, in his eyes, 'based on the need to remove Britain's last hope for continental support ... Once this mission is completed, we will have a free hand, especially with air and naval arms, to bring Britain down finally.' However, he continued: 'If we ... do not achieve rapid, decisive success, it is possible that the tension current in the occupied area may increase and allow Britain an intervention opportunity ... The important issue is the sudden execution of the Barbarossa operation ...'[17]

Not only did Operation Barbarossa have to succeed, it had to succeed rapidly. Without rapid German success, the Allies would have time to build their production capability and Germany would be drawn into a conflict it was not prepared for. They had already carried out the Blitz on Great Britain with inadequate aircraft types; an Avro Lancaster could carry 10 tons of bombs, the German medium bombers only 2–3 tons. Imagine the effect if the positions had been reversed.

There were already some doubts about the German production methodology. The Germans spread manufacturing across a great number of companies, such as Argus and BMW, and Junkers in the case of aero engines. All required their own logistical support and training. There were also myriad research projects into turbo-jet engines, rocket engines and unmanned aircraft. Were they simply too advanced and inquiring for their own good, and did the diversification render effective focus impossible? Were they already spreading themselves too thinly in technology terms? In 1940, only one year into the war, Göring had decided: 'All other long-range programmes are to be examined again'[18] – in part owing to a shortage of raw materials. The replacement and development of the early aircraft types was proving difficult. The new Messerschmitt Me 210, Me 410 and the Junkers Ju 188 were proving to be unreliable in trials, and they were not being produced with a protracted Russian campaign in mind.

Werner Baumbach summarised the weakness in this approach to production:[19] 'In the effort to meet all the demands of the forces, even the smallest special request was fulfilled and a very large number of small lines, with idiotic sub-division, were produced. Complete confusion took the place of rational order. Everyone made everything.'

It is highly unlikely that Hess chose to make his flight for the above reasons alone. However, it is possible that, in combination with concerns about military leadership and equipment, or the stated desire not to be drawn into a protracted conflict, real doubts had started to emerge about German invincibility. The consequences of defeat did not stand scrutiny. Hess knew this. If he was sure of German victory he would not have flown to Britain.

The British Blockade

The role of the British blockade of Germany in the First World War is well known. Imposed at the start of that war, German imports by 1915 had fallen to 55 per cent of their pre-war level and exports to 53 per cent.[20] Controversially perhaps, the blockade was not finally lifted until March 1919. The imposition of a similar blockade in 1939 is not so well known, but its impact was just as far-reaching.

Naval blockades and their effects were certainly not new, but were potentially controversial in legal terms. Indeed, there is evidence that Goebbels was investigating the legal position concerning the blockade, looking at what it might allow Germany to do in order to alleviate its impact. His diary, 26 February 1941: 'Legal judgment: not only are we not duty-bound to feed the populations of the occupied territories, but we can even requisition provisions there. An important argument in the controversy over the blockade.'

It was not just the belligerent nations that were affected. Similarly, it was not just the military, of course. Women and children, young and old, rich and poor, all were affected to a greater or lesser degree. On 4 September 1939, Winston Churchill, then First Lord of the Admiralty, had instigated the British Naval Contraband Control system, according to which every merchant vessel entering British-controlled waters was subject to examination. Three European offices were established for the purpose: Weymouth, Kirkwall and Gibraltar. Essentially, the British had re-imposed the blockade of 1914–19.

Immediately, the Royal Navy went into action. British submarines were positioned off the Elbe and Jade estuaries, and others between Norway and the Shetland Islands. The Humber Force and Home Fleet mounted regular patrols off Norway, initially hoping to intercept the *Bremen*, flagship of the German merchant navy. They failed, the *Bremen* eventually berthing in Murmansk.

Between 3 and 28 September 1939, some 108 merchant ships were stopped, with 28 being being ordered to Kirkwall for inspection. On 10 September, whilst engaged on blockade duties off the Norwegian coast, the British submarine HMS *Triton* tragically torpedoed the submarine HMS *Oxley* in the first friendly fire incident of the war. Between 11 and 16 September 1939, the Royal Navy laid 3,000 mines off the Straits of Dover. From October 1940, the British naval force was joined by the former Polish submarines, *Orzel* and *Wilk*, both having broken out from the Baltic.

The German mobilisation and the stepping up of the economy were good for business; many countries complained about the disruption to their trade and were calling the British action illegal. The blockade was very effective, especially after the intensification of early 1940, and the complaints grew as almost any cargo could be seized for assisting the German war effort. The aggressive nature of this collective action should not be underestimated. In the First World War the blockade had brought Germany to her knees, with estimates of the resultant deaths of between 400,000 and 750,000. The privations of the 'Turnip Winter' (1916–17) are well recorded. Interestingly, in 1939 no public announcement was made, the Royal Navy just went ahead and imposed the blockade. Similarly, its instigator, Sir Frederick William Leith-Ross (1887–1967) is hardly known in Britain. We believe that Leith-Ross, in instigating the blockade, was responsible for an act of war as aggressive as sending the British Expeditionary Force (BEF) to France and one which would fundamentally limit Germany's ability to wage war.

Germany had, of course, anticipated this course of action. Herman Göring was put in charge of the *Vierjahresplan* (Four Year Plan), devised to increase domestic production to meet the demands of war and reduce the dependence on imported goods. As time went on, this production failed to keep pace with demand and, increasingly, the plan assumed quotas of production from the eastern conquests. As Josef Goebbels recorded on 29 March 1941: 'The Ukraine is a good grainstore. Once we are entrenched there, then we can hold out for a long time. With this, the Eastern and Balkan questions will finally be settled.' On 1 May: 'Meat is going to have to be cut by 100 grammes per week from 2 June. The Wehrmacht is too well off and is using up too much of the available ration. Per head, three times that allowed to the civilian population. We can hope to get by so far as bread is concerned, as long as there is no problem with the harvest … If we have to go through a third year at war, then we shall consume the last reserves of bread. But nevertheless we are better off than England in many respects. But our situation is by no means rosy. I now face the question of how I am to put this over to the public.'

The British declaration of war and the effective naval blockade left Germany's industrial heartland in the Ruhr vulnerable to attack and potentially starved of raw materials. Hitler had to secure his borders to the west and break the British naval stranglehold. From 1938, the Westwall (Siegfried Line) fortifications were strengthened and defensive airfields were built nearby, but now circumstances demanded attack. Hitler drove over his neighbours to secure supplies and neutralise the chance of attack by Great Britain and France. In turn, he could then apply his own blockade against the supply lines across the Atlantic and neutralise the British threat.

When *Mein Kampf* was being written in Landsberg prison during 1923, the memory of the devastating effects of the Great War blockade was fresh in the minds of Hitler and Hess. If Germany were to go eastwards, no western blockade would be effective as the necessary raw materials could be obtained without any interference from British sea power. As Hitler told Carl Burckhardt in August 1939: 'I need the Ukraine, so that no one is able to starve us again, like in the last war.' Lizzie Collingham quotes Corni and Gies, 'Lebensraum would make Germany truly self-sufficient and immune to blockade and this would eventually enable Germany to challenge British and American hegemony.' The British geographer H.J. Mackinder, had realised this as far back as 1904, with his 'Heartland' theory.[21]

However, in May 1941 the invasion of Russia had yet to take place. Hess may well have been fearful of the consequences, but it is more likely that he would have been already mindful of the effects the British blockade was already having. Notwithstanding the effect on military production, there had already been a cut in the German bread ration by 600 grammes (g) in July 1940. In June 1941, the meat ration was cut by 400g. By 1944, a German civilian was eating 40 per cent less fat, 60 per cent less meat and 20 per cent less bread than in 1939.[22] In addition, the blockade restricted the importation of nitrogen, an important component of artificial fertiliser, vital for increasing agricultural production.

Sure enough, to compensate, food was taken from the occupied countries and ordered from Germany's allies, and as a consequence many in the donor countries starved. By early 1941 there were signs that food supply was becoming a serious problem. Foreign labour was being imported into Germany to work in factories and on farms; there were far more mouths to feed.

Herbert Backe, Walter Darre's assistant at the Ministry of Agriculture was diligently calculating the effect on food demand should the planned invasion of the Soviet Union proceed. He had calmly reported that it would be likely that 4.2 million Slavs would have to starve if German troops and civilians were to be fed from the areas anticipated to be captured. It is very likely that Hess would have been aware of this eventuality.

It would therefore appear that the effect on raw materials and food when moving from a peaceful economy to a wartime one had not been fully appreciated, or more likely, the terrible consequences of such an action had been ignored and seen as a part of the strategy. Hitler's plans assumed success and his continuing strategy relied on it. It does not take much for such plans to unravel. Did Hess and others have growing doubts about such strategy? Was the situation in Germany on a real knife-edge?

The Jewish Issue

Some authors have theorised that Hess flew in an attempt to bring the war to an end so as to prevent the Holocaust[23]. They cite the fact that a German Foreign Office report had proposed Madagascar as a potential refuge, but then blamed Britain and France for the abandonment of the plan owing to their occupation of the island. The Gerhard Engel diaries quote Hitler considering Madagascar as a refuge in February 1941, but then states, 'He [Hitler] had pondered on many other ideas which were not quite so nice.'[24]

We do not believe the above and suspect that Hess, the Deputy Führer, would have simply conformed to the party line. However, it is quite likely that Hess would be uncomfortable with the knowledge of the impending brutality that Hitler saw as part of the strategy to conquer the Russian homelands. At Nuremberg, Keitel and Jodl were condemned to death, in part for their acquiescence to the *Kommandobefhl* (Commando Order), which dealt with the establishment of German Army control in occupied Russia. The British prosecutor, G.D. Roberts, quoted from the order: 'All resistance is [to be] punished, not by legal prosecution of the guilty, but by the occupation forces spreading such terror as is alone appropriate to eradicate every inclination to resist.'[25] In other words, brutality was strategy. The order was directly conveyed through and to the army. As Laurence Rees writes: 'An atmosphere was thus created in which appalling brutality was to be expected.'[26]

In March 1941, Himmler had told twelve *SS-Gruppenführers* that the purpose of the campaign was to reduce the indigenous population by some 30 million.[27] Hess knew of these terrible plans through Rosenberg and Himmler. There are pictures of Hess and Himmler at a *Volksdeutsche Mittlestelle* (Ethnic German – VOMI) conference, dated March 1941, which dealt specifically with the resettlement of Germans in occupied areas. As the 'conscience of the party',[28] did this knowledge weigh heavily on his shoulders? Hess had signed the 1935 Nuremberg Race Laws and during his trial at Nuremberg it was deemed likely that he was aware of the atrocities committed in Poland between 1939 and 1940. Were they a step too far?

The Timing of Barbarossa

As discussed above, it is generally accepted that Hess knew of the plan to invade Russia. It had been formally approved as policy on 18 December 1940, in Führer Directive 21. Originally it was timed to commence on 15 May 1941. This date would allow for anticipated progress before winter, and before the wet season and the impassable muddy roads. It would yield the vital 1941 harvest at a critical

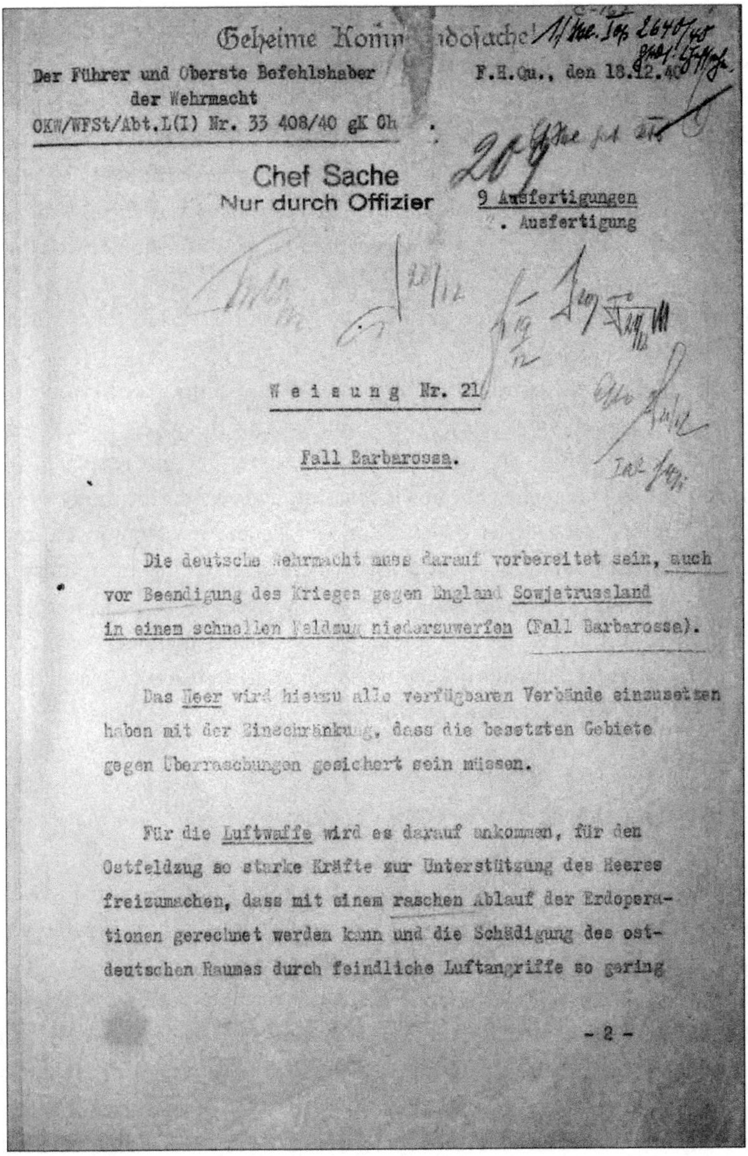

Geheime Kommandosache!

Der Führer und Oberste Befehlshaber der Wehrmacht

OKW/WFSt/Abt.L(I) Nr. 33 408/40 gK Ch.

F.H.Qu., den 18.12.40

Chef Sache
Nur durch Offizier

9 Ausfertigungen
. Ausfertigung

W e i s u n g Nr. 21

Fall Barbarossa.

Die deutsche Wehrmacht muss darauf vorbereitet sein, auch vor Beendigung des Krieges gegen England Sowjetrussland in einem schnellen Feldzug niederzuwerfen (Fall Barbarossa).

Das Heer wird hierzu alle verfügbaren Verbände einzusetzen haben mit der Einschränkung, dass die besetzten Gebiete gegen Überraschungen gesichert sein müssen.

Für die Luftwaffe wird es darauf ankommen, für den Ostfeldzug so starke Kräfte zur Unterstützung des Heeres freizumachen, dass mit einem raschen Ablauf der Erdoperationen gerechnet werden kann und die Schädigung des ostdeutschen Raumes durch feindliche Luftangriffe so gering

- 2 -

Fall Barbarossa.

stage from June until September. If the Soviets got the chance to harvest the grain it would be quickly transported east, and anything they could not harvest or move could be easily destroyed by fire. If the harvest was lost, the conquered lands would yield little or nothing for a whole year.

The planners set about their task moving vast armies of men and machinery eastwards. The British soon realised what was happening through Ultra intelligence and informed Stalin; being unsure, Stalin countered by moving some divisions westward, thus heightening German nervousness still further.

However, during the spring of 1941, the German Army was already engaged in the Balkans and this is the reason now accepted by most for the decision to delay the invasion until 22 June – thirty-eight days later. This delay was later to have profound consequences. (For a complete analysis of the reason for the delay, see *Zitadelle* by Mark Healy.)

Rudolf Hess would spend the winter of 1941 in Camp Z at Mytchett Place, a country house near Camberley, Surrey, England, so the progress of Operation Barbarossa was beyond his influence. Nine months earlier, in the spring of 1941, he was desperately concerned about the invasion. This was by far the greatest military project that Nazi Germany would undertake and it was almost a step into the dark. German intelligence was poor as to the size of Soviet military forces and, to an extent, there was no plan B. As we have seen, Hitler did not have the equipment for protracted war and knew it. The order demanded '*einem schnellen feldzug*' (a quick field campaign). Given the timetable already in place, the need for a western peace was becoming critical.

Nuclear Weapons

Without wishing to state the obvious, the Second World War eventually became a race to build a usable nuclear bomb. Whichever side won the race would win the war and set the post-war agenda for the world.

In the spring of 1941, an independent analysis of the respective progress made by Germany on the one side and the Allies on the other would place the Germans as clear leaders in the race. Since the celebrated 'radium-barium-mesothorium-fractionation' experiment of December 1938, the German chemist, Otto Hahn, was at the forefront of research into nuclear fission. However, when dealing with pure chemistry, even of such international importance, Hahn's next step had been to publish his findings in the magazine *Naturwissenschaften* (*Natural Sciences*) on 22 December 1938. The genie had escaped from the bottle.

By the spring of 1939, the race had begun in earnest. Two German scientists, Professor Harteck and Doctor Groth, had already written to the German War

Office, referring to, 'The newest development in nuclear physics, which, in our opinion, will probably make it possible to produce an explosive many orders of magnitude more powerful than the conventional ones ...'When war was declared in September 1939, Germany already had an office devoted to the military application of nuclear fission.The British had retaliated only by trying to buy as much uranium as was available on the world market.

By 1940, the Germans were experimenting with heavy water ($2H_2O$ or D_2O) as a means of moderating a chain reaction in a pile with uranium. Given the newness of the initial discovery, rapid progress was being made. However, by the spring of 1941, no real prospect of a workable bomb yet existed. Hitler knew of the research work, as presumably did Hess. In the autumn of 1940, the Minister of the Post Office (whose department was funding some of the work) had personally told him of the possibilities of making a workable bomb.

Thereafter, there was a degree of bluff.The Allies knew that the Germans were making progress, but did not know precisely how much.They also knew that the Belgian uranium stockpiles had been taken during the May 1940 invasion and that production of heavy water had been increased at the Norsk Hydro plant in Rjuken, Norway. Churchill's experts assured him that the Germans were not close to a bomb because technically they could not be, but no one knew for sure. If the Germans believed that they were close, did this underpin Hitler's confidence in winning what was seen by many as an unwinnable war with Russia? We believe it significant that Hitler (and Hess) chose to play on this uncertainty.When Hitler attended the Reichstag on 4 May 1941, just six days before the Hess flight, he observed that '... the scourge of modern weapons of warfare, once they were brought into action, would inevitably ravage vast territories.'

As will be described later, when Hess was in captivity, if he wanted attention, he too would speak of the bomb. He knew the British would want to know the reality of German nuclear production. Hess knew that there was no German nuclear bomb and he may have wondered if there ever would be. Did he know that Hitler was not holding any aces?

Know Thine Enemy

In arriving at the decision to fly to Scotland, Hess must have considered the position of the enemy. If he concluded that he would have been shot on arrival then there would be little point in flying. On balance, he must have believed that the enemy was ready to consider peace. From a German perspective, the following factors must have come into play:

– The Germans had failed to gain air supremacy over Great Britain in 1940. Any invasion would, therefore, be a very bloody affair and the Germans knew it.

– Despite an almost nightly attack on the cities of Great Britain, the Blitz of 1940–41 had failed to bring the government to the negotiating table.

– There was little evidence of defeatism within the wider British population and what little had manifested itself had been effectively censored.

– Churchill had made little secret of his strategy, to hold out until the US entered the war. This was beginning to work with the Destroyers for Bases treaty of September 1940 and the Lend-Lease agreement being signed on 11 March 1941.

– Whilst most US citizens saw these two treaties as a way of support without involvement, they were clear demonstrations as to whose side the US was on, in her quest to be the 'Arsenal of Democracy'. These treaties were well publicised and the Germans were certainly aware of their existence. The threat of a war with the US was looming ever larger. A war that rational Germans knew they could not win.

– A sizeable number of influential British politicians did not wish to side with the US and instead saw a European alliance against Communist Russia as a preferable option. But such politicians were not in power.

The problem facing Hess was two-fold in this respect. Firstly, to make sure his approach was to the correct part of the political establishment; secondly, to ensure that it was in a position to entreat. The Churchill government had consistently made its position clear and Hess had to make sure he was not dealing with them.

It is unlikely that any one of the factors listed above alone made Hess take off. But for the first time since the Nazi accession to power, he was unsure of the outcome of a Nazi act of aggression. The stakes were too high and Hess, it is argued, was seeking to 'de-risk' the action by neutralising Great Britain. Subsequent events proved that he was quite correct in his fears for the *Ostfront*, but in spring 1941 he was ignorant of the outcome of Operation Barbarossa; at the same time he knew of some of the means to be employed in the assault. Few knew just how much pressure the Hitler government was under and how risky was their situation. Gerhard Engel wrote on 18 December 1940: 'I am convinced that the Führer still does not know what will happen. Distrustful of his own military leaders, uncertainty about Russian strength, disappointment over British stubbornness continue to preoccupy him.'[29]

That is why Hess felt he had to leave, pushed by his concerns over the perilous state of his country and his Führer, and influenced by the positive signs from across the English Channel that offered him the possibility of success.

3. THE BRITISH POSITION, SPRING 1941

Whereas in Germany, despite a number of solo assassination attempts, Hitler's position was still unassailable, in democratic Great Britain the same cannot be said of Churchill. While he epitomised the spirit of resistance to the British people, there were many in Parliament and the wider governing classes who were questioning his defiant stance.

The military position is reasonably well known. Since Churchill assumed office on Friday 10 May 1940, the following key events had occurred:

- France and the Low Countries were lost in June 1940.
- Greece was lost in April 1941.
- Yugoslavia was lost in April 1941.
- Victories and losses in North Africa. Typically, victories against the Italians and losses against the Germans.
- Machinations designed to keep Spain and Turkey neutral.
- The victory in the Battle of Britain, which prevented or deferred the German invasion.

In short, Great Britain had lost all its main European allies and, realistically, would not be able to mount an invasion of Europe without significant foreign assistance. There were still British Empire troops to call upon from Australia, India and New Zealand, but the Empire was also coming under pressure in the Far East from an expansionist Japan, aided and abetted by Germany.

Night by night, the German Luftwaffe was proving Stanley Baldwin's prediction that the bomber will always get through. Progressively, major industrial towns and ports were being attacked, and devastating damage was being inflicted. Air defences, whilst improving, were still seemingly unable to prevent what were essentially massacres by aerial bombardment. Press censorship was necessary to prevent the worst becoming common knowledge.

The story was similar at sea. German U-boat crews christened this time *Die Glückliche Zeit* – the happy time. From June to October 1940, over 270 Allied ships were sunk; the major difficulty for the German commanders was being able to locate the convoys. Germany was doing to Great Britain what she was doing to Germany, only more effectively. On 26 November 1940, Churchill had written to Roosevelt: 'Were this diminution to continue at this rate, it would be fatal.' Britain was on the ropes, possibly waiting for the knock-out blow.

In the First World War, the British did not impose food rationing until 1918, but now acted quickly and effectively. Petrol was rationed in September 1939, followed by basic foodstuffs in January 1940. Some claimed that, because of rationing, nutritional standards actually rose. There was no starvation. Shortages perhaps, but certainly not starvation on the scale witnessed in mainland Europe. Rationing also imposed, to an extent, a sense of 'fair play' in that everyone was affected. The maintenance of the food supply, while initially imperilled, helped to preserve civilian morale. (Rationing eventually came to an end as late as 1954.)

The Political Position

The British political position was very much a reflection of the British military position. Simplistically, those in England with much to lose were naturally worried that they might lose it. Churchill was in charge, the war was going badly and, therefore, Churchill came under pressure.

Given the military position there seems to have been only two possible strategies at this time: do as Churchill did and try to hold out until the US joined the war; or accept a peace settlement with Germany. Neither strategy was simple. The Churchill strategy, while wholly honourable, would mean the eventual transfer of power from the British Empire to the US. Some in Great Britain resented that thought. It would also inevitably lead to further massive loss of life. The second strategy meant a pact with the devil, and who knew what the future might hold if Germany was then successful against Soviet Russia? It could just be a deferral of the first strategy. Aiding the decision-making process was the fact that Churchill knew of the German intent to invade Russia, making the 'hold out and see what happens' strategy more attractive.

A further complication was that the royal family were half German and saw Germany as a natural ally, albeit preferably without Hitler as leader. They were certainly in the 'those with much to lose' camp. The Battle of Britain had ensured, at the very least, that an invasion attempt would be a bloodbath with an unpredictable outcome. This victory had at least bought Churchill more time to court the US, and his overtures had started to pay dividends.

The British Constitution

In order to understand the political options further, a brief note on the British Constitution is necessary. Great Britain has no written constitution; it has no written *modus operandi*, and instead, government is based largely on precedent and conventions, the most important of which is that the sovereign should act on ministerial advice.[30] However, the extent of the sovereign 'acting on advice' has, over the years, been very much a moot point. Rodney Brazier gives examples where the monarch has acted independently of ministerial advice: the 1903 trip to Paris by Edward VII, arranged without informing the government; the implied threat of veto during the Irish Home Rule debates of 1912–14; and the choice of Stanley Baldwin as prime minister in 1923. There are also the 'reserve powers' the sovereign has accumulated over the years. They are rarely used and, indeed, only ever considered in times of constitutional crisis. Although, as Rodney Brazier states: 'Rules and powers which are part of the common law do not become extinct merely through lack of use.' So what are these powers that seem to be a reflection of a time before 1688, or even 1649?

Helpfully, the Labour government of 1997–2010, in a moment of reforming zeal, made a list of the royal prerogatives in 2003, presumably with a view to their abolition. (The Labour MPs were reacting to the fact that Tony Blair had gone to war with Iraq without a vote. Constitutionally, he did not need to.) Amongst others, the powers included the appointment and dismissal of ministers; the summoning, prorogation and dissolution of Parliament; royal assent to bills; the appointment and regulation of the civil service; the commissioning of officers in the armed forces; and directing the disposition of the armed forces in the UK. In foreign policy: the making of treaties; declaration of war; deployment of armed forces overseas; recognition of foreign states; and the accreditation and reception of their diplomats.[31] So in a time of constitutional crisis, the King or Queen could, in theory, act virtually independently of the government of the day.

This is the reason that Hess was obtaining books on the British Constitution in April 1941. He could request the monarch to invoke the royal prerogative, dismiss the prime minister and, presumably, appoint in his place a prime minister who would act in accordance with the King's wish – to make a peace treaty with Germany. Exceptionally, it would appear that the King could make peace with Germany without recourse to Parliament at all, but that would potentially be a wholly empty gesture as the government would continue (at least in the short term) to control the armed forces. If the King were to act in this way, he would need to be sure of a viable governmental alternative (or eventual government support), and secondly, be persuaded that the British people would back the action.

There had been a precedent; William IV in 1834 had been the last monarch to appoint a prime minister against the will of Parliament.

However, if there was either a lack of parliamentary support or general support from the population at large, the King would look a fool, and in the worst case, civil war was possible. The monarchy would in all probability come to an end and the British war effort undermined.

We now believe that this is why Hess flew. He had been led to believe that this would happen on his arrival. His was the gesture to act as the catalyst to the above sequence of events. He was not looking for the Duke of Hamilton, he was looking for King George VI. The Duke of Hamilton, or another duke, was to be the link, though a duke cannot invoke any part of a peace process.

The constitutional position of a duke is also worthy of comment. Hess had to make contact with his chaperone as quickly as possible and meanwhile keep out of the hands of the British government. This requirement explains much of his behaviour after landing at Floors Farm, which will be described later.

We have known since *Motive for a Mission* was published that the primary 'link man' between Hess and the Duke of Hamilton was actually Albrecht Haushofer, who knew both extremely well.[32] There has also been a debate for some while as to whether Hamilton met Hess in 1936.[33] In the Public Records Office at Kew, file AIR 19/564 deals with the subject. Apparently, there is evidence that the duke went to Hess' home for lunch whilst in Berlin (the day after the Vannsittart function), and James Douglas-Hamilton was trying to establish the veracity of the evidence.

We are not sure it actually matters. Hess did not abscond because he believed the Duke of Hamilton could actually force a peace between Great Britain and Germany. He left because he desperately needed a duke, or member of the peerage, as part of the constitutional process he sought to invoke.

On 12 April 1643, the title of the Duke of Hamilton was created while King Charles I was at Oxford. Quite why is not particularly obvious, as the first duke seems to have flitted in and out of favour with the King.[34] He was finally executed in 1649 following his capture by Cromwell at the Battle of Preston in 1648. A biography of the First Duke is called *Captain Luckless*,[35] which does seem to characterise the Ist Duke of Hamilton well.[36] Titles are of course part of the control system of the establishment, even more so in the days before 1649. The government of Tudor England has been described as a partnership between the monarch and the landed classes. However, Britain being Britain, various privileges survived the change to a constitutional monarchy in much the same way as we have already established in the section pertaining to the monarch.

These rights or privileges are listed as being: trial by the House of Lords (abolished in 1948); freedom from arrest (so as not to prevent the peers' ability to advise the monarch); and access to the sovereign.

The latter was necessary as part of the governmental process of England in the Middle Ages. Then it was formally recognised as one of the four bodies of advisors to the King: the Privy Council, Parliament and the Judiciary and the Great Council (being composed of the peerage).

In 1765, William Blackstone, a barrister and academic wrote: ' … it is usually looked upon to be the right of each particular peer of the realm, to demand an audience of the King, and to lay before him, with decency and respect, such matters as he shall judge of importance to the public weal.'[37]

Amongst the photographs that are routinely published in books on Hess is the one showing the Duke of Hamilton's brother and Andrew Elphinstone playing the accordion to the Princesses Elizabeth and Margaret.[38] Clearly the two families were very well acquainted, which is not surprising given that the various Dukes of Hamilton have been the Keepers of Holyrood Palace since 1646. The Duke of Hamilton is often described as the premier peer in Scotland.

In June 1953, the Duke of Hamilton played an important part in the Service of Dedication of the newly crowned Queen at St Giles Cathedral, Edinburgh. Therefore, the Duke of Hamilton, or another duke, was constitutionally an ideal target for Hess to meet, notwithstanding the fact that they may have met previously. He knew the King in both formal and informal capacities; he was the premier peer in Scotland and, as a peer, held a right to access. In theory, he held all the cards if, for example, Parliament did not wish him to meet with the King (right of access) or if they wished to place him under arrest for whatever reason (freedom from arrest). Whether in practice the government would respect these rights is, of course, a matter of debate. There is no doubt that they existed. It is also pertinent to note that there are five 'ranks' of peers, with dukes heading the list, followed in order by marquis, earl, viscount and baron. Clearly, the Duke of Hamilton was (and is) very much in the 'premier league' of peers, particularly as, in addition to the dukedom, he held a multitude of other titles, including some English titles, so as to ensure his eligibility for the English-based House of Lords.[39] In a letter to his wife, dated 9 May 1948, Hess tried to describe his role in the flight as that of a 'Parlementar', which is translated as 'an officer bearing a banner of truce'. Hess confirmed that he was 'self-appointed' in the role, but had expected to be treated as a 'Parlementar' should be treated. This is all very well, but what (or who) gave Hess the idea that he might be treated as such? The review of the British Constitution has shown:

– The King could *in extremis* appoint a new prime minister.

– The King could *in extremis* make a peace settlement, or truce.

– A duke has a right of access to the King.

– Hess believed he had the diplomatic rights pertaining to a truce bearer.

The conclusion is that, constitutionally, Hess was quite able to achieve what he set out to do, 'Parlementar' or not.

Churchill's Isolated Position in Parliament

The 1941 Parliament was already extraordinary in that it reflected the results of the 1935 general election, held some six years previously. Eventually, it was to run for ten years, through to the spring of 1945.

Its leader, Winston Churchill, had not been elected by the population; he had taken over in May 1940 from Neville Chamberlain. At the time, many in the Conservative Party would have preferred Lord Halifax, but this had not taken place for reasons that are still not wholly clear. It should be mentioned that, constitutionally, the King could have appointed Halifax in preference to Churchill had he so chosen, but instead followed Chamberlain's recommendation.

The only advantage Churchill had over his rivals was the power of rhetoric. The military position was bleak, but Churchill galvanised the nation, with his personal popularity never falling below 75 per cent in the country at large. It is difficult to see how anyone else could have achieved the same. Halifax was certainly not an orator.

In Parliament, however, things were quite different. In 1935, the Conservatives represented 63 per cent of the House of Commons, with Stanley Baldwin the leader. He was elected on a manifesto of economic recovery and housing. He is also quoted as saying: 'There will be no great armaments'. Like Chamberlain, his successor, he tried to deal with the growing threat of Nazi Germany through business-like discussion. Both Baldwin and Chamberlain came from a business background.

Obviously, in Britain there could scarcely be a bigger contrast between the position in May 1935 and that experienced in the war-torn spring of 1941. The population was seemingly quite content with the transition from Baldwin to Chamberlain, and then to Churchill, but in Parliament things were different. In May 1940, when Churchill had become prime minister, Sir Henry 'Chips' Channon, an ardent Chamberlain supporter, had written: 'We were all sad, angry and felt cheated and out-witted.' This response is unsurprising. Churchill had spent the latter years of the 1930s openly criticising the Baldwin and Chamberlain governments, and making enemies in the process. However, by July 1940 the military position was no worse than it had been after the fall of France, and Channon recorded: 'He [Churchill] is at the very top of his form now and the House is completely with him, as is the country ...'

At the beginning of 1941, the mood once again changed. Military setback after military setback had occasioned Churchill to shuffle and blame generals; by the early spring of 1941, Channon was speculating: 'Is Winston preparing to throw Eden over if the going gets too hot?'

On 7 May 1941 Churchill called for the parliamentary debate on the conduct of the war to be treated as a vote of confidence. Despite being attacked by Lloyd George, the truth was that, whilst there was opposition to Churchill, there was little effective, organised opposition. Halifax, Beaverbrook and Chamberlain (up to his death) had been neutralised and silenced by their government appointments and Lloyd George was losing his powers and support. He spoke poorly on 7 May 1941. Robert Menzies, another potential threat, had problems in his native Australia and had to return to Canberra. Despite Lloyd George in particular, Churchill won the vote by 447 to 3. 'A triumph on paper but in reality the Government has been shaken and both Anthony and Winston know it,' recorded Channon. So while there were other opponents and attacks, Churchill's position was safe for the time being.

Another potential threat came from within; writer Johnathan Pile has researched the role of Sir Joseph Ball, an MI5 agent and Chamberlain supporter, and makes the convincing case that he also was scheming against Churchill during the late 1930s, largely in support of Chamberlain, his sponsor.

In early 1941, Churchill had few friends politically and there were various groups waiting for him to fail. Some were in favour of a negotiated peace, but they failed to show their hand. Whoever was in charge could only choose to wage war from a very weak position or chance a Nazi peace settlement and all it might entail. It really was an invidious position. Churchill had chosen to drink from the poisoned chalice whilst others merely waited to see what might occur. Moreover, any peace settlement would appear a complete *volte-face* to the population of a country who had recently been told 'we will fight on the beaches' and 'give us the tools and we will finish the job'.

Churchill and the Monarchy

As with some in Parliament, Churchill had also not endeared himself to the monarchy. In 1936 he had actively supported the Duke of Windsor, who had badly 'fallen out' with King George VI following the abdication. His support for Edward was based on his utmost belief in the institution of monarchy and he had briefly contemplated the idea of standing against the Baldwin government as the leader of a 'King's Party'. His wife, Clementine, wrote: 'You are Monarchical No. 1 and value tradition, form and ceremony.'

This is hardly surprising given Churchill's background. The abdication crisis essentially saw a victory of Parliament over the monarchy, which was in danger of finally being neutralised after some 300 years of wrangling with Westminster.

Parliament had removed the troublesome Edward VIII and replaced him with George VI, who appeared to be more tractable than his elder brother.

What is also not wholly surprising is that, since Edward VIII's abdication, the monarchy's foreign policy position was at the opposite extreme to Churchill's. The King had obviously approved of Chamberlain's actions following the Munich Agreement and, as a consequence, Chamberlain had become the first commoner to be invited onto the Buckingham Palace balcony (in what was later described as the most unconstitutional act of the century). Since the abdication, the two Windsor matriarchs, Queens Mary and Elizabeth, had regained or gained their power bases. Queen Mary's famous quip of 'backing the wrong horse' was well known in connection with Britain's stance in the First World War. The younger Queen's view of Churchill had verged on hatred. Queen Elizabeth was also a close friend of Lord Halifax, Churchill's main rival in May 1940. Lord Halifax's wife, Lady Dorothy, acted as Lady of the Bedchamber to Queen Elizabeth, who would certainly have preferred Halifax as prime minister. Documents on this particular relationship are still withheld by the Bodleian Library in Oxford.[40] Robert Bruce Lockhardt later recorded: 'George VI did not like WSC. He was an admirer of Chamberlain and was one hundred per cent pro-Munich.'

The British and the Nuclear Bomb

Given the parlous military position in the spring of 1941, the possibility of a nuclear weapon was perhaps one means of salvation, if it could be delivered quickly enough. Knowledge of the enemy's capabilities in the same field was vital. If Germany had the A-bomb or was building such a weapon, the game was over and a peace settlement would be the only logical solution.

The book *Most Secret War* by R.V. Jones is an excellent record of the British reaction to the German need for heavy water in the period 1942–43. The earlier period is better dealt with by the controversial David Irving, who writes in *The Virus House*: 'By the end of June 1940 ... Germany's position in the nuclear race was impressive and alarming: she had little heavy water, but she had the heavy water factory; she had thousands of tons of very high grade uranium compounds; she had the cyclotron nearing completion; she had her body of physicists ... and she had the greatest heavy chemical engineering industry in the world.'

In early 1941, it seems that the British were still attempting to ascertain what was possible and what was not. Germany was well ahead in the race. An Allied nuclear weapon was years away, but how far advanced was Germany?

The spring of 1941 saw Britain at the nadir of her fortunes and the situation seemed desperate. If Germany were to have the 'bomb', the future was decided.

The British prime minister, whilst still popular with the nation, was politically isolated, disliked and distrusted by both the monarchy and establishment alike. The monarchy was still bitter following the 1936 abdication crisis, when the government had forced the King to abdicate without consulting Parliament.

But was there enough effective opposition to effect change? Could the Royalists/Chamberlainites mount one last challenge and force a compromise peace without recourse to the government? Constitutionally, it was possible.

4. COMMUNICATIONS
[31.08.40–06.11.40]

Having described the conditions prevalent in Britain and Germany in the spring of 1941, we return momentarily to August 1940, to the genesis of the Hess flight. We believe that Richard Overy summarises the post Battle of Britain position well: 'The Battle matters because it prevented German invasion and conquest and kept Britain in the war. This achievement was worthwhile enough. Nine European states (ten, counting Danzig) had failed to prevent German occupation by the summer of 1940, with the grimmest of consequences.'[41] Nevertheless, some historians have raised serious doubts about the traditional story of the battle, which gave birth to the myth of a united nation repelling invasion and gave iconographic status to the Spitfires and 'the Few' who flew them.

There is another history to be discovered behind the popular narrative, however. The effort to uncover it has already challenged some of the most cherished illusions of the battle story. Take, for example, the generally accepted view that the battle prevented German invasion of southern Britain. Documents on the German side suggest that this was not so. Invasion, it can be argued, was a bluff designed to force Britain to sue for peace; in the summer of 1940, Hitler's eyes were already gazing eastwards, where there lay real 'living-space'.

The Royal Air Force did not repel invasion for the simple reason that the Germans were never coming. This interpretation has prompted some historians to suggest that Britain should have taken the chance of peace with Hitler and let the two totalitarian states bleed each other to death in Eastern Europe. Behind this argument lies still more revision.

The picture of a firmly united and determined people standing shoulder to shoulder against fascism has been slowly eroded by the weight of historical evidence. The British were less united in 1940 that was once universally believed. Defeatism could be found, side by side with heroic defiance. Churchill's government included powerful voices urging a search for peace in the summer of 1940, just like the appeasers of the 1930s.

Peter Fleming, in his book *Invasion 1940*, speculates as to the precise date that Hitler called off any notion of invasion. He concluded: 'It suggests that between 8 and 14 September Hitler dismissed from his mind the idea of an opposed landing on the English coast. (He may conceivably have dismissed it earlier; the deliberate compromising of his objectives in clandestine broadcasts at the end of August suggests this.)'[42] We therefore suspect that Hess also knew this and this explains why, at the end of August 1940, he put in motion the sequence of events that eventually led to his flight in May 1941. Obviously, had the invasion taken place, no action would have been necessary. As it was, he now knew that the invasion was not going to happen, so took alternative action. Even as early as 14 August 1940, Hitler had stated: 'We must see what the Luftwaffe can do, and await a possible general election.' An entry on 14 August in the war diary of the German Naval Staff recorded: 'Whatever his final decision, the Führer wants the threat of invasion of Britain to persist.'

The authors believe the following letters are vitally important in that they document the thought processes and sequence of events that started the affair. So we reprint them here, together with our notes. The references shown are those of the National Library of Congress, Washington, USA. This sequence of events started only once the military option had been effectively ruled out:

C109/C002185-87
Dr Karl Haushofer to Dr Albrecht Haushofer
Munich, September 3, 1940

Dearest Albrecht: Cordial thanks for your letter of the 29th from the Hotel Imperial in Vienna. I had almost a vague premonition that you might be there.

If you composed your birthday letter to me in the air raid cellar, I could have reciprocated this kind service on the night of the 1st and 2nd because I promised your mother when I left the mountain cabin to go down when the alarm sounded and consequently spent 1½ hours in exercise and gymnastics.

For, as with you, everything has changed with us too. Through Lisa's sudden departure, which you witnessed, mother's trip to the Hart became unnecessary. Because her stomach and knee both took a turn for the worse, she remained at the Alpine cabin and, only because everything was so arranged, let me go down to the valley alone from the 31st to the 3rd. But I was rewarded, for it brought me a meeting with Tomo[43] from 5.00 o'clock in the afternoon until 2.00 o'clock in the morning, which included a 3-hour walk in the Grunwalder Forest,[44] at which we conversed a good deal about serious matters. I have really got to tell you about a part of it now.

As you know, everything is so prepared for a very hard and severe attack on the island in question[45] that the highest ranking person[46] only has to press a button to set it off. But before this decision, which is perhaps inevitable, the thought once more occurs as to whether there is really no way of stopping something which would have such infinitely momentous consequences. There is a line of reasoning in connection with this which I must absolutely pass on to you because it was obviously communicated to me with this intention. Do you, too, see no way in which such possibilities could be discussed at a third place[47] with a middle man, possibly the old Ian Hamilton[48] or the other Hamilton.[49]

I replied to these suggestions that there would perhaps have been an excellent opportunity for this in Lisbon at the Centennial,[50] if, instead of harmless figureheads,[51] it had been possible to send well-disguised political persons there. In this connection, it seems to me a stroke of fate that our old friends, Missis [sic] V.R., evidently, though after long delay, finally found a way of sending a note with cordial and gracious words of good wishes not only for your mother, but also for Heinz and me and added the address.

Address your reply to: Miss V Roberts, c/o Postbox 506, Lisbon, Portugal. I have the feeling that no good possibility should be overlooked; at least it should be well considered.

This letter is astonishing. Karl and Albrecht Haushofer are discussing the European situation and the necessity for a German peace, and father Haushofer tells his son of 'a stroke of fate' – Mrs Roberts, their 76-year-old English friend, has 'finally found a way of sending a note'!

In May 1940, the Treachery Act had made it a capital offence in certain circumstances to help the enemy, and so be under no illusion as to the potential consequences of this 'stroke of fate'. Mrs Roberts was perhaps one step away from treachery. It also appears to us that this letter seems to be very much a *fait accompli*. Karl is effectively telling his son to go ahead and make the contact. There does not seem too much debate; at this stage the objective seems to be a meeting in a neutral country 'to discuss possibilities'. There is no mention of a flight to Scotland! The next letter:

C109/C002188-89
Rudolf Hess to Dr Karl Haushofer at present at Gallspach[52]
September 10, 1940

Dear Friend: Albrecht brought me your letter, which at the beginning, besides containing official information, alluded to our walk together on the last day of August, which I, too, recall with so much pleasure. Albrecht will have told you about our conversation, which beside *volksdeutch*[53] matters, above all touched upon the other matter, which is so close to the hearts of us both. I reconsidered the latter carefully once more and I have arrived at the following conclusion:

Under no condition must we disregard the contact or allow it to die aborning. I consider it best that you or Albrecht write to the old lady, who is a friend of your family, suggesting that she try to ask Albrecht's friend whether he would be prepared if necessary to come to the neutral territory in which she resides,[54] or at any rate has an address through which she can be reached,[55] just to talk with Albrecht.

If he could not do this just now, he might, in any case, send word through her where he expected to be in the near future. Possibly a neutral acquaintance, who had some business to attend to over there anyway, might look him up and make some communication to him, using you or Albrecht as reference.[56]

This person[57] probably would not care to have to inquire as to his whereabouts only after he got there or to make futile trips. You thought that knowing about his whereabouts had no military significance at all; if necessary, you would also pledge yourselves not to make use of it with regard to any quarter which might profit from it. What the neutral would have to transmit would be of such great importance that his having made known his whereabouts would be by comparison insignificant.

The prerequisite naturally was that the inquiry in question and the reply would not go through official channels,[58] for you would not in any case want to cause your friends over there any trouble.

It would be best to have the letter to the old lady with whom you are acquainted delivered through a confidential agent of the AO to the address that is known to you. For this purpose Albrecht would have to speak either with Bohle or my brother. At the same time the lady would have to be given the address of this agent in L. or if the latter does not live there permanently, of another agent of the AO who does live there permanently, to which the reply can in turn be delivered.[59]

As for the neutral, I have in mind; I would like to speak to you face-to-face about it for some time. There is no hurry about this since, in any case, there would first have to be a reply received here from over there.[60]

Meanwhile let's both keep our finger crossed. Should success be the fate of the enterprise, the oracle given to you with regard to the month of August would yet be fulfilled,[61] since the name of the young friend and the old lady friend of your family occurred to you during our quiet walk on the last day of that month.

With best regards to you and to Martha.

Yours, as ever,

R[udolf] H[ess]

Can be reached by telephone through: Linz-Gallspach A.

This second letter introduces a second option. The first option is very much the letter to Mrs Roberts. We have the introduction of a neutral intermediary (unnamed as yet). Thereafter the letter essentially becomes a 'to do' list.

C109/C002190-04
Memorandum by Dr Albrecht Haushofer
Berlin, September 15, 1940

TOP SECRET
ARE THERE STILL POSSIBILITIES OF A GERMAN-ENGLISH PEACE?
On September 8, I was summoned to Bad G.[62] to report to the Deputy of the Führer on the subject discussed in this memorandum.[63] The conversation which the two of us had alone lasted 2 hours. I had the opportunity to speak in all frankness.

I was immediately asked about the possibilities of making known to persons of importance in England Hitler's serious desire for peace. It was quite clear that the continuance of the war was suicidal for the white race.[64] Even with complete success in Europe, Germany was not in a position to take over inheritance of the Empire. The Führer had not wanted to see the Empire destroyed and did not want it even today. Was there not somebody in England who was ready for peace?[65]

First I asked for permission to discuss fundamental things. It was necessary to realise that not only Jews and Freemasons, but practically all Englishmen who mattered, regarded a treaty signed by the Führer as a worthless scrap of paper. To the question as to why this was so, I referred to the 10-year term of our Polish Treaty, to the Non-Aggression Pact with Denmark signed only a year ago, to the 'final' frontier demarcation of Munich. What guarantee did England have that a new treaty would not be broken again at once if it suited us? It must be realised that, even in the Anglo-Saxon world, the Führer was regarded as Satan's representative on earth and had to be fought.

If the worst came to the worst, the English would rather transfer their whole Empire bit by bit to the Americans than sign a peace that left to National Socialist Germany the mastery of Europe. The present war, I am convinced, shows that Europe has become too small for its previous anarchic form of existence; it is only through close German-English co-operation that it can achieve a true federal order (based by no means merely on the police rule of a single power), while maintaining a part of its world position and having security against Soviet Russian Eurasia. France was smashed, probably for a long time to come, and we have the opportunity currently to observe what Italy is capable of accomplishing. So long, however, as German-English rivalry existed, and in so far as both sides thought in terms of security, the lesson of this war was this: every German had to tell himself, we have no security as long as provision is not made that the Atlantic gateways of Europe from Gibraltar to Narvik are free of any possible blockade.[66] That is: there must be no English fleet. Every Englishman, must, however, under the same conditions, argue: we have no security as long as anywhere within a radius of 2,000 kilometres from London there is a plane that we do not control. That is: there must be no German air force.

There is only one way out of this dilemma: friendship intensified to fusion, with a joint fleet, a joint air force, and joint defence of possessions in the world – just what the English are now about to conclude with the United States.[67]

Here I was interrupted and asked why, indeed, the English were prepared to seek such a relationship with America and not with us. My reply was: because Roosevelt is a man, and represents a *Weltanschauung* and a way of life, that the Englishman thinks he understands, to which he can become accustomed, even where it does not seem to be to his liking. Perhaps he fools himself – but, at any rate that is what he believes.

A man like Churchill – himself half American – is convinced of it. Hitler, however seems to the Englishman the incarnation of what he hates, that he has fought against for centuries – this feeling grips the workers no less than the plutocrats.

In fact, I am of the opinion that those Englishmen who have property to lose, that is, precisely the portions of the so-called plutocracy that count, are those who would be readiest to talk peace.

But even they regard a peace only as an armistice. I was compelled to express these things so strongly because I ought not – precisely because of my long experience in attempting to effect a settlement with England in the past and my numerous English friendships – to make it appear that I seriously believe in the possibility of a settlement between Adolf Hitler and England in the present stage of development. I was thereupon asked whether I was not of the opinion that feelers had perhaps not been successful because the right language had not been used. I replied that, to be sure, if certain persons, whom we both knew well, were meant by this statement, then certainly the wrong language had been used.[68] But at the present stage this had little significance. I was then asked directly why all Englishmen were so opposed to Herr v. R. [Ribbentrop]. I conceded, that, in the eyes of the English, Herr v. R., like some other personages, played, to be sure, the same role as Duff Cooper, Eden and Churchill in the eyes of the Germans. In the case of Herr v. R., there was also the conviction, precisely in the view of Englishmen who were formerly friendly to Germany that – from completely biased motives – he had informed the Führer wrongly about England and that he personally bore an unusually large share of the responsibility for the outbreak of war.

But I again stressed the fact that the rejection of peace feelers by England was today due not so much to persons as to the fundamental outlook mentioned above.[69]

Nevertheless, I was asked to name those whom I thought might be reached as possible contacts.

I mentioned among diplomats, Minister O'Malley in Budapest, the former head of the South-eastern Department of the Foreign Office, a clever person in the higher echelons of officialdom, but perhaps without influence precisely because of his former friendliness toward Germany; Sir Samuel Hoare, who is half-shelved and half on the watch in Madrid, whom I do not know well personally, but to whom I can at any time open a personal path; as the most promising, the Washington Ambassador Lothian, with whom I have had close personal connections for years, who as a member of the highest aristocracy and at the same time as a person of very independent mind, is perhaps best in a position to undertake a bold step – provided that he could be convinced that even a bad and uncertain peace would be better than the continuance of the war – a conviction at which he will only arrive if he convinces himself in Washington that English hopes of America are not realisable.

Whether or not this is so could only be judged in Washington itself; from Germany not at all. As the final possibility I then mentioned that of a personal meeting on neutral soil with the closest of my English friends: the young Duke of Hamilton, who has access at all times to all important persons in London, even to Churchill and the King.[70] I stressed in this case the inevitable difficulty of making a contact and again repeated my conviction of the improbability of its succeeding – whatever approach we took.

The upshot of the conversation was H's statement that he would consider the whole matter thoroughly once more and send me word in case I was to take steps. For this extremely ticklish case and in the event that I might possibly have to make a trip alone – I asked for very precise directives from the highest authority.[71] From the whole conversation I had the strong impression that it was not conducted without the prior knowledge of the Führer, and that I probably would not hear any more about the matter unless a new understanding had been reached between him and his Deputy.[72]

On the personal side of the conversation I must say that – despite the fact that I felt bound to say usually hard things – it ended in great friendliness, even cordiality. I spent the night in Bad G., and the next morning still had the opportunity, on a walk together in the presence of the Chief Adjutant, to bring up all the *Volksdeutsch* questions from the resettlement in all parts of Europe to the difficulties as to personnel in the central offices in Berlin – which resulted in H's direct intervention.

A[lbrecht] H[aushofer]

This comprehensive memorandum is an excellent resumé of the actual thought processes that September. What it does not do, however, is to describe how a peace is to be achieved. We suspect Albrecht already realises it is an unattainable goal whilst Hitler is in power.

C109/C002179-202
Dr Albrecht Haushofer to his Parents
Berlin, September 19, 1940

Dear Parents: I am sending you enclosed herewith some important documents: First, T.'s. Letter to Father.

Secondly, my answer to T., which has already been sent and, I hope, has your subsequent approval.

Thirdly, the draft of a letter to D.,[73] which I will keep to myself and not show to anyone else. I request that you examine it to see whether it might involve any danger for the woman who may transmit it.[74] I really believe that it sounds harmless enough. I have inserted the reference to the 'authorities' over there purposely as a safeguard for the transmitter and recipient. So I should like to have your honest opinion and any corrections. Fourthly a report of what I said on the 8th in G., as an accounting before history (save till the last).[75]

The whole thing is a fool's errand, but we cannot do anything about that.[76] According to our latest reports the treaties of union between the Empire and the United States are about to be signed.[77]

Best Wishes,
ALBRECHT

Enclosure 1
TOP SECRET
My Dear Herr Hess: Your letter of the 10th reached me yesterday after a delay caused by the antiquated postal service of Partnach-Alm. I again gave a thorough study to the possibilities discussed therein and request – before taking the steps proposed – that you yourself examine once more the thoughts set forth below.

I have in the meantime been thinking of the technical route by which a message from me must travel before it can reach the Duke of H[amilton]. With your help, delivery to Lisbon can of course be assured without difficulty. About the rest of the route we do not know. Foreign control must be taken into account; the letter must therefore in no case be composed in such a way that it will simply be seized and destroyed or that it will directly endanger the woman transmitting it or the ultimate recipient.

In view of my close personal relations and intimate acquaintance with Douglas H[amilton] I can write a few lines to him (which should be enclosed with the letter to Mrs R., without any indication of place and without a full name, an A. would suffice for signature)[78] in such a way that he alone will recognise that behind my wish[79] to see him in Lisbon there is something more serious than a personal whim. All the rest, however, seems to be extremely hazardous and detrimental to the success of the letter.

Let us suppose that the case were reversed: an old lady in Germany receives a letter from an unknown source abroad, with a request to forward a message whose recipient is asked to disclose to an unknown foreigner where he will be staying for a certain period – and this recipient was a high officer in the air force (of course I do not know exactly what position H. holds at the moment; judging from his past I can conceive of only three things; he is an active air force general, or he directs the air defence of an important part of Scotland, or he has a responsible position in the Air Ministry.)

I do not think that you need much imagination to picture to yourself the faces that Canaris or Heydrich would make and the smirk with which they would consider any offer of 'security' or 'confidence' in such a letter if a subordinate should submit such a case to them. They would not merely make faces, you may be certain! The measures would come quite automatically – and neither the old lady nor the air force officer would have an easy time of it! In England it is no different.

Now another thing. Here too I would ask you to picture the situation in reverse. Let us assume that I received such a letter from one of my English friends. I would quite naturally report the matter to the highest German authorities I could contact, as soon as I had realised the import it might have, and would ask for instructions on what I should do myself (remembering I am a civilian and H. is an officer).

If it should be decided that I was to comply with the wish for a meeting with my friend, I would then be most anxious to get my instructions if not from the Führer himself, at least from a person who receives them directly and at the same time has the gift of transmitting the finest and lightest nuances – an art which has been mastered by you yourself but not by all Reich Ministers. In addition, I should very urgently request that my action be fully covered – vis-a-vis other high authorities of my own country – uninformed or unfavourable.

It is not any different with H. He cannot fly to Lisbon any more than I can! Unless he is given leave, that is unless at least Air Minister Sinclair and Foreign Minister Halifax know about it.[80] If, however, he receives permission to reply or to go, there is no need of indicating any place in England; if he does not receive it, then any attempt through a neutral mediator would also have little success.[81]

In this case the technical problem of contacting H. is the least of the difficulties. A neutral who knows England and can move about in England – presumably there would be little sense in entrusting anyone else with such a mission – will be able to find the first peer of Scotland very quickly as long as conditions in the Isle are still halfway in order. (At the time of a successful invasion all the possibilities we are discussing here would be pointless anyway).

My proposal is therefore as follows:

Through the old friend I will write a letter to H. – in a form that will incriminate no one but will be understandable to the recipient – with the proposal for a meeting in Lisbon. If nothing comes of that, it will be possible (if the military situation leaves enough time for it), assuming that a suitable intermediary is available, to make a second attempt through a neutral going to England, who might be given a personal message to take along. With respect to this possibility, I must add, however, that H. is extremely reserved – as many Englishmen are toward anyone they do not know personally. Since the entire Anglo-German problem after all springs from a most profound crisis in mutual confidence, this would not be immaterial.[82]

Please excuse the length of this letter; I merely wished to explain the situation to you fully.

I already tried to explain to you not long ago that, for reasons I gave, the possibilities of successful efforts at a settlement between the Führer and the British upper class seem to me – to my extreme regret – infinitesimally small.

Nevertheless I should not want to close this letter without pointing out once more that I still think there would be a somewhat greater chance of success in going through Ambassador Lothian in Washington or Sir Samuel Hoare in Madrid rather than through my friend H.[83] To be sure, they are – politically speaking – more inaccessible.

Would you send me a line or give me a telephone call with final instructions? If necessary, will you also inform your brother in advance? Presumably I will then have to discuss with him the forwarding of the letter to Lisbon and the arrangement for a cover address for the reply in L[isbon].

With cordial greetings and best wishes for your health.

Yours, etc

A[albrecht] H[aushofer]

Enclosure 2
Draft Letter to D.H.[84]

Mr dear D ... Even if this letter has only a slight chance of reaching you – there is a chance and I want to make use of it.

First of all, to give you a sign of unaltered and unalterable personal attachment. I do hope you have been spared in all this ordeal, and I hope the same is true of your brothers. I heard of your father's deliverance from long suffering; and I heard that your brother-in-law Northumberland lost his life near Dunkerque. I need hardly tell you how I feel about all that ...

Now there is one thing more. If you remember some of my last communications before the war started you will realise that there is a certain significance in the fact that I am, at present, able to ask you whether there is the slightest chance of our meeting and having a talk somewhere on the outskirts of Europe, perhaps in Portugal. There are some things I could tell you, that might make it worthwhile for you to try a short trip to Lisbon – if you could make your authorities understand so much that they would give you leave. As to myself – I could reach Lisbon any time (without any kind of difficulty) within a few days after receiving news from you. If there is an answer to this letter, please address it to ...

C109/C002203
Dr Albrecht Haushofer to Rudolph Hess
September 23, 1940

My dear Herr Hess: In accordance with your last telephone call I got in touch with your brother [Alfred] immediately. Everything went off well, and I can now report that the mission has been accomplished to the extent that the letter you desired was written and dispatched this morning. It is to be hoped that it will be more efficacious than sober judgement would indicate.

Yours, etc
H[aushofer]

C109/C002204-05
Dr Albrecht Haushofer to Dr Karl Haushofer
Berlin, September 23, 1940

Dear Father: I am enclosing the copy of a short letter of serious content, which perhaps had better be kept by you than by me. I have now made it clear enough that in the action involved I did not take the initiative ...

Now to the English matters. I am convinced, as before, that there is not the slightest prospect of peace; and so I don't have the least faith in the possibility about which you know. However, I also believe that I could not have refused my services any longer. You know that for myself I do not see any possibility of any satisfying activity in the future ...

Best regards to both of you.
Albrecht

That appears to be the end of the exchange of letters. A few things emerge: Hess and Hitler had been discussing the need for peace following the failure to gain air supremacy over Britain in summer 1940; Hess spoke with Karl Haushofer about the same issue; Haushofer mentioned Mrs Roberts and her recent contact. Albrecht Haushofer is also consulted, and whilst not convinced of success goes along with his master's (and father's) idea of a letter; he makes it clear to Hess and his father that he feels it unlikely to succeed; a secondary idea of an intermediary to meet with Hamilton is also mooted; and the letter is sent, via the Lisbon PO Box. These letters were taken by US authorities at the end of the war and microfilmed in Alexandria, Virginia, in 1949.

Copies were also distributed to the other major archives and the original papers returned to Germany in 1958. So they have been in the public domain for a long time. We are surprised that they do not appear to have been analysed in any detail previously, apart from in the book *Motive for a Mission* by James Douglas-Hamilton.

Mary Violet Roberts (1864–1958)

After describing the world situation in May 1941, the prospects for world domination and the immense stakes that the major players were playing for, it may seem odd to take time to describe a lady who in 1941 was already 77 years old and who particularly enjoyed walking her 'Scottie' dog and bottling gooseberries. However, the more we consider the role that Mrs Roberts played, the more convinced we become that she is, in fact, a key to understanding the Hess affair, simply because her involvement was wholly non-governmental (indeed, it is hard to conceive of anyone more non-governmental!). Hess and Haushofer had used Mrs Roberts as a conduit precisely because of this. It was an attempt to negotiate a peace outside the usual government channels. Had Hess and Haushofer wanted to negotiate with the British government then there would not be a need for the drama of letters and flights to Scotland. That's what diplomats were for, albeit diplomats that had failed in this instance.

We believe that the existence of the correspondence involving Mrs Roberts is evidence that Hess and Haushofer were trying to reach persons outside the government (or dissenters within it), persons who, nonetheless, were apparently quite capable of instigating the changes that Hess desperately sought. After the flight Mrs Roberts was investigated by MI5, surely evidence that they too were unsure as to her actual role.

Who was Mary Violet Roberts and why did she became embroiled in the Hess affair? In many ways she was an ideal, but very unlikely, intermediary. (Mrs Roberts was responsible for our initial interest in the Hess affair, many years ago. David Irving had stated that Mrs Roberts was the daughter-in-law of Field Marshal Lord Roberts. This is impossible. Lord Roberts' unmarried son was killed at Colenso in 1899.)

Mary Violet Roberts was born 5 September 1864 in Ferozepore, India, and baptised on the 25th of the same month. Her father was Patrick Maxwell, at that time a captain in the Bengal Staff Corps. Patrick had joined the Bengal Army as a cadet on 31 January 1845 and had progressed to the rank of captain, late of the 37th Native Infantry, and deputy commissioner in the Punjab at Googaira. Her mother was Louisa Sarah, née Bell of Tasmania. They had married in 1853.

Patrick Maxwell's cadet papers show that his father had to give his consent for his son to follow a career in the army. His father, William, was described as: 'William Maxwell, Merchant of Dargavel, Glasgow.' Dargavel is no more than 20 miles from where Hess crashed and has an obvious similarity to Dungavel, the so called 'Hess target'. William Maxwell had married Mary Campbell of Possil Park, which in 1834 was described thus:

> It was then far away from the noise and smoke of the city, and stood among fine old trees. With its beautiful gardens, its grassy slopes, and its clear lake, Possil formed as delightful and retired a country residence as any in the county.

Clearly, here was a family of substance. Dargavel House was the ancestral home of Mary Violet Roberts. Dating from around 1580 the house is still standing, though currently part of the 2,500 acre estate of the former Royal Ordnance Factory. Once the largest in Europe and so secret that it did not appear on Ordnance Survey (OS) maps, the site has now been decommissioned and is awaiting planning permission so that it can be developed. The house is described thus:

> John Maxwell of Dargavel was the second son of Sir Patrick Maxwell of Newark and his wife Helen, a daughter of Sir Neil Montgomery of Lainshaw. In 1516, John obtained grant for the lands of Dargavel from the Earl of Lennox. Dargavel Castle is a 'Z' plan tower house; it consisted of a rectangular central block of three floors and a garret with two large round towers on opposite corners. The Maxwell armorial stone with a stag's head crest on the east gable is dated 1584 but this is likely to represent some additional building work on the structure as it was greatly extended since its original construction. The whole house was reconstructed and extended in 1849 in the Scottish Baronial style by the architect David Bryce … The Maxwells of Dargavel were involved in the feud between the Montgomerys and the Cunningham family that embroiled this part of the lower Clyde Estuary. The principal line of the Maxwells failed

in the early part of the nineteenth century and the heiress married John Hall of Fulbar who took the additional name of Maxwell. The Hall-Maxwells of Dargavel were a prolific family and many of the sons became notable military men. The First World War however claimed three of the last laird's sons and two of his grandsons. The barony was sold between the two world wars and the house and its gardens and parkland were taken over by the Government for the Bishopton Rl Ordnance Factory. The old house is now deep inside this secret area, apparently again much altered.

Again, evidence of wealth and status. Further research revealed that the Maxwells seem to originate back to Caervalerock Castle, Dumfries, in around 1270. Clearly the Maxwells were well connected and, indeed, appeared to be an even older family than the Hamiltons. We should not, therefore, be too surprised to learn that, in 1638, Elizabeth, the daughter of James Maxwell, married William, 2nd Duke of Hamilton.

In 1864, the Maxwell family was in India, eight years away from returning to England. In 1872, Patrick retired to Bath, Wiltshire, with the rank of major general. The family lived in a large house at 19 Pultney Road. Mary therefore spent her formative years in the west of England. She also had a brother, Louis.

In the late 1880s, Mary began her courtship with the senior mathematics teacher from the nearby Bath College. Herbert Ainslie Roberts was born in 1864. Academically gifted, Herbert had attended Gonville and Caius College, Cambridge, graduating in 1887. His elder brother, Ernest Stewart, was also exceptionally academically gifted, becoming the Master of Gonville and Caius from 1903 to 1912.

Mary and Herbert married in 1894 and moved to Cambridge in 1898, Herbert initially becoming a mathematics coach. The couple were not poor, Mary being the principal beneficiary of her father's will when he died in July 1906. In addition to a specific bequest, Patrick also gave his daughter the proceeds of a marriage settlement that had been received in 1853, when he married her mother, Louisa Sarah.

By the time of his father-in-law's death in 1906, Herbert had become secretary to the recently formed (1899) Cambridge Appointments Board. It was this position that was to earn Herbert his reputation, described thus in 1932: 'It is hardly too much to say that Roberts achieved the greatest bit of constructive work of a not strictly academic character done in Cambridge by a single individual in the last 25 years.'

The Roberts' were becoming comfortable and in 1912–13 they commissioned the then fashionable Mackay Baillie Scott to design and build a 'Sussex-style farmhouse of mock Tudor design'. It is a lovely house and still stands to this day.

Of far more relevance to this story is that around this time the Roberts family became acquainted with the Haushofer family, a friendship that lasted for the next forty years at least. How the two families met we are still not sure (even after twenty years of trying to find out), but we do know that H.A. Roberts was secretary to the Cambridge Appointments Board, the Indian Civil Service Studies Board and the Foreign Service Students Committee. They may, therefore, have met through his work. E.S. Roberts may have introduced them through his important position at Gonville and Caius. In 1899, Karl Haushofer travelled to England and met with Joseph Chamberlain. This appears to coincide with the visit of Kaiser Wilhem to England in a British-inspired attempt to improve relations. On 14 August 1925, Mary and Herbert met Albrecht Haushofer. The diary entry says: '*Die Bekanntschaft mit der Familie R. datierte aus der Vorkriegszeit*' ('The acquaintance with the family R. dated from before the war').

So the friendship was certainly longstanding and durable. It also transcended the generations. Karl and Martha Haushofer had two boys, Albrecht and Heinz, while Herbert and Mary Roberts had one son, Patrick. Albrecht was born in 1903, Patrick in 1895. Not surprisingly, given the family backgrounds, both sets of children were also academically gifted. Patrick went to Eton aged 13, then Trinity College, Cambridge, before joining the Foreign Service in 1919. Albrecht spent his formative years in Munich and graduated in history and geography from the University in 1924, aged 21. Heinz studied as an agronomist. The Haushofer archives in Koblenz detail various meetings with the younger Roberts who, at the time, was rapidly progressing through the diplomatic ranks:

11.6.1925 – *Patrick Roberts zum Mittagessen, tee u.abend essen.*
14.8.1925 – *Mr & Mrs Roberts viel bei mir. Roberts mit Albrecht um ½ I fort.*

Patrick obviously met up with his parents and their German friends prior to leaving the Berlin Embassy for Warsaw (he started there on 15 August 1925).

Later on, the families' meetings are less well documented and the authors are very grateful to Andrea Schroder Haushofer, who provided a copy of the visitor's book at the family estate, *Hartschimmelhof*. The Roberts' visits are recorded, but the copy of the book appeared to have been written up in hindsight. All the entries are in the same handwriting, the same colour ink and it seemed to be to have been done after the event. Nevertheless, the Roberts' are recorded as having visited the Haushofers in 1925 and 1926. In 1932, Herbert Ainslie Roberts died and, in 1934, the Haushofers visited London, Cambridge and Oxford. In 1936, Albrecht visited the family alone.

By 1936, when the main events of the story start to unfold, the two families' friendship had passed down to the two sons. By 1936, Karl Haushofer was 67 years old. Mary Roberts was 72 years old and was living with her high-achieving son, Patrick, in Athens, Greece, while he was working at the British Embassy. He was, by that time, chargé d'affaires in Athens.

In 1937, Mary Robert's world was shattered. Patrick was involved in a car crash at Ikali, north of Athens, and died shortly afterwards. Mary returned to England and was living in London with her nephew, Walter Roberts, at 36 Queen's Gate, Kensington, when probate was granted in 1938. Eventually, she returned to Cambridge and lived in Wilberforce Road.

However, we suspect none of the family members anticipated the roles they were about to play in world history, particularly Mary Violet Roberts, who was at that time more worried about who was going to keep her Cambridge lawn cut.

Reaction to the Haushofer Letter

Hitler and Hess were now under immense pressure. Operation Sealion had been called off or postponed in early September 1940; the planning for the May 1941 Operation Barbarossa had already been instigated in July 1940[85]; and the clock was ticking. Britain had still to be neutralised, yet despite the setbacks, the defeats and apparent hopelessness of their position, there was no settlement, and little real hope of one. The US was still neutral, but for how much longer?

Rudolf Hess had some ideas; unconventional, certainly, but at least some ideas. The German Foreign Office had failed to date, in much the same way as the Luftwaffe, and on 23 September 1940, Albrecht Haushofer had sent the first letter to the Duke of Hamilton.

If Britain would not come to the peace table voluntarily, she would have to be blasted into attendance: the 'Blitz of Britain' was about to commence.[86] As we have seen, the sequence of letters started after Karl Haushofer's walk in the forest with Rudolf Hess at the end of August 1940. He apparently mentioned the fact that after a 'long delay' a letter had been received from their old family friend. Members of the Roberts family have stated that Mrs Roberts definitely did not leave England during the Second World War. This is not particularly surprising, given that she was 76 years old in 1940, but it does raise the question (among others) as to why she gave her address as PO Box 516, Lisbon. It appears that Hess[87] thought she was in residence there,[88] but this is not the case.

In this connection we highly recommend *Undercover Addresses of WW2*, published by Chavril Press. First printed in 1992 by the Entwhistles of Abernethy, Scotland, it details the means by which postal services operated during the war, in particular between belligerent nations. Mrs Roberts did nothing else other than make use of the services legally open to her (and anyone else) after the outbreak of war. The British government felt it right that families and friends could continue to correspond. However, to avoid accusations of collaboration, rather than use the General Post Office (GPO), the company of Thomas Cook Limited was used. The company was already providing a similar service to the Canadian government.[89] In January 1940, a service commenced, based in what was then neutral Holland. Obviously, the events of May 1940 then made Holland far from neutral and so, from June 1940, the service moved to neutral Lisbon, which at that time was becoming known as 'the gateway to Europe' for that very reason.

Thomas Cook subsequently used the PO Box number 506 to pass millions of letters between the UK and friends and family in Germany and occupied Europe. Eventually, inhabitants of the Channel Islands and prisoners of war would become the most common users. Thomas Cook even placed advertisements in *The Times* newspaper to promote the service. However, along with the service came a strict series of rules. While not illegal to correspond with persons abroad, all such letters would be subject to the scrutiny of the censor. Below is a list of the specific rules pertaining to this postal service:

Communications must be clearly written (without erasures) and should not exceed two sides of a normal sheet of notepaper. Only one letter may be placed in one envelope.

Letters and envelopes must omit the sender's address. They must refer only to matters of personal interest.

No reference may be made to any town (other than Lisbon), village, locality, ship or journey. No indication may be made that the writer is not in Portugal.

Mention of a letter received from or written to the enemy or enemy-occupied territory is not permitted.

Each letter must be placed in an open unstamped envelope, fully inscribed to the addressee, who should be asked to address any reply to your full name, care of Post Office Box 506, LISBON, Portugal. Poste Restante addresses are not permitted.

The open envelope containing the letter should be placed in an outer stamped envelope and sent to THOS. COOK & SON LTD, Berkley Street, Piccadilly, London, W1 together with a memorandum plainly written in BLOCK LETTERS containing the name and full address of the sender.

The communication to THOS. COOK & SON LTD, must enclose a postal order value 2s [shillings] which fee will cover the postage of one envelope containing one communication to the neutral country, also of a reply (if any) from the neutral country to Messrs Cook's Head Office in London. An additional fee is payable for airmail.[90]

We believe this document explains how Mrs Roberts communicated with her old friends the Haushofers. She could only write in a personal manner. She follows the instructions, pays her two shillings and the letter is sent. She probably posts the outer envelope in Cambridge, addressed to Thos. Cook, London. She cannot give an address on the actual letter, other than the return address in Lisbon. This explains the impression given that she was actually in Lisbon, an impression that her German friends apparently believed. We should not perhaps be too surprised at their ignorance; the service had only just started (June 1940) in Lisbon. It may well be that the 'long delay' was simply occasioned by the fact that Mrs Roberts did not pay the extra money for airmail.

The system does not imply intelligence involvement in any way. The reason that the letters were to be left open was so that the censor could read them before despatch. It was, therefore, almost an inevitability that any 'dubious letters' would be found out and (at the least) returned to the sender.

The exact same thing happened to the Haushofer letter of 23 September. An Auslands agent posted the reply back to PO Box 506, Lisbon (apparently Hess's brother), but the letter was opened by the British censor and retained. Realistically, it never stood a chance, but we do not think that the Haushofers perhaps understood the system. Hess thought Mrs Roberts really was in Lisbon.

We do know that the censor eventually forwarded the letter to RAF intelligence, which was then keen to try and get the Duke of Hamilton to attend a meeting with Haushofer in the spring of 1941. We also know that the Duke of Hamilton was very careful as to how he was seen in assisting in this approach.[91] We also suspect that Mary Roberts sent a further letter, as there is an envelope in the Bundesarchiv dated 6 May 1941.

However, we now do not believe that the Roberts letter was anything other than friendly greetings, simply because otherwise it would have been stopped by the censor. If Mrs Roberts was really taking part in intelligence-inspired, international intrigue, would she really rely on the Thomas Cook service? It is also quite right to say that we do not know for sure, because the letter has yet to surface. It does not feature on the microfilms, but it may possibly still be in the Haushofer private archive in Germany. It cannot be deemed to be contentious, or the censor would have stopped it before it left the UK, or Thomas Cook would not have sent it as it contravened Rule 2.

Moreover, given the suppression of some documentation concerning the Hess affair, we are surprised that the series of letters first entered the public domain as early as 1949. If they really were the third party evidence of intelligence intercepts, we doubt they would have been released that early. So, we have changed our view.

In his book *Hess: The British Conspiracy*, John Harris made the case that the letter was the stimulus for a forged exchange, masterminded by the British intelligence community. This we still believe likely, albeit playing only a part in the scheme. Ernst Bohle, head of the Auslands organisation under Hess, has talked of translating letters from Hess to the Duke of Hamilton as late as January 1941, thus suggesting a continuation of the September 1940 correspondence. Harris went on to explain the link between Mrs Roberts and the intelligence community through her nephew, Walter Stewart Roberts (who was a member of SO1) and her son, Patrick, who, until his death in 1937, was a very well-connected and important Foreign Office official.

We are now sure that, while the German response was certainly the intended opening round of an attempted non-governmental peace approach, it never stood a chance.

5. THE SEQUENCE OF EVENTS LEADING TO THE FLIGHT (06.11.40–10.05.41)

In the Public Records Office, Kew, there is a letter dated 22 November 1940 from MI5 to the Foreign Office, asking if the September 1940 letter from Albrecht Haushofer to The Duke of Hamilton (sent via Mary Violet Roberts) could be forwarded to the Duke of Hamilton.[92] This appears to follow a censor's report dated 6 November 1940, following the interception of the letter on 2 November. Further copies of the report were sent to MI5, the Foreign Office and the Inter-Services Research Bureau.

The first part of the Haushofer/Hess plan had disastrously failed. The written letter plan had not worked, largely because of a German misunderstanding of British wartime postal conventions. Not a wholly inexcusable mistake. However, it had the effect of alerting the British intelligence services to the fact that the Haushofers were trying to arrange a meeting between the Duke of Hamilton and Albrecht. That was perhaps the most important implication.

The second approach, plan B, was now to commence. Cue the 'neutral interme-diary' that was propsed in the Haushofer letter.[93] Cue also the British secret services, now fully alerted as to what was potentially going on and between whom.

The Hess letter to Haushofer, dated 8 September 1940, stated: 'Possibly a neutral acquaintance, who had some business to attend to over there anyway, might look him up and make some communication to him, using you or Albrecht as refer-ence.' This seems clear. Someone known to Albrecht and Karl Haushofer would be instructed to 'look up' the Duke of Hamilton when in Britain. (Ironically, this was just the role that Hess sought for himself in May 1941.)

This is exactly what we believe happened, except that British intelligence ser-vices were now standing behind the Duke of Hamilton, looking over his shoulder, waiting for this second approach to be made. Moreover, the Duke of Hamilton knew very well that British intelligence was aware of the Haushofer approach when he was eventually given the copy of the letter. So his 'card was marked' we would say. (If indeed it needed marking).

We suspect that Hamilton was already 'signed up' for a 'sting' way before RAF intelligence, or T.A. Robertson and the XX Committee, or MI5, got round to really addressing the issue; quite possibly without his being aware of his pre-cise role. This is why Hamilton was perturbed in the extreme when the RAF intelligence department did get round to interviewing him in early 1941.[94]

They were too late. British intelligence, a completely different department was already at work. The potential for blunders had just increased, with two operations simultaneously mounted. We know that the RAF intelligence department was not involved in the flight. There is a letter from RAF intelligence, dated 13 May 1941, making it clear that they did not know about it.[95] James Douglas-Hamilton makes the convincing case that his father was not shown the Haushofer letter until March 1941,[96] and also makes it clear that the duke was frustrated that the letter had gone unanswered for seven months when he complained to the Air Ministry on 28 April 1941.

You will remember that the Haushofer letter to Mrs Roberts of 23 September had been copied to three intelligence departments: MI5, the Foreign Office and the Inter-Services Research Bureau. The latter was simply a cover name for the Special Operations Executive (SOE). The receipt of a copy of this letter, so John Harris assumed, confirmed an operation by this branch of British intelligence, eventually leading to the May 1941 flight.

SOE was, to an extent, a purely wartime political creation, so as to keep Labour Party coalition partners happy. Ever since the 1920s, the Labour Party, not without good reason, had been suspicious of the Intelligence Services, largely on account of the fact that they were staffed (as they assumed) almost exclusively by Right-wingers. SOE was a trade-off against a Labour Party demand for more control of the established services. As a result, in June 1940, Hugh Dalton, the bright but volatile Minister of Economic Warfare, was given overall political control of SOE, which took as its basis the old 'Section D' organisation.[97]

SOE was then split into two parts: SO1 (for words) and SO2 (for deeds). As recounted in *Hess: The British Conspiracy*, SO1 was based around Woburn Abbey, Bedfordshire and relied upon an assortment of ex-journalists, such as Sefton Delmer, and ex-'city types', such as Leonard Ingrams, to come up with a highly unconventional, but nonetheless successful, black propaganda department.

John Harris speculated that it was SO1 that was responsible for luring Hess to England. He based this viewpoint largely on the fact that its financial director was none other than Walter Stewart Roberts, the nephew of Mary Violet Roberts, whose role has already been described. It all seemed rather nepotistic, particularly when he discovered that two beneficiaries in the will of Mary Roberts were Sir Anthony Bevir and Sir Edward Playfair.[98]

We do not yet now why but Walter Stewart Roberts saw fit to change his name to Walter Stewart-Roberts by deed poll. When his aunt died in 1958, her death appears not to have been recorded anywhere. It is tempting to wonder if these events are related. However, we now think that, while SO1 certainly had the capacity to come up with such a scheme, we suspect that Claude Dansey had beaten them to it (or stolen the idea) and had already started to do the work.

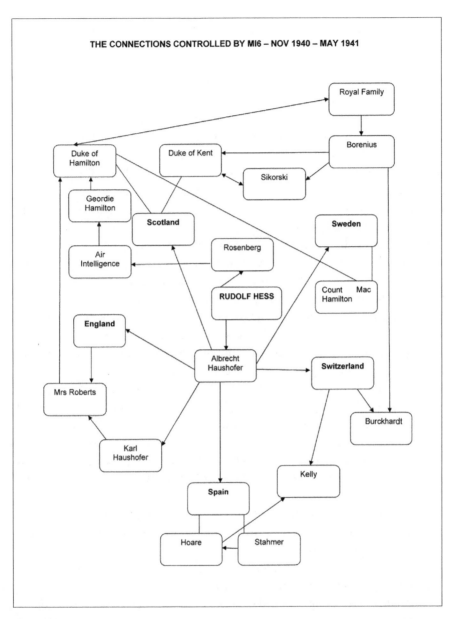

THE CONNECTIONS CONTROLLED BY MI6 – NOV 1940 – MAY 1941

Connections.

It is also recorded that Dansey, being an 'old school' SIS man, detested SOE, seeing them as amateurs. Consequently, we think it unlikely that he would have welcomed collaboration with this newly formed organisation. So, to the involvement of Dansey and MI6, Carl Jacob Burckhardt provided the much needed non-governmental conduit.

Carl Jacob Burckhardt: the Neutral Intermediary?

Carl Burckhardt (1891–1974) was a Swiss academic and historian who came to international attention in 1937 when he became the last (as it turned out) League of Nations High Commissioner for the Free City of Danzig. Previously he had spent periods as a university professor and a Swiss diplomat, and it was in the second role that he plays his part in this particular series of events. Given his experience in European power politics of the late 1930s, and his acquaintance with the key players, he would seem to be the obvious choice for Hess' wish for an 'independent neutral intermediary', as stipulated in his letter to Albrecht Haushofer in early September 1940. His subsequent actions and letters would only confirm this viewpoint

His task as High Commissioner for the Free City of Danzig from 1937–39 was almost impossible. The Free City of Danzig was a creation of the much-maligned Treaty of Versailles in 1919. Throughout the 1930s, Hitler's Germany had placed the wholly artificial creation under severe political pressure. Between 90–95 per cent of the population was of German descent, in a city that was geographically in the middle of newly reconstituted Poland. Burckhardt took over the 'poisoned chalice' two years after the previous incumbent, Irishman Sean Lester, had resigned in 1935 on account of the German pressure.

In 1939, Germany invaded and the city was incorporated into the Third Reich. However, the role that Burckhardt had played in the two years of his tenure had been universally acknowledged. Significantly, he became well known to the foreign offices of the leading European players. According to *Meine Danziger Mission*,[99] the book he wrote on his enforced retirement, glowing testimonials were received from, amongst others, Viscount Halifax, Baron Weizsacker and the British Ambassador to Switzerland, David Kelly.

Equally significant, just before the invasion of Poland, Burckhardt was summoned to Berchtesgaden to meet with Adolf Hitler. A transcript of part of the conversation is given below.

Danzig league chief's report to Britain, 16 August 1939:
We landed in Salzburg, stopped briefly to eat, and then took a car to the Obersalzberg. Perched on the great height of the 'Berghof', up the spiralling roadway, past the so-called 'Tea House,' sat the 'Eagle's Nest' of the leader of all the Germans.

Here is a confirmed report that I made in Basel [Switzerland] on August 13, 1939 to the representatives of Lord Halifax and Minister Georges Bonnet – Roger Makins and Minister Pierre Arnal – about the visit and conversation that I had with the Dictator.

Beginning of the Conversation

Hitler: 'I hope you had a comfortable flight. My Condor aircraft is not as fast as the Douglas, but it is more solid and useful as a military aircraft. It holds up better against gunfire. You have had a stressful week. I know that you have done your best to find a peaceful solution (Hitler's friendly expression changed here into a menacing mask) but that all of your work has been ruined by the Poles. I have suggested to [Albert] Forster that he work through the representatives of the League of Nations (*Völkerbund*). I do not prefer this approach, but I must be extra sure that the League of Nations is handled correctly as concerns the Saar and Danzig Questions (i.e., Hitler was referring to plebiscites here). I stress that Forster has proceeded according to my instructions because I know that this organization is objective. Despite economic repression and threats, Forster has not acted excessively. The Poles, however, who are still members of the League of Nations, I believe, have not made any effort. Last Friday (the day the Polish ultimatum arrived); I would have been satisfied with a telephone call from them. The Poles knew that talks were possible. They did not have to send a note (i.e., formal document).'

Burckhardt: 'Then the negotiations have broken down over some details.'

Hitler (looking annoyed): 'This is unfortunate at such a serious moment. Two days before the matter came to a head; Chodacki received instructions from Beck to take steps to bring matters under control. He made a grave telephone call. During which, [Arthur] Greiser has told me, that certain measures were to be taken against [German] border officials; Beck broadcast all of this to the press. (Hitler then became furious.) The press said that I had lost the war of nerves, that threats were the correct way to deal with me, that we had given way, because the Poles had stood firm; that I had been only bluffing the year before, and that Polish courage, which the Czechs didn't possess, had called my bluff. I have seen idiotic statements in the French press that I have lost my nerve, but that the Poles have retained theirs.' (Hitler became so bitter that for a few moments he was unable to speak.)

Burckhardt: 'You give these journalists too much credit, if you take their comments so seriously. A Reich Chancellor should stand above such trifles.'

Hitler: 'I cannot do that. Because of my origin as someone who rose from the working class, because of the way I rose [to power] and because of my character, I cannot see these things in another light. These statesmen must understand this and reckon with it, if they wish to avoid a catastrophe. It is not true that the British government has no influence over the press. The press is silent when the government wishes it. (Hitler's voice rose to a crescendo.) The State Secretary will summon the Polish ambassador and say to him 'the hour has come'. That is the answer to ultimatums and to the lost war of nerves. If the slightest incident occurs, I will smash the Poles so completely that not a single trace of Poland will be found afterwards. Like a lightning bolt I will strike with the full power of my mechanised army, the power of which the Poles have no idea. Mark my words.'

… 'How can they (i.e., the English) attack me? Via the air? People try to impress me with numbers and demonstrations of armaments, particularly aerial armaments. (Hitler laughed hysterically.) I laugh because I am the specialist in armaments, not the others. Their air force! England has 135,000 men, France 75,000. I have 600,000 in peacetime and 1,000,000 in wartime. My flak is the best in the world, as I demonstrated in Spain. The Russians, and we know them better than do most other people, hundreds of our officers have trained in Russia, have no offensive strength and will not haul the chestnuts of others out of the fire. A nation does not murder its officers if it plans to wage a war. We defeated the Russians in Spain. The Japanese have also defeated them. (Hitler states scornfully) One cannot give us goose pimples by talking about the Russians. (Hitler now states calmly) All of this talk of war is stupidity and it makes people crazy.'

'*What then is the question? Only that we need grain and timber. For the grain I need space in the east;* for the timber I need a colony, only one [colony]. We can survive. Our harvests in 1938 and in this year were excellent. We can survive, in spite of the triumphant cries of others that we will starve. We have achieved these harvests thanks to the persistence of our people and above all due to the use of chemical fertilizers. However, one day the soil will have had enough … What then? I cannot stand by and let my people starve. Am I not better off then in putting two million men on the battlefield, than in losing them to starvation? Perhaps there are still among the apostles of humanity (i.e., those who seek peace at any cost), those who remember 1919. I do not want to repeat that. I will not repeat that. Free trade, open borders, that is all practical, we had these things. However when everything depends upon those masters of the seas (i.e., the English), when we can be brought low by a blockade, then it is my duty to create a situation whereby by my people can live off of their own fat. That is the only question, the rest is insanity.'

'I do not harbour any romantic aims. I have no wish to rule. *Above all I want nothing from the West; nothing today and nothing tomorrow.* I desire nothing from the thickly settled regions of the world … All of the notions that are ascribed to me by other people are inventions. *However, I <u>must have a free hand in the east</u>. To repeat: it is a question of grain and timber, which I can find only outside of Europe.'*
Burckhardt: 'I came here because of Danzig. I am not inclined to discuss other matters. A new war will usher in the end of civilization. That is a great responsibility [to bear] for the future. It is better to live in honour than to take such a responsibility upon oneself. The stronger one is, the longer he can be patient.

The more honour a man has the more attacks he can fend off. Someone once said to me that Germany's strength lies in being patient when it comes to the Polish and Danzig Questions.'

Hitler (in a serious tone): 'That is very important. (Turning to Forster) We must mention this to Ribbentrop.'

Burckhardt: 'I am fully convinced that this problem can be solved via negotiations and that the Western Powers are prepared to talk.'

Hitler (in a serious tone): 'Why then do they incite the Poles to boast about their ultimatums and to send ultimatums to us!'

Burckhardt (speaking pointedly): 'This is not worth discussing. London and Paris exercise a moderating influence in Warsaw. The Danzig Question is very simple. It is a matter of a complex of international laws that can no longer be violated through one-sided pressure, through force, or through the threat of force.'

Hitler (slamming his fist on the table): 'Talks! But on what basis? Do you remember the disarmament talks? I made a generous offer to the Poles. In March I wanted, after I removed the threat of war with Czechoslovakia from my southeast flank, to put out two burning issues: Memel and Danzig. Every time I took a step, and this is borne out by history, I found England and France in my path. What then can I do?...'

(There was a long pause. Hitler then stood up and offered to take me on a tour of the property)

Hitler (walking on the road outside of the building): 'How happy I am when I am here. I have had enough trouble. I need my rest.'

Burckhardt (stating suggestively): 'You are expressing the sentiments of the entire world. You more than anyone has the chance to give the world the peace and quiet it needs.'

Hitler: 'No, it is not so. (Hitler dismissed Forster and stood there nervously while speaking softly.) Because I recognise that England and France are inciting Poland to war, in which case I would rather have war today than tomorrow; to lead it this year rather than next year. Surely, however, one should attempt to find a way out? If the Poles leave Danzig at peace, if they do not attempt to hoodwink me with falsified maps, then I can wait. However, a condition is that I must stop the suffering of our minority in Poland. No one believes me but I have ordered that sensational cases (e.g., castrations, etc.) not be mentioned in the press. They enrage public opinion very much. However, I cannot hold back the truth for much longer. The limits of patience have been reached. I am able to bring forward victims, for example in the South Tyrol. Yet no one gives me any recognition for this, instead they shriek: '[that is] unjust and inhumane!' I can bring forward political victims too, but everything has its limit.

'I did not always know it, but I know now, that England and France belong inseparably with one another. That is the nature of things. I do not intrigue against this situation, which is quite different from those others who intrigue against my friendship with Italy. I fought in the trenches for four years against England and France and I recognise the courage of both of these peoples. Yet there is something about the Anglo-Saxons (and the Americans) that separates them deeply from us [Germans]. What is it?'

Burckhardt: 'Perhaps it is their fidelity when faced with obligations?'

Hitler: 'One can interpret that in different ways. We recognise our deeds for what they are. They are hypocrites. I can cite examples.'

Burckhardt: 'Paix – Pax – Pacts, these words all have the same root, as do the words peace (*Friede*) and joy (*Freude*). With the Germans it is always a case of the sense [of a word].'

Hitler: 'We are an ethnic nation [*Volksstaat*], the English an Empire. We are an [organic] body, England is an association …'

Burckhardt: 'Forster told me that I should ask you a question – should I allow my children to remain in Danzig?'

Hitler: 'Anything can happen in Danzig any day now, but only if the Poles will it to be so. I believe that your children would be better off in Switzerland. I have enjoyed seeing you. You come from a world that is alien to me. However, I have fought for a peaceful solution. I have great sympathy for another man, Lord Halifax. Many people have spoken badly of him to me, but my favourable first impression remains. I believe that he is a man who sees things in a very measured way and who also wants a peaceful solution. I hope to see him again someday.'

'At the moment [I was leaving], before Hitler turned to go back into the Main Room, he had said to me: 'I would like, before it is too late, to speak to an Englishman who can speak German.' I responded, 'Sir Nevile Henderson speaks fluent German, from what I hear.' However, Hitler shook his head, 'That does not make sense,' he said, 'he is a diplomat who does not have a keen mind, I would like to speak with a man like Lord Halifax. But he can no longer come in person. How are things with Marshal Ironside?'[100] I hear good things about him. Will you tell this to the English?'

Burckhardt added afterward that this final comment of Hitler's was later reprinted by the English in a report following Burckhardt's meeting with Roger Makins[101] and Pierre Arnal[102] in Basel, Switzerland on 13 August 1939.

However, this comment was left out of the French version of his report. Burckhardt claims that this occurred for the following reason:

[We, the English, the French, and myself] had a standing and firm agreement that no one was supposed to know of the meeting I had with the two diplomats at my home in Basel. To my great astonishment, however, Minister Arnal was called to the telephone while I was in the middle of my report. Alarmed, I asked, 'What is the meaning of this? It was a precondition of our meeting that no one was to know of it!' Arnal reassured me, 'The only one who knows is our ambassador in Bern. Only he can call me here, and Arnal left the room. During his absence I expressed to Mr. Makins Hitler's wish to meet with Marshal Ironside.

Yet as soon as Arnal returned, what he told me made my transmission of Hitler's wish for a final contact with the English moot. 'The ambassador,' Arnal explained, 'shared with me the news that the entire event of your visit to the Obersalzberg will be published in *Paris Soir*; and that the report will be so sensational it includes certain untrue elements, among which is the claim that Hitler handed you a letter to Neville Chamberlain in which he asks the Prime Minister to join the Germans in a pact against Russia.

This news brought to nothing the hopes that I had for my conversation at the Obersalzberg ... The writer of this ludicrous article was a young journalist. ... As I later learned, on the morning of 11 August he had attempted to enter my office. A secretary had received him and told him that I had gone on a hunting trip in Austria ... He then went around the city [of Danzig] and met with a number of people, asked questions, and learned that the airstrip had been closed since noon. He then went directly to the airstrip and spoke there with a Polish official who told him that the High Commissioner, escorted by the Gauleiter [of Danzig – Forster], has climbed into the private plane of the Reich Chancellor (Hitler) and flown away. The remaining parts of the report were a combination of this news and the fantasies of the young reporter.

Lastly, Burckhardt reported: 'Yet another thing was missing from the reports of Makins and Arnal, perhaps the most remarkable com ment made to me by the Chancellor. Hitler had said to me on that August 11th.'

Everything I undertake is directed against Russia. If the West is too stupid and too blind to comprehend this I will be forced to reach an understanding with the Russians, turn and strike the West, and then after their defeat turn back against the Soviet Union with my collected strength. I need the Ukraine and with that no one can starve us out as they did in the last war.

Following the meeting [with Makins and Arnal] I was so defeated by the indiscretion [that had been shown], that I had not reported this final and surprising comment of the Chancellor; it had seemed so completely improbable [that Hitler had said this] as to be part of an hallucination.

We believe this report to be important for a variety of reasons. Firstly, it shows the relationship between Hitler and Burckhardt; Burckhardt certainly does not appear to be 'star struck'. Secondly, it appears that the conversation was intended for British consumption; and thirdly, the foreign policy objectives appear to be a case study directly from the Haushofer/Mackinder school of geopolitics.

Hitler was not to be disappointed. As soon as Burckhardt got back to Basle, he made his report and forwarded it to Viscount Halifax, Foreign Secretary in the Chamberlain government. The report was published in the *Daily Telegraph* newspaper:

A REPORT FROM CARL J. BURCKHARDT, HIGH COMMISSIONER OF THE LEAGUE OF NATIONS, ON HIS MEETING WITH ADOLF HITLER ON AUGUST 11, 1939.

Viscount Halifax, the Foreign Secretary, received a message yesterday from Prof. Burckhardt, League High Commissioner in Danzig, recording the tenor of the conversation he had with Herr Hitler at Berchtesgaden on Friday.

This information, as I predicted yesterday, is being treated by the Foreign Office as strictly confidential, seeing that the interview was sought by Herr Hitler, through a personal invitation to Prof. Burckhardt with a request that the matter should be treated in this way.

There is, however, full authority for stating that neither through Prof. Burckhardt, nor any other source, has the British Government received any proposals for a settlement of the Danzig question.

I can also reiterate that the League High Commissioner did not deliver any message from the British Government.

Indeed, it seems unlikely that he had any opportunity to do so, for it is learned that his interview with Hitler lasted only thirty minutes. The bulk of this was occupied by the German Chancellor in expressing his views on the Danzig situation and asking questions on the circumstances in which local incidents had arisen. Had the interview taken the form of an exchange of views, Professor Burckhardt would have been in a position to give Hitler a precise re statement of the British viewpoint that any attempt to change the present status of Danzig by force, or the threat of force, which Poland felt compelled to resist, would immediately call into play the British and French guarantees of armed support.

Buying Time

At the same time, he could have added, Britain would naturally welcome any peaceful solution of the Danzig problem acceptable to all parties concerned, but particularly to Poland, of whom further concessions were being demanded by Germany. Such a statement would, in effect, have been no more than a restatement of Britain's attitude, as already publicly voiced by the prime minister and foreign secretary.

Professor Burckhardt was in a position to know that there had been no change in this attitude. But it seems improbable that he was invited to express any opinion on such matters, and these circumstances account for the fact that no special importance was attached to the incident. The visit is regarded as no more than an item in the general development of events; a development which was expected to proceed in a variety of forms, both militarily and diplomatically, during the next few weeks.

It now appears that, in inviting Burckhardt to Obersalzberg, Hitler had essentially initiated 'governmental' peace proposals with the West, even before the Polish invasion had been launched. The usual messages were all relayed to Burckhardt: the need to go east for resources, and the wish for co-existence etc. These were to become the themes of the mantra that now formed the basis of the 'peace feelers' season that was about to start following the Polish invasion.

The next we hear of Burckhardt is in July 1940, when this time he is seen to be approaching the British cabinet. On Wednesday 10 July 1940, the War Cabinet met at 10 Downing Street, London. Present were Churchill, Chamberlain, Attlee, Halifax and Greenwood. Also in attendance were Lord Simon, General Dill, John Anderson, Duff Cooper, Viscount Caldecote and A.V. Alexander.

After dealing with matters concerning evacuation, home defence and the Far East, Minute 5 dealt with 'Germany: plans and intentions'. It reads: 'A telegram had been received from our Minister in Switzerland (No. 365) giving an account of a conversation which a traveller, recently returned from a visit to Berlin, had had with various personages in Germany. The War Cabinet agreed with the foreign secretary's view that no reply should be sent to this telegram.'

A bland statement one might think, until one reads the copy of the telegram attached to the minutes. Burckhardt was now the acting Head of the International Red Cross, based in Geneva, Switzerland.

Decypher. Mr. Kelly, (Berne).
8th July, 1940.
D. – 1:35 a.m., 9th July, 1940.
Ra 7:25 a.m., 9th July, 1940.
No. 365
IMPORTANT
Secret and Confidential.
M. Paravicini asked me today to meet Dr. Carl Burckhardt, Acting President of the Red Cross, who has just returned from a visit to Berlin on mission regarding

Red Cross relief for refugees in France. Baron Weiszacker had sent an aeroplane for him and he stayed three days.

2. After begging me to treat his communication with the utmost discretion Dr. Burckhardt said he was given opportunity for long individual conversations with Gauleiters, one General and Weiszacker himself. All four told the same story.

3. Hitler had returned to his old idea and hesitated – before attacking England because he still clung to the hope of working arrangement with the British Empire as hinted at in his recent interview in Belgium with the American journalist Carl von Wiegand. He wanted a European Federation and felt this would be 'difficult without British co-operation. There were some 'local demands' of Italy which he was bound to support but in general he wanted 'a white peace like Sadowa' (two of the talkers used this formula). The General said that while they were confident of their ability to defeat England they realised that it might involve much greater sacrifices than had the defeat of the French army, most of whom had put up a very poor show and fought half-heartedly.

4. Each of the four had insisted that he was expressing his personal opinion but one of them had asked Doctor Burckhardt whether there was any chance of his having Red Cross business in England when he might see if there was any hope of a 'reasonable arrangement'.[103] Doctor Burckhardt said he could not do so but would talk to an English friend in Switzerland.[104]

5. The Doctor assured me that (a) his Red Cross mission was very important and not a cover for these conversations and (b) German Government really were hesitating with the preparations for an attack on England and they were willing to call it off if they could do so without the loss of face.

6. He said that he felt sure that this was not due to weakness but to a faint hope of avoiding further sacrifices involved, although he also said that he had watched Hitler's triumphal entry into Berlin and felt that there was no spontaneous enthusiasm.

7. I told Dr. Burckhardt (as I already had on the previous occasion), that I thought that our distrust of Hitler, apart from anything else, was a fatal obstacle to any peace. He said that he fully appreciated this but had thought it his duty to Switzerland to inform me of his conversations. He had hesitated about telling me 'because it would be most disastrous for him personally if any of this obtained any sort of publicity.'[105] Whatever we might think he begged that his report should be treated as absolutely secret.

8. It is very important for our own position here that his wish should be respected as he is most influential here and if he were made to look foolish, my own position and reputation for discretion would be compromised.[106] The situation is difficult enough.

9. Burckhardt mentioned casually that he would have to return to Berlin shortly about the refugee problem.

10. Presumably we shall have no thought of compromising on any such lines but if it is important for us to gain time I venture to suggest that it might be better to leave me without instructions rather than to return a flat negative.

If then Dr. Burckhardt should again approach me before returning to Berlin it will show us that he was really being sounded while the Germans will be left guessing as to whether His Majesty's Government are taking their talk seriously or not. So long as secrecy is maintained complete silence on our part can in no way weaken our war effort while it may weaken that of the enemy by causing hesitation.

We believe that this is significant. Firstly, in that the telegram was discussed at all by the War Cabinet, and secondly, that no reply was sent, according to Minute 5. What was not minuted was whether the telegram was then forwarded to any other departments for discussion, action or debate.

A British policy is also becoming established: the need to buy time. By not giving Burckhardt a reply, the War Cabinet were doing this by allowing him to say quite honestly that he did not know the British response. The other theme that is starting to appear is that Britain cannot make peace whilst Hitler is in charge. 'We' do not trust him (but 'we' do trust the Americans). So, the above telegrams and reports give some idea as to the standing of Carl Burckhardt in July/August 1940 when the Hess/Haushofer non-governmental peace mission begins. Burckhardt was extremely well connected with both sides in the conflict, but in a strictly guarded and protected, non-governmental way. The non-political status of the International Red Cross demanded that it should be so. Clearly Burckhardt could do nothing that would impinge on its principles. To do so could compromise the organisation terminally; a not unrealistic prospect given that the League of Nations had also recently disappeared. Burckhardt was playing with fire, a fact he clearly recognised.

In 2007, when we travelled to Geneva, the Burckhardt archivist made it plain to us that Burckhardt had extensively sifted through the archives after 1945 so as to preserve his history of neutrality. The future of the International Red Cross was possibly at stake.

We have already described the Thomas Cook mail service that Mrs Roberts made use of in the autumn of 1940. Perhaps unbeknown to her, she actually had a choice; the Red Cross had also initiated its own service, but only allowed a maximum of twenty-five words at a time. The Philatelic Society described it thus:

Following the declaration of War in September 1939 the International Committee of the Red Cross obtained specific agreement from the British,

French and German Governments for short messages to be exchanged between members of the same family living in belligerent countries as un-interned civilians. Such messages were only to be exchanged via the offices of the International Red Cross Committee in Geneva.

The British Chief Postal Censor approved the new scheme which was introduced in London from 11th December 1939 and extended to provincial centres within a year. ... All messages had to be sent via a Bureau and censorship was strict. At first restricted to relatives and fiancées, this limited communication was soon extended to include friends.

Message forms from the United Kingdom were routed from the Red Cross Bureau to the ICRC in Geneva using various routes as the war situation required. ... Overall messages are known to have taken up to nine months to complete their round journey although the average journey was around four to five months.[107]

Therefore, Carl Burckhardt had direct access to a mail service should he need to communicate in that way. However, he also had other, far more direct routes through third parties.

Burckhardt, Roman Battaglia and British Intelligence

Carl Jacob Burckhardt was a confidant of both the British and German governments, at the highest levels, in the period both prior to and after the declaration of war in September 1939. However, one discovery we stumbled across concerning Burckhardt was very much the most unexpected of this period of research. So unexpected that, when first discovered, we were convinced of a plot the scale of which, even to our conspiratorial minds, was far beyond that originally suspected. The accepted view was certainly brought into doubt.

When Rudolf Hess crashed, the basic sequence of events is broadly agreed: taken to the Baird farmhouse, offered tea, the Home Guard arrives, taken to the local Scout hut and then interrogation. Stephen Prior quite properly raises other questions concerning the initial apprehending of Hess and asks why Hess apparently gave his Iron Cross medal to one of his captors.[108] This issue is dealt with later.

However, the basic facts seem to be consistent with a typical apprehension of an enemy airman: some confusion, some 'pulling rank' and some adherence to procedure. The whole process has been likened to a classic *Dad's Army* episode and we are content that this display of British ineptitude is indicative of the fact that Hess was not expected in that particular area that night. We are also content that the actions of most of those involved were the actions of those who were not expecting to be drawn into the Hess affair. Except possibly for Roman Battaglia.

Roman Battaglia has been known about for some time. He was the Polish consulate who interrogated Hess for two hours in the Scout hut in Giffnock.[109] Peter Padfield makes the point that he was not even originally requested; his landlord at Newton Mearns, Mr Fairweather, was ill in bed so Battaglia attended in his place.[110] However, the discovery we were to make initially transformed our view of the 'off-duty diplomat' into something quite different.

Roman Roger Adam Maria Guido Battaglia was born in Vienna in 1903, the son of Roger Battaglia, 4th Baron Forst (1873–1950), a reasonably famous diplomat and politician in the days of the Austro-Hungarian Empire. The family was ancient, originally coming from Venice. He was well educated, graduating from the University of Cracow in 1927 as a bachelor in law. From there he joined the Polish Foreign Ministry and worked in Warsaw, Paris, Warsaw again and then, from 1935 to 1939, Danzig. On 4 March 1937, he married Aniela Kleber whilst stationed at Danzig.[111] The reader will perhaps wonder if Battaglia's postings had coincided with those of Patrick Roberts, Mrs Roberts' diplomat son, but we do not think so as the timings are different.

However, the Danzig posting most certainly did coincide with another major protagonist in the Hess affair, Carl Jacob Burckhardt.[112] Most of the books written about Hess detail the visits to Burckhardt in the spring of 1941 by, amongst others, Albrecht Haushofer, Tancred Borenius and, possibly even, Samuel Hoare.

Our hearts started to beat faster. Within a couple of hours of arrival Hess was being interviewed by an acquaintance of one of the men that had acted as a conduit and facilitator to his making the flight! We had to find out more about Battaglia.

This proved difficult in the extreme, which made us excited and suspicious in equal measure. The Sikorski Institute in London held a brief resumé of his career as above, but in 1945 it listed him as going to France.[113] After that the trail went cold. We searched death registers on the Internet; again, nothing. Wondering if there might still be Battaglias in Vienna, we learned that a Mrs Battaglia worked at the Art Museum in the city.

We e-mailed the museum and were surprised (though probably should not have been) to receive an e-mail from Jakub Forst-Battaglia, the recently retired Austrian Ambassador to Estonia and husband of the lady at the museum. He told us that Roman's father had died in near poverty in the Soviet bloc and that Roman, he thought, had migrated to Canada.[114] He did not think there were children. Helen Cara, the long-suffering personal assistant to John Harris, was travelling to Canada on holiday to visit relatives and was coerced into making searches whilst in Toronto; again, to no avail.

While on the Battaglia trail, we also noticed that a file was being suppressed at the PRO, Kew, but after a Freedom of Information application we eventually obtained access.[115] Originally embargoed until 2049, this dealt with an application for British citizenship in November 1946. Thinking that this must be significant, we rushed to Kew.

The trip was disappointing. While repeating much of the biographical information we had gleaned from Jakub Forst-Battaglia and the Sikorski Institute, the main purpose of the file was to record the various searches that the Home Office had made prior to approving the application for citizenship in January 1948. There was not any mention of 'Hess involvement'.

MI5 even replied: 'There was nothing recorded'.[116] This is strange, given that there were (and are) MI5 files from 1941 specifically dealing with how Battaglia had got so close to Hess in the Scout hut at Giffnock.[117] The police also gave Battaglia a clean report, save for the fact that Mrs Battaglia had been fined ten shillings for 'fraud on the railway' in December 1945.

But then the important discoveries started to come in: firstly, we discovered that it was likely that Roman Battaglia had died in Toronto, Canada in 1967–68. In 1967, a Roman Battaglia was listed as living at 76 Quebec Avenue, and in 1968 the listing had changed to solely Angela Battaglia. Battaglia had apparently been employed as a travel agent in the city and had established his own company, Caniaga Travel.[118] It appears, therefore, that Battaglia had successfully applied for citizenship in 1946–48 and then subsequently migrated to Canada.

Secondly, the Battaglia's travelled to Geneva in May/June 1945 for a holiday.[119] An odd choice, or an opportunity to meet up again with Carl Burckhardt, who, as Head of the International Red Cross, still worked in the city?

Thirdly, the Burckhardt link became stranger. We travelled to Geneva, some sixty-six years later in the summer of 2007. While there we met the very helpful keeper of part of the Burckhardt archive, who warned us that the files were spread across various locations and that Burckhardt had been 'very careful' about what was allowed to remain and what was removed.

It was, therefore, with the expectation of failure that we embarked on a search of his archive, hoping for, but not expecting, the evidence of a link between Burckhardt and Battaglia. We were amazed to discover a listing at the University of Basle for a 1938 letter between the two parties. After many attempts to gain approval from the modern-day guardian of the Burckhardt papers, we received a scanned copy of the original letter, together with further copies of two later letters, dated 1939 and 1940.[120] This was where matters became more bizarre. The two later letters were actually part of a dialogue from Angela Battaglia to Burckhardt requesting money! The 1938 letter:

Le 15 Novembre 1938

Cher Monsieur Battaglia,
Conformement à notre conversation téléphonique, je vous transmets avec la letter à
Monsieur le Ministre Chodaki, une letter au Ministre des Finances de la Republique
Polonaise et une annexe provisoire, dont je vous ferai parvenir l'eventuelle rectification.
    En vous remerciant de l'amiabilité que vous apportez à l'expedition de cette affaire, je
vous exprime, cher Monsieur Battaglia, l'expression de mes meilleurs sentiments.

To: Monsieur le Conseiller de Legation Dr.R.Battaglia
Commissariat General de la Republique de Pologne, Dantzig

Dear Mr Battaglia,

As we discussed on the telephone, I am sending you, along with the letter to the
minister Mr Chodaki, a letter to the Minister of Finance for the Polish Republic
and a provisional schedule, the final version of which I will send on to you.
    I thank you for your kindness in this matter and send you my best regards

To: Diplomatic Advisor Dr R. Battaglia
Commissariat Général of the Polish Republic, Danzig

This discloses a degree of friendship. The two men speak on the telephone and
they jointly deal with an issue between Mr Chodaki,[121] and the Finance Minister
of Poland. Burckhardt signs off with yours faithfully/yours sincerely. It also gives
an indication of the level at which the two men were operating. This was high
diplomacy at the epicentre of 1930s world politics that were rapidly approaching
their climax.
    The 1939 letter is very different in tone: it is from Mrs Battaglia to Burckhardt
and tells us a lot about how world events had shifted against the Battaglia family
in the intervening twelve months.

29-11-1939

Monsieur le Haut Commissaire,
Après une longue hesitation je me suis decidé de m'addresser à vous, puisque les circon-
stances tout à fait exceptionnelles, dans lesquelles je me trouve, me permettent de vous
priez de bien vouloir m'aider dans la situation très difficile de ma vie au présente ... je
n'ai pas besoin de vous décrire Monsieur le Haut Commissaire tout ce que j'ai souffert et
m'apporté dès le jour, où j'étais obligée de quitter Dantzig, puisque certainement vous le

savez. Maintenant nous sommes en France, où mon Mari s'est engagé comme volontaire à l'armée polonaise qui se forme en Bretagne, et moi, je vie dans une petite ville au bord de l'Atlantique dans des conditions tres modèstes – Puisque en quittant la Pologne, nous n'avons pas pu nos ne rien prendre avec nous, et mon Mari est au camp d'instruction au commencement et comme simple soldat … et ne gagne rien alors notre situation materielle est très difficile et penible. C'est pour cette raison que je me permets de m'adresser à votre grande volonté Le Haut Commissaire en vous priant bien sincèrement de bien vouloir nous prêter un peu d'argent pour cette période si dure de notre vie. Naturellement la grandeur de cette somme dépende tout à fait de votre bonne volonté. Monsieur Le Haut Commissaire, et vous pouvez être tout à fait sur que dès que notre situation va s'ameliorer, nous ferons tout notre possible pour vous rendre cette somme avec notre plus grand reconnaissance-

Croyez moi aussi Monsieur le Haut Commissaire, que si je m'adresse à vous avec cette grande prière, c'est vraiment notre … est très difficile, et je suis persuadé que vous allez me comprendre …

En attendant votre aimable reponse et avec toute ma confiance, je vous envoie Monsieur le Haut Commissaire mes salutations les plus distinguées.

Angela de Battaglia
Les Sables d'Olonne (Vendee)
45 Quai G Clemenceau
France

Dear High Commissioner,

After hesitating for some time, I have resolved to contact you. The altogether exceptional circumstances I find myself in mean that I must take the liberty of asking if you would help me in the very difficult situation that is affecting my life at the present time … I need not describe to you, Sir, everything that I have suffered and borne since the day I was forced to leave Danzig, for I am sure you already know. We are now in France, where my husband has joined the Polish Army that has been forming in Britain, and I am living in a small town on the Atlantic coast on very limited means – since on leaving Poland we were unable to bring anything with us, and my husband has just started at the training camp as an ordinary private … and earns nothing, so our financial situation is difficult and frustrating. It is for this reason that I venture to appeal to your goodwill, Sir, by asking you, in all sincerity, if you would lend us a small amount of money in this difficult period of our life. Naturally the size of this loan is entirely at your discretion, Sir, and you can be entirely confident that as soon as our situation improves we will do everything we can to repay the sum, with all of our gratitude.

Please also believe, Sir, that if I am writing this petition to you it is truly [because our situation] … is very difficult, and because I am convinced that you will understand.

I await your response with every confidence, and send you my best regards.

Angela de Battaglia

The 1940 letter:

Sables d'Olonne Vendee
15-1-1940
45 Quai Clemenceau

Cher Monsieur Le Haut Commissaire – je vous demande bien pardon, que je suis si en retard avec ma réponse, mais j'ai l'impression, et ça me fait une grande peine que vous n'avez pas assez de confiance en nous-

Si, je me suis adressé à vous Monsieur, c'est que vous étiez à Dantzig, que vous avez bien connu moi et mon mari, aussi son travail et sa valeur personnelle, et j'étais persuadée que vous allez bien comprendre la grande difficulté de notre vie actuelle –

Je comprends très bien que notre situation est tout à fait differente maintenant, mais à present je peux vous assurer Monsieur, qu' encore au courant de cette année j'aurai la possibilité de vous rendre votre aimable service, puisque dans quelques mois je vais commencer à travailler dans notre Ministere des Aff.Etr à Angers … A cause de celui je peux m'adresser encore une fois à vous monsieur en vous priant de tout mon coeur de bien vouloir me prêter encore 4 milles francs; ils me sont undispensables, puisque je me trouve sans aucune réserve, et je suis obligée de m'acheter une bonne machine à écrire et de m'occuper un peu de ma santé et de mes choses …

Je vous donne ma parole d'honneur que je vous rendrai cette somme de 6 (six) milles francs, dans 6 mois (je pourrais verser à votre conto mille francs chaque mois) – dès le commencement de mon travail au Ministère –

Vous êtes monsieur le seul homme à qui je peux m'adresser avec cette prière. Je vous serai infinissement reconnaissante et croyez moi Monsieur que j'ai vraiment énormement besoin de l'argent parce que même pour une femme c'est une chose infinissement penible et difficile de prier pour cette raison –

Je vous envoie Monsieur mes respecteuses et sincères salutations.

Angela De Battaglia

Dear High Commissioner – please accept my apologies that my reply is so late, but I feel, and it pains me, that you do not have sufficient faith in us.

My reasons for approaching you, Sir, were that you were in Danzig, you knew me and my husband, his work, and our reputation well, and I was sure that you would appreciate the great difficulties of our life at this time.

I fully understand that our circumstances are completely different now, but I can assure you, Sir, that even in the course of this year I will have the opportunity to repay your kind gesture, as in a few months I will start work in our Ministry of Foreign Affairs … in light of this, may I once again approach you and ask you, from the bottom of my heart, to please lend me another 4,000 francs; it is imperative, as I have no funds, and I must buy myself a good typewriter and take care of my health and other matters.

I give you my word that I will repay you this sum of 6,000 francs in six months (I can transfer 1,000 francs a month into your account) after I start my job at the ministry.

You are, Sir, the only man of whom I can ask this favour. I will be eternally grateful, and please believe, Sir, that I am really in great need of this money, for, even for a woman it is infinitely distressing and difficult to have to beg for this reason.

I send you, sir, my sincere and respectful regards.

Angela De Battaglia

Once again the letters are wholly consistent with the Home Office file that records Battaglia's postings while in Britain. According to the file, the Battaglias fled to France when Poland was invaded in September 1939. As the 1939 letter reveals, they went to Angers, near Paris, which had become the temporary base for the Polish government in exile. Mrs Battaglia appears to have resided at Les Sables d'Olonne, on the coast, some 160km from Angers. It was from 45 Quai Clemenceau that she corresponded with Carl Burckhardt.

In June 1940, her husband had left France for England with the Polish Army. He is described as a 'simple soldier'. On 1 July 1940 he took up residence at 'Faside', Newton Mearns, Renfrewshire, Scotland (Landlord: Mr Fairweather) and it was from this address that he travelled to Giffnock Scout hut on the night of 10 May 1941. 'Faside' is a large house on Ayr Road, Newton Mearns, the owners of which became the Barr family of Irn-Bru drink fame.

He had by this time been seconded from the army to the Polish consulate in Glasgow, being recorded as the assistant consul, working from 91 Hill Street, Glasgow.[122] Technically, he was the honorary consul as he was still in the army, but in January 1941 he was discharged on the grounds of ill health. However, he remained in Glasgow. Is this just a cover story for a transfer to Polish intelligence?

His role was recorded as liaison between the Polish government and the Department of Health in Scotland, together with a more suitable role as assistant legal advisor to the Polish Foreign Office. It appears that his main role consisted of dealing with the mass of Polish refugees that were making their way to Britain following the Fall of France.[123] Is there perhaps a synergy between this role and that of the Red Cross?

In October 1941, five months after the Hess affair, he was transferred to London and resided firstly at 49 Hallam Street in Mayfair and then, after 1943, in Acton and Ealing. When making his application for citizenship, he was residing at 111 The Avenue, Ealing, in a house he co-owned with a Mieczyslaw Habibcht. Battaglia was working for the BBC, having left the Polish government because 'he was not in sympathy with political changes in Poland'.[124]

We do not know when he was re-united with his wife. Clearly, in November 1939 and January 1940 she was residing on the Atlantic coast of France under threat of impending German occupation. Perhaps the reunion was the purpose of the recorded holiday to France in May 1945. Perhaps they had already been reunited in Scotland or London. Perhaps the holiday's purpose was to repay a debt to Burckhardt. We simply do not know. In September 1945, Battaglia was earning the sum of £580 per year from the BBC, so presumably he could afford to repay the debt.

So a leading Polish diplomat, a close friend of Burckhardt and Sikorski, is the first person to interview Hess on arrival.[125] We even began to wonder if the Hess affair was a Polish initiative.

There is another aspect of the Burckhardt story that belies the image of the stuffed shirt diplomat. Diana Cooper, who was at the time married to Alfred Duff Cooper (1890–1954), embarked on a love affair with Carl Burckhardt during 1938/1939. At the time, Diana was married to the recently resigned First Lord of the Admiralty,[126] Duff Cooper, who eventually became Minister of Information in the wartime coalition. In August 1938, Diana Cooper had travelled with her husband on board the Admiralty yacht, HMS *Enchantress*, to the Baltic. Danzig was a port of call and it was there that she renewed her acquaintance with Burckhardt.[127] The affair appears to have continued throughout 1939 and Ziegler notes that Burckhardt came to London in October 1939. We think this affair with a married woman, the wife of an eminent British politician, paints a different picture of the very formal Swiss historian.

Burckhardt as the Intermediary

Switzerland in wartime was, as always, the country where deals were done, where the belligerents on both sides could meet, talk and frequently double cross each other. (*Colonel 'Z' – The Secret Life of a Master of Spies*)[128]

In August 1939, as described, Carl Burckhardt was summoned by Hitler, directly reporting back to the British. In October, he visited Britain, after which he returned to Geneva to take up his professorship at the Graduate Institute of International Studies.

We will reflect upon two unlikely visitors that made their way to Geneva during late 1940/early 1941. As well as his professorship, Burckhardt maintained close associations with the International Red Cross, also based in Geneva. From reading *Dunant's Dream*, it appears that Burckhardt and Lucie Odier master-minded the organisation and structure of the Relief Committee.

Visitor No. 1 was Professor Tancred Borenius.

The diaries of former German Ambassador to Rome Ulrich von Hassell were published as early as 1948,[129] in an attempt to demonstrate to the recently victorious peoples of the Western Alliance that not all Germans were pro-Nazi and pro-Hitler. The diaries were seen as part of the post-war healing process.

Ulrich von Hassell (1888–1944) was executed following the failed July 1944 attempt on Hitler's life. His diaries from 1938 to the date of his death record the various approaches that were made to Nazi Germany through various countries and persons in an attempt to forge a peace. His January 1941 entry records the fact that Carl Burckhardt had 'looked [him] up in Geneva' to tell him that 'very recently' Tancred Borenius had come to him to explain, 'apparently on behalf of English officials, that a reasonable peace could still be concluded'. The use of the word 'apparently' is intriguing. The author had doubts.

We believe this visit was the real catalyst for the Hess flight, not the earlier 'Roberts letter' as the Germans would, or should, have anticipated that any 'ghosted reply' would have been intercepted by the censor. A direct approach was both necessary and vital. It was really the only way that a non-governmental peace approach could be efficiently communicated in time of war, orchestrated by Dansey/MI6 or not. We should also record that the visit by Frank Foley to Lisbon took place at the same time as Borenius would be travelling to Geneva. This may or may not be related.

The 1948 edition of the Von Hassell diaries described Tancred Borenius as having 'very intimate connections with …' (deliberately left blank). The 2011 edition is much more forthcoming by disclosing: 'He has very intimate connections with the Royal House (principally the Queen).' This raises the question as to who Tancred Borenius claimed to be representing. Was he even appearing to be an emissary of the British royal family?

Carl Tancred Borenius (1885–1948) was born at Viipuri, Finland, modern Vyborg, Russia. He died at Coombe Bissett, near Salisbury in Wiltshire, UK. He was an Italian renaissance scholar, art dealer and art magazine editor. Borenius was the son of Carl Borenius, a member of the Diet of Finland (the legislative assembly 1808–1906). After receiving his Ph.D from Helsingfors in 1909, he moved to London where he published a version of his dissertation, *Painters of Vincenza* (1909). The same year he married Anne-Marie Rüneberg, granddaughter of the Finnish poet J. L. Rüneberg. Roger Fry became a close friend, providing him entré into the art circles of London. He was appointed lecturer at University College, London, in the position vacated by Fry. When Finland achieved independence, he acted as secretary of the diplomatic mission (1918) and later as representative of Finland in London (1919). From 1922–47, he was Durning-Lawrence Professor at University College. Borenius' opinion on art was highly valued in England. After admission to the Burlington Fine Arts Club, he contributed many articles to the *Burlington Magazine*, and was the editor from 1940 to 1945. By then, Borenius was no longer considered reliable on attributions at Sotheby's (and considered himself too grand to do the work of cataloguing) and was replaced in 1945.

Borenius was 'non-governmental'. He relied on direct contact and, as such, was also beyond direct governmental control, or the illusion of direct governmental control. He could not be censored and, because of his Finnish nationality, could travel relatively unhindered through occupied Europe. He was the ideal messenger to the 'neutral intermediary' (Burckhardt) that Hess was suggesting in his letter of September 1940 to the Haushofers. Why else is a 56-year-old Finnish art expert travelling through enemy-occupied Europe in 1941 in order to visit Carl Burckhardt?

Lars Ulrich, known as Peter, was the son of Tancred Borenius.[130] According to Peter, his father's wartime trip had caused some later amusement in the Borenius household on two accounts: firstly, because he had been asked to deliver a 'book' to Burckhardt; and secondly, he had been given a poison pill the size of a golf ball. The family thought that Borenius would choke on the pill long before the supposed poison would take effect. Borenius had apparently passed through Geneva on his way to Italy. He also said that he had been given the book by Claude Dansey, prior to his departure. Claude Dansey was the deputy head of MI6, who were in the process of rebuilding their credibility following the loss of their 'Passport Office System' of intelligence at the outbreak of the war.[131]

Much later we also spoke to Aurelia, the granddaughter of Tancred Borenius. She was very kind and added to our knowledge of her intriguing ancestor. The brief CV reproduced above does not really do justice to Tancred Borenius. His granddaughter says he was extremely well connected, a brilliant raconteur, but wholly impractical; he could not drive for instance. Osbert Lancaster, in a *Daily Mail* cartoon, portrayed him as a rather plump eccentric. He thoroughly enjoyed mixing with, cultivating and advising the upper classes. He became art advisor to the Harewood Family (Viscount Lascelles, 6th Earl of Harewood had married Princess Mary, the only sister to Princes David, Albert, Henry, John and

George, in 1922), but this certainly does not appear to be his only commission from the rich and famous in 1930s England. We also now have the intriguing connection to the Queen, via the Von Hassell diary.

He acted for the Methuen Family[132] of Corsham Court in north Wiltshire, and the National Portrait Gallery hold photographs of Borenius with Phillip and Ottoline Morrell,[133] prominent members of the 'Bloomsbury Set'. He catalogued the porcelain collection of Frederick Leverton Harris[134] and occasionally acted as a dealer, buying and selling works of art for the rich and formerly rich. Borenius cultivated royal connections; in 1922 he sent the Duke and Duchess of York a copy of his latest book, *Travels in Italy*, as a wedding present. In 1936, Prince George and Princess Marina visited Wiltshire, staying at Wilton House over the weekend of 11/12 July. On the Saturday, it was recorded that the couple met Tancred Borenius in Salisbury Close.

Two weeks later, he was presented to the King, this time in a diplomatic capacity. Aurelia Borenius told John Harris that, as he grew older he, not unnaturally, rediscovered his political energy, largely on account of what was happening in Eastern Europe. In 1939, his sister had to abandon the family home in Wiborg and escape from the invading Russian forces.

On 7 December 1937, the Duke of Kent was the principal guest at the Anglo-Finnish Society. Tancred replied to the duke's toast. In 1940, he was recorded as a member of the Executive Committee. On 23 September 1941, he addressed the Royal Institute for International Affairs at Chatham House on the subject of 'The Eastern Frontier of Finland and the East Carelian situation'.[135] It will be remembered that Albrecht Haushofer had also addressed the institute in 1937. In May 1939, he attended a reception at the Swedish legation. Baron Knut Bonde was also recorded as being present.

A year later, we suspect he briefly returned to the art world. On 19 May 1940, nine days after the German invasion of the Low Countries, there was a major art sale in London. The Duke of Kent purchased 'The Altieri Claudes', two classical Italian paintings by Claude Lorraine from the late seventeenth century. The duke paid £3,990 and £840 respectively for the two paintings that were previously sold for £6,090 and £1,785 in 1884. The proximity of the Wehrmacht to London perhaps had a depressing effect on 1940 prices. We do not know for sure that Borenius was involved in the purchase, but given that the two men certainly knew each other by this time, and the paintings were exactly in Borenius' sphere of expertise, it is certainly not inconceivable that he was involved. In 1947, the executors of the duke's estate sold the paintings for a healthy profit.

Tancred Borenius' sister had married into a Polish family and, given his dislike of all things Russian, Borenius became Honorary Secretary General of the Polish Relief Fund; the headquarters of the fund was at 10 Grosvenor Place, London, SW1.

On 1 May 1940, the magazine of the British College of Nursing recorded Tancred Borenius bidding farewell to a group of Canadian Poles embarking on a foreign mission.

This organisation was clearly substantial. The British government had contributed £100,000 in clothing and other forms of relief. It was through this organisation that Borenius came to meet and know General Sikorski. It must also say something about Borenius that the Honorary Secretary General of the Polish Relief Fund was not Polish.

However, as Ulrich von Hassell records, when Burckhardt met with Borenius in Geneva, Borenius went through and recited the usual peace demands: restoration of Holland and Belgium, some kind of Poland etc. Then came the inevitable stumbling block: '... one was highly reluctant to make peace with Hitler. The main reason, one simply can't believe a word he says'. Hassell continued, 'The English Consul General had also told Burckhardt the same thing.'

We have already stated how Lars Borenius had told the authors that, before embarking to Geneva, his father had been briefed by Claude Dansey and given a book to deliver, together with the impractical suicide pill.

Why the pill for a visiting art historian? We can only conclude that he was in possession of information that would render the use of the pill necessary were he to be captured. How did he travel to Switzerland? If he was travelling independently, then the only route available to him would be England/Lisbon/Spain/Vichy France/Switzerland. We have already considered if Frank Foley was helping his passage.

Stockholm was too dangerous. Fast air flights in and out only commenced in late 1941 and the subsequent travel through Germany would be fraught. We really cannot see Claude Dansey arranging to drop Tancred from an aircraft, and even if he did, this immediately implies a government-sponsored approach, which is exactly not what was intended. All governmental peace feelers had failed.

However, we now believe that MI6 had arranged passage for Tancred, through the only route available to him. Was he accompanied all or part of the way?

The Role of Claude Dansey

Claude Dansey was described to John Harris by Lars Borenius, as being the man that had briefed his father prior to the Geneva trip in 1941. Dansey (1876–1947) was the epitome of a British Secret Service agent. Devious, untrustworthy, according to Hugh Trevor Roper: 'Dansey was an utter shit ...'[136] Dansey had endured a strange childhood under a dominant father, had many siblings and was allegedly assaulted when aged 16 by one of Oscar Wilde's lovers. However, 'shit' or not, he rose to become the deputy head of SIS, or MI6. At the end of the war, he was showered with honours from around the world, and Anthony Read and David Fisher make the case that, while deputy to Stewart Menzies, it was Dansey who was the real 'power behind the throne'. An Intelligence Officer since 1900, he was certainly astute enough to realise that the traditional European 'Passport Office' system made MI6 very vulnerable to the effects of invasion, which is precisely what happened in 1940.

Consequently, throughout the 1930s he had effectively established an alternative, the 'Z' system. The 'Z' system relied on individual intelligence gathering, often using established businesses as a 'front'.

Nigel West[137] deals with this method of working and details some 'front' companies: Menoline Limited; H. Sichel & Sons (wine merchants); Lamnin Tours (holidays); and Sir Geoffrey Duveen & Company.

It was this last company that aroused our interest, as Nigel West/Rupert Allason described the company as 'International Fine Art Dealers': precisely the same title as used by Tancred Borenius. Geoffrey Duveen was actually a practising barrister and nephew to Lord Duveen, having recently left the art dealing company. Duveen's office was adjacent to that of Claude Dansey on the eighth floor of the north-west wing of Bush House, together with the other 'front companies' that Dansey and MI6 hid behind.

The art dealing company had made significant amounts of money by selling European art to wealthy US citizens in the latter part of the nineteenth and first half of the twentieth century. The archives of the company are well catalogued and are housed at the Getty Research Institute, Los Angeles. Microfilm 466 (208) is a copy of Box 353, which holds the correspondence between Borenius and the company.

Borenius was well known to the Duveens. For instance, on 9 July 1938, Geoffrey and Tancred both attended an exhibition of twentieth-century German art at the Burlington Galleries. On 3 May 1938, they had attended the opening night of the opera 'Die Zauberflote' at Covent Garden. *The Times* newspaper recorded that Borenius had 'completed the Royal party'. Borenius was more of an academic than Duveen and, together with Bernard Berenson, was used to authenticate or attribute, with varying degrees of success. Typically, Borenius would catalogue works that Duveen would then buy and sell on.[138]

So, we can clearly demonstrate a link between Borenius and a company associated with MI6. We should also not forget that Carl was the grandson of Jacob Burckhardt (1818–1893), the famous art historian of art and, indeed, Carl himself initially studied art history at university. It does appear that art certainly was, *prima facie*, a common thread that bound the attendees at the 1941 meeting.

However, when living in Switzerland between 1934 and 1936, Dansey was not interested in art. Some time in 1934/35, Dansey had apparently been thrown out of the Intelligence Services on account of some financial irregularity, but this now seems to have been a cover whilst he was in the process of building a parallel intelligence system, well away from the constraints of the traditional 'passport control'.

Switzerland was an ideal choice for a base and Dansey worked quickly. Soon there were offices in Basle, Geneva, Zurich, Lausanne and Lugano. This time the information gathering would be based on people and businesses, not control systems. Many of the notable intelligence successes eventually came via the Swiss offices, such as the 'Lucy Ring' and the contact with Admiral Canaris. As Read and Fisher state: 'Dansey's most important station – particularly in the early part of the war – remained Switzerland.'

At the outbreak of the war, Dansey returned to London, partly to chaperone Menzies, partly to pick up the pieces after the Venlo affair finally blew the pre-war network apart. Dansey was in Britain during January 1941, so he was able to brief Tancred Borenius.

However, who was Tancred really delivering messages for? We now think it likely that the 23 September Haushofer/Hamilton letter was answered by MI6 on behalf of Hamilton, probably doing no more than suggesting that Borenius come to Geneva to meet with Burckhardt for further discussions. The Borenius/Burckhardt meeting had to be pre-arranged, particularly in the middle of a war.

Had Claude Edward Marjoribanks Dansey and his organisation already made contact with Carl Burckhardt? Given the interception of the Haushofer letter, was Albrecht Haushofer also on the payroll of His Majesty's government? Chatham House worked closely with MI6;[139] Haushofer was a frequent visitor to Britain throughout the 1930s and his true views of the Führer and the Nazis would have been known to a number of high-ranking Britons. Switzerland in 1940/41 was crowded with SIS agents. Would it really be so surprising if, in another century, when the PRO reluctantly release some MI6 files from the Second World War, we learned that Borenius, Burckhardt and Haushofer were actually British agents? We do not think so.

Albrecht Haushofer and his Travels, Spring 1941

Much detail is known about Albrecht Haushofer, our second traveller, and yet very little is known about his true motives. Both works by James Douglas-Hamilton centre on him and his role in the affair.[140] We have already recorded Haushofer's pre-war meetings with the Marquis of Clydesdale (as he was then known) and the Roberts family. By giving Haushofer the prominence in the affair he does, James Douglas-Hamilton inevitably implies his father played a prominent role in the affair, which he then tries to downplay. This seems odd. We would now like to centre on his role as the 1940/41 messenger/middleman/roving reporter: in part, a German equivalent to Tancred Borenius; in part an advisor to the German deputy leader. There are similarities between the two men: Borenius, we believe, was probably delivering a set of proposals to Burckhardt in 1941, for onward transmission to Germany. Haushofer, in turn, was happy to receive and forward them to Hess, but knew enough already to suspect that, ultimately, they would never work. The interesting question is whether he allowed, or even encouraged, Hess to continue, knowing that his mission was never going to succeed.

What we do know is that Albrecht Haushofer had been very busy in the spring of 1941. We have already seen how he was instrumental in the exchange of correspondence in September 1940, instigated by Rudolf Hess. From 2–5 February 1941, Albrecht had visited Stockholm. It will be remembered that the Duke of Hamilton was at Lesbury, Northumberland, from 25 January–4 February 1941. Also, Tancred Borenius had been recently despatched to Geneva, which we assume was also at the middle/end of January 1941.

It is far too easy to speculate on what was happening here, so we will allow the reader to consider the possibilities. We have yet to discover how Borenius travelled to Switzerland, but assume it must have been via Lisbon, Spain and Vichy France. Of possible relevance in this regard is the fact that Frank Foley, head of the German section of MI6, flew to Lisbon on 17 January 1941 with his secretary, returning on 1 February.[141] It would appear possible that Foley was either helping Borenius on his way, or attending a meeting himself. Between 21 and 24 February, Haushofer was with Hess. On 10 March, he met Von Hassell in Berlin. From 12–15 April, he was back with Hess in Berlin, and again on 26 April, this time accompanied by his father.

Two days later, on 28 April 1941, he met Carl Burckhardt in Geneva. There is also speculation as to whether he had met Samuel Hoare in Spain (and/or Geneva) in April 1941, but Haushofer's protégé Stahmer certainly had. Lord Halifax was also in attendance, if Stahmer is to be believed.

Whether Haushofer (and indeed Hess) had met with Hoare and Halifax in Spain we will have to wait until 2017 to know, as the relevant files are currently embargoed. In any event, Haushofer's almost manic travels (in the middle of a war) indicate frantic activity. Doing what?

We know from letters to and from his parents that, while he felt the flight was a 'fool's errand', he was pleased with the 28 April meeting. Whether this was because he thought he could convince Hess to fly – for whatever motive or reason – we may never know.

Finally, there is the behaviour of the Nazi leadership in the days leading up to the flight. It is well reported that Hitler and Hess met on 4 May 1941, just before Hitler was to make a major speech to the Reichstag. According to Franz Lutz's later interrogation reports, [142] Hitler materially changed the contents of the speech to accommodate the implications of a telephone call from Karl Haushofer, who was in Berlin. It is unlikely that we shall ever know the precise edits that were made, but a review of the speech is enlightening.

While appearing to be a justification of the 1941 German position, it is actually a vitriolic attack on Winston Churchill, the man who stands between Hitler and peace with the West. Hitler spoke of 'Churchill, one of the most hopeless dabblers in strategy ... He, the most bloodthirsty or amateurish strategist that history has ever known ... The gift Mr. Churchill possesses is the gift to lie with a pious expression on his face and to distort the truth until finally glorious victories are made out of the most terrible defeats.'

On one level, this attack can be wholly understood, but we now wonder if the speech was directly aimed at that part of British society that could actually influence the position by their actions. The speech is basically saying, 'get Churchill out of the way' and we can have peace. We suspect that Hitler might well have meant it.

After the speech had been delivered in Berlin, Hess left for Augsburg by overnight train and met Albrecht Haushofer the following Monday morning, 5 May 1941. No doubt the recent meeting with Carl Burckhardt was high on the agenda. On 9 May, Hess requested that Alfred Rosenberg fly to Munich the next day. We know that the two men lunched together, prior to Hess's departure later that afternoon.

The book *Secret and Personal* by F. W. Winterbotham details the close friendship of these two men. They were seen as 'old comrades', as their friendship went back to before 1923, in the formative days of the Nazi Party. Hess and Rosenberg were seen as the thinkers; Hitler, the implementer. *Secret and Personal* also details the channel established between Rosenberg and Winterbotham, via Baron William de Ropp. Winterbotham states: 'Hitler seemed to have a soft spot for airmen ... there was still some glamour attached to the fliegers.'

It seems that the final luncheon meeting was for one of two reasons: either a matter of discussing what was possible in terms of peace, or more likely, Alfred Rosenberg was being used as a communication channel to whoever in England was furthering the negotiations – real or imagined.

Finally, we have the story of Hermann Göring phoning Adolf Galland, the Luftwaffe fighter ace who was stationed on the French coast, and asking that he shoot Hess down. Apparently this call was at 10.00 p.m., on the evening of 10 May 1941 and begs the question as to how Göring knew about the 'solo flight'. If the head of the Luftwaffe knew of Hess' intentions, who else knew? It now appears to us to be a foolish notion that Hess acted alone in making the flight to Britain.

PART 2

THE AIRCRAFT FOR THE FLIGHT

Part 1 of this book has dealt with the rationale and motivations behind Rudolf Hess' decision to fly to Scotland in May 1941. It has drawn on such documentation that is available to piece together the sequence of events from 31 August 1940– 10 May 1941.

There is still an incomplete paper trail. Some British Foreign Office files dealing with meetings in Madrid in early 1941 are still withheld. Royal papers are outside the scope of the Freedom of Information Act, and our most recent request to see the papers Hess brought with him simply produced a listing that we had already obtained from the PRO search engine. The 1941 diary of the Duke of Hamilton is apparently missing and there is confusion about the number of Hess' maps given to the family.

We are particularly concerned that the recent 'official history' of MI6 makes no mention of the Hess affair, despite John Harris having been told of Claude Dansey's involvement by Lars Borenius. Furthermore, the 2004 partial publication of Kay Foley's diaries also place MI6 firmly in the spotlight, in particular with regards to her husband, Frank, and his role in the Rudolf Hess story.

Indeed, the 2013 auction, in the United States, of a MI6 file, taken by Sir Maurice Oldfield (Head of MI6 1973–78) to prevent its destruction, does raise serious issues as to the accountability of the security services. (The file failed to reach its $750,000 reserve.)

If the evidence is not as yet forthcoming from these bodies, for whatever reason, alternative evidence will have to be obtained from sources that are currently available and to which access is allowed. This is not evidence of any 'conspiracy theory', but is merely stating a fact. In Part 2, we now concentrate on the flight, to try and garner such clues from the technical aspects as to provide evidence of the 'character' of the flight.

The authors firmly belive that an analysis of the aircraft, flight and the background shows yet again the Hess flight was anything but a 'solo mission'. It was extremely well planned, as it needed to be, and required considerable input from various German agencies if it was to succeed. This input alone raises obvious questions as to the level of German involvement. We start this alternative analysis by examining the aircraft.

6. THE HESS AIRCRAFT

Doubts have surrounded the identification of the Hess aircraft ever since the crash on the night of 10 May 1941. At 2225hrs, Mr G.W. Green, head observer at Royal Observer Corps (ROC), Chatton (Post 30/A3), Northumberland, correctly observed the silhouette of a Messerschmitt Bf 110, heading fast inland from the North Sea. He reported the observation to his Durham control, which duly passed on the information to No. 13 Group, RAF Fighter Command. The controller 'Considered it to be a ridiculous report and thought that the aircraft might be a Dornier 17'.[1]

This opinion was vented because a Bf 110 was known to not have the range to return to Germany. Quite how the alternative conclusion was reached, that the aircraft was Dornier 17/215, may also require scrutiny, as its range (it also was a twin-engined aircraft) was little different to that of the Bf 110.

However, the aircraft that Mr Green had identified was a Bf 110, manufactured by the *Messerschmitt Aktiengesellchaft* in Augsburg, Bavaria. The *Bayerische Flugzeugwerke AG* (BF) had been taken over by Messerschmitt in July 1938, though designs such as the 109 and 110 retained their 'Bf' nomenclature on account of the date of their earlier initial design. It was only later, when Messerschmitt AG submitted designs under its own name that the 'Me' descriptor was solely used.[2]

In the spring of 1935, the *Bayerische Flugzeugwerke*, along with the Junkers, Focke-Wulf and Henschel companies, had been invited to tender by the RLM for the design and production of a 'new high-speed bomber', armed with just a single machine gun and able to carry a 500kg bomb load at a speed of 311mph. The prototype Bf 110 V-1 was first flown from Augsburg airfield on 12 May 1936.

In order to properly analyse the flight that Rudolf Hess undertook, five years after the initial flight of this aircraft, it is important to establish the precise type and model of the Bf 110 that was used. It is only after this identification that one can then try to establish exactly what was and what was not possible.

The last of the type, the Bf 110 G-4, was produced between October and December 1943. The specification of this last aircraft was naturally very different to the 1936 prototype. The prototype had two Junkers Jumo 210A engines, whereas the G-4 was fitted with the much more powerful Daimler-Benz supercharged engine. The Jumo engine produced 680hp,[3] the DB 603E engine 1,800hp.[4] Precise identification is therefore vital, as fuel consumption and range varied dramatically.

Bf 110 fuselage, showing the remnants of the Siemens K4ü autopilot mechanism.

Most early authors on the Hess affair are a little vague. We have already recounted how in *Attack Warning Red* (the history of the Royal Observer Corps, published 1976), Derek Wood tells how even the basic Bf 110 identification was challenged. In 1954, Ilse Hess described the aircraft as: 'The then most modern type of pursuit aircraft, the Me110.' In 1962, James Leasor describes it as 'A Me110, flying at 180mph.'[5] In 1986 Wolf Hess: '... his Me110.'[6] In 1971 James Douglas-Hamilton: 'Messerschmitt 110.'[7]

In 1979, Hugh Thomas created a media storm when he suggested that Hess, then in Spandau, was not the same Hess that arrived in Scotland in 1941. As is now well known, he cited the fact that the Hess in Spandau was apparently missing some scars brought about by a gunshot wound that he had received in the First World War.[8] Having made the case that the real Hess had been murdered en route, Thomas then went on to analyse the flight by the performance of the aircraft. Unfortunately, he gets the production type wrong; speculating on a type D (but in fairness, not ruling out an E).

The next step forward then came in 1993, when Lord James Douglas-Hamilton had a second attempt in explaining the affair in *The Truth about Rudolf Hess*. Douglas-Hamilton commissioned Roy Conyers Nesbit, an expert on Second World War aviation, to write an introduction to the book, specifically dealing with the flight. In the introduction the aircraft is described as 'a Messerschmitt Bf 110, radio code VJ+OQ, works number 3869.'

This contradicts Hugh Thomas, who quoted the *Werknummer* (works number) as 3526. We now believe that new evidence has come to light that proves the Hess aircraft that crashed in Scotland to be a Bf 110E/2-N, works number 3869, radio code VJ+OQ.

The first piece of new evidence is contained within the excellent book *Zerstörer* by John Vasco and Peter D. Cornwell.[9] At the end of the book is a schedule of losses. On 18 August 1940, a Bf 110C is recorded as having crashed, being shot down off Clacton, Essex, by Pilot Officer Gray of No. 54 Squadron. The pilot, Hubert Luttke, and his radio operator/observer, Herbert Brillo, were both killed. The works number of the Bf 110 is given as 3526.

Most written works cite the fact that Hess had tested a number of Bf 110 aircraft prior to the flight in May 1941. It would appear that the aircraft with the works number 3526 was not the Bf 110 in which he made his flight, but simply an earlier test aircraft. This machine had subsequently crashed.

Roy Conyers Nesbit also quotes the flight diary of Helmut Kaden, a Messerschmitt test pilot. His diary clearly shows that works number 3869 is the 'Hess maschine'. It should, however, be noted that this description is written in a different hand to the rest of the diary.

The second piece of evidence is in *Messerschmitt Bf 110/Me210/Me410* by Heinz Mankau and Peter Petrick.[10] This detailed record of development recreates production records. The originals were apparently lost in a bombing raid on Augsburg in 1944. This shows that aircraft 3526 was produced as part of a batch (numbered 3487–3563) at the MIAG works between May and July 1940.[11] Being the thirty-ninth out of a batch of seventy-seven aircraft, it is quite likely that this was the machine built in June that crashed in August 1940.

Similarly, we are told by the authors that number 3869 was built at the Messerschmitt works, Augsburg between October and December 1940, as part of a batch (3817–3889). This seems to agree with Roy Conyers Nesbit's assertion that Hess chose his final aircraft around Christmas 1940. This viewpoint is given further weight when Mankau and Petrick list the Bf 110 prototypes. The prototype with works number 3862 is given the delivery code of VJ+OJ. It was listed as being a Bf 110 E-1. Sequentially:

3863 becomes VJ+OK
3864 becomes VJ+OL
3865 becomes VJ+OM
3866 becomes VJ+ON
3867 becomes VJ+OO
3868 becomes VJ+OP
And 3869 becomes VJ+OQ, which is the Bf 110 that crashed in Scotland.

The aircraft was a Bf 110E, taken straight from the production line. Roy Conyers Nesbit gives the production date of 3869 as 21 November 1940. After a few weeks of air testing, the aircraft would be placed on a delivery availability list. According to Conyers Nesbit, again quoting Helmut Kaden, the Messerschmitt test pilot, Hess, chose 3869 and thereafter did not fly another Bf 110.

Rudolf Hess had acquired his aircraft.

A Precise Specification

Roy Conyers Nesbit and George van Acker completed their 1999 identification of the aircraft by carefully detecting that, in certain pictures of the crash site, the fuselage revealed a groove running along the top, front to back. This groove carried a control cable, operated from the rear cabin, which allowed a *Schlauchboot* (inflatable dinghy) to be released from a storage area at the end of the fuselage. The fuselage was especially extended to facilitate this modification, albeit only on two types of Bf 110, the D-3 and E-2.

In addition, the fuselage (which is currently at the Imperial War Museum, Duxford, while its London site is being refurbished) has a vent on the starboard side to allow fresh air to the *Kabinenheizanlage* (cabin heating system). The heating system had been re-introduced on the Bf 110E. Therefore, by a process of elimination, the aircraft was identified as a Bf 110E-2/N.

The 'N' designation is a classification of the type of Daimler-Benz DB 601 engine used to power the machine. As well as an alphabetic type descriptor, it also means the engine was configured to run on 100 Octane, C3 fuel. The 'N' is marked on the engines in white paint and would have been similarly marked on the fuel fillers to avoid potentially dangerous mistakes when refuelling.[12] Correspondence between Messerschmitt AG and the *Generalluftzeugmeister* reveals that the DB 601N engines were in short supply during October/November 1940 and that the Bf 109 should have priority. The Bf 110 was to be fitted with the earlier (and less powerful) DB 601A engine. The fact that the Hess aircraft was fitted with the DB 601N engine would appear to show an anomaly in the then current production regime. We have no evidence to indicate influence from any particular outside agency in this decision.

Engine and Carburation

Apart from the fledgling turbo-jet engines of 1940/41, the Daimler-Benz DB 601N was one of the most modern, sophisticated and powerful engines in world aviation.

The DB 601 was developed from the earlier DB 600 series of Daimler–Benz aero engines designed in the early 1930s. By late 1940, the engine had been developed to give the following power statistics: at ground level, 1,159hp at 2,600rpm; at 6,890ft altitude, 1,253hp at 2,600rpm. The British-built Rolls–Royce Merlin XX, which had been in production since July 1940, produced 1,480hp at 3,000rpm.

Both Daimler–Benz and Rolls–Royce were developing their engine power output by the use of supercharging, whereby air is pressurised prior to entering the combustion chamber. The use of 100 Octane fuel was also being developed. The British had found that 100 Octane fuel consequently generated much higher operating temperatures and so had developed a water/glycol mix to cool the engine more efficiently. If the engines were allowed to run too lean (fuel-to-air mixture) the pistons in the engine could be damaged, with disastrous consequences.

However, there were two main differences: firstly, the German engine was an inverted design, with remote oil sumps; and secondly, the method of carburation was different. The British (at that time) preferred to use a carburettor, whereas the Daimler–Benz engine was equipped with Bosch PZ 12 HP 110/19 *Einspritzpump* (fuel injection). The Imperial War Museum has one of the original fuel injectors from the Hess aircraft.

Eventually, the British fitted a fuel-injection system, but in late 1940 it was felt that the carburettor would produce a denser (and therefore more combustible) mixture. However, the Germans chose direct injection, the advantage being that engine performance was not affected by gravitional (g) forces.

This difference in approach soon had practical implications. The Rolls–Royce Merlin engine would cut out owing to the carburettor emptying during high g-force manoeuvres. (This problem was eventually remedied in part by the insertion of a disc in the fuel lines. Named after its inventor, Beatrice 'Tilly' Shilling, the simple device was duly called 'Miss Shilling's Orifice.')

The Bosch PZ 12 HP 110/19 fuel-injection system is essentially a carefully engineered metering device. It receives low pressure fuel from the lift pump and injects it at high pressure into the combustion chamber just prior to ignition. The nomenclature is as follows: P – injection pump; Z – self-drive shaft; 12 – twelve-cylinder engine; H – series designation; P – separate suction chamber; 110 – pump piston diameter (11mm); 19 – type number.

To calculate the fuel consumption, one must know the engine revolutions required for the various stages of flight. Aero engines are not used like those in automobiles; they tend to be run at a more constant rate of revolutions than the automobile engine with its rapid acceleration, followed by deceleration and braking. Once an aircraft reaches optimum altitude, the pilot sets the engine revolutions for cruising speed, the optimal speed in terms of engine and overall aircraft performance.

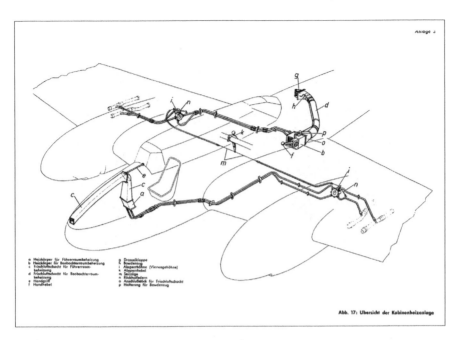

Heating system.

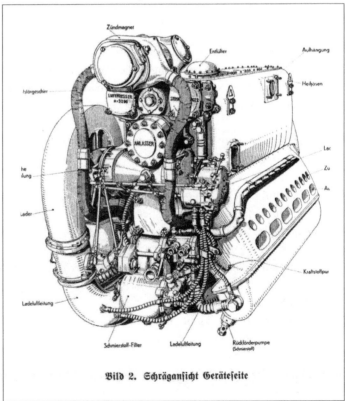

DB 601 engine.

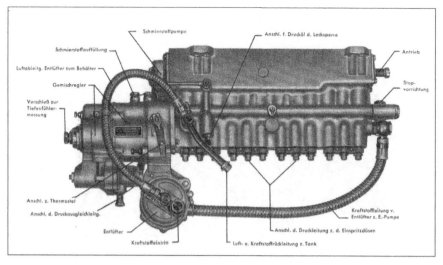

Injection pump.

Daimler-Benz expressed the various engine speeds and power for the DB 601N as follows:

A – *Start und Rotleistung* (start and warm up) – 2,600rpm (1,159hp).
B – *Steig und Kampfleistung* (climbing and combat power) – 2,400rpm (1,006hp).
C – *Dauerleistung* (maximum continuous power) – 2,400rpm (957hp) (with reduced inlet manifold pressure).

The company also expresses a theoretical fuel consumption figure for each of these engine speeds:

A – 215 grammes per unit of power per hour.
B – 210 grammes per unit of power per hour.
C – 205 grammes per unit of power per hour.

Consequently, if we now multiply the engine power by the fuel consumption:

A – 1,175 PS at 215 = 252kg per hour.
B – 1,020 PS at 210 = 214kg per hour.
C – 970 PS at 205 = 198kg per hour.

100 Octane fuel weighs 6lb per gallon. This equates to 2.72kg per gallon, or 4.54 litres. Therefore:

A – 252/2.72 x 4.54 litres per hour = 420 litres x 2 engines = 840 litres per hour.
B – 214 /2.72 x 4.54 litres per hour = 357 litres x 2 engines = 714 litres per hour.
C – 198/2.72 x 4.54 litres per hour = 330 litres x 2 engines = 660 litres per hour.

These figures are based on specific fuel consumption, which is a theoretical measurement. By way of further verification, the authors were able to obtain from the Deutsches Museum in Munich a *Flugstrecken* (Route planner) issued by the Luftwaffe, Rechlin. Unfortunately, this deals with the DB 601A, the immediate predecessor of the DB 601N engine.

The DB 601A engine was a slower revving engine, with less power and no necessity for 100 Octane fuel. However, the comparable fuel consumption figures (given in terms of litre per hour) were:

A – Not given.
B – 139 gallons per hour (630 litres per hour).
C – 145 gallons per hour (660 litres per hour).

It is also pertinent to note that the lift pump (which draws fuel from the aircraft tanks to the engine) has the stated *Grosste einspritzmenge* (maximum flow capacity) of 165 gallons per hour. The computed consumption figures are comfortably within this limit.

The Bf 110 had four fuel tanks, two in each inboard wing section, between the cockpit and the engine. They were coated with a rubber compound in an attempt to make them self-sealing if hit by enemy bullets.

From this specification, and from other sources,[13] we do not believe there is any contention over fuel capacity. Two 57-gallon tanks plus two of 82 gallons were in the wings, giving a total fuel capacity of 279 gallons (1,270 litres). This appears to have remained unaltered through the various types, B to G.

Basic Duration and Cruising Speed

As to basic duration, we have already established that, using Daimler-Benz source information, the fuel consumption of the DB 601N not surprisingly varies with engine revolutions. If the engine is flown using *Dauerleistung* (maximum continuous power), the fuel is consumed at between 132/145 gallons (600/660 litres) per hour, dependent upon altitude. Consequently, the basic Bf 110 would typically have sufficient fuel for around two hours, if flown as fast as possible. The higher power/revolutions were only used for short bursts, such as when in combat and during take-off.

I. Leiſtungs= und Verbrauchsangaben DB 601 N u. P mit hydrauliſcher Laderkupplung bei Verſtell=Luftſchraube.						
Flug-höhe km	Leiſtungsſtufe	Ladedruck ata	Leiſtung PS	Drehzahl U/min	Kraftſtoffverbrauch	
					g/PSh	Spielr. g/PSh
0	Start- u. Notleiſtung	1,35	1175	2600	215	+10
0	Steig- u. Kampfleiſtung	1,25	1020	2400	210	+10
0	Dauerleiſtung	1,15	910	2400	205	+10
5,5	Start- u. Notleiſtung	1,35	1190	2600	215	+10
5,4	Steig- u. Kampfleiſtung	1,25	1060	2400	210	+10
6,1	Dauerleiſtung	1,15	970	2400	205	+10

Schmierſtoffverbrauch: 5—9 1/h

Fuel consumption chart.

Clearly, the Bf 110 pilot did not fly using 'maximum continuous power' at all times. The Luftwaffe technical department at Rechlin also gave figures for *Grossteflugstreken* (longest flight plan), essentially the most economical cruising speed. Instead of 2,200rpm, the engine would be run at a lower speed. Figures are given for 2,000rpm, 1,800rpm and 1,600rpm, albeit at different altitudes. At the lower engine revolutions, consumption fell, but so did airspeed. At an altitude of 16,400ft at 2,000rpm, the consumption fell to 106 gallons (480 litres) per hour. At 1,600rpm, consumption was 79 gallons (360 litres) per hour. This appears to make perfect sense. Like any engine, the more that is demanded of it, the more fuel it consumes.

Consequently, we need to see the Hess flight in terms of consumption, speed and time, in order to understand what was and what was not possible.

If the 279 gallons (1,270 litres) of fuel were consumed at *Grossteflugtreken* rates, then there was enough fuel for around three hours. However, at 'maximum continuous power' at an altitude of 16,400ft and with engines running at 2,400rpm for 298mph, fuel consumption was sufficient for barely two hours. At *Grossteflugstreken* rates, the Hess aircraft was at an altitude of 16,400ft and travelling at between 228 and 261mph, with the engines running at 1,600rpm.

The Use of Auxiliary Fuel Tanks

This is vital to an understanding of the Hess flight, as it defines what was and what was not possible. As analysed above, the basic Bf 110 could fly for between two to three hours, based on the standard specification of 279 gallons (1,270 litres). However, there is a considerable weight of evidence that the Hess plane was fitted with auxiliary fuel tanks, a common enough device to lengthen potential flight duration.

It should be stated that the use of such tanks was not ideal. Any additional weight attached to the underside of a plane would affect its handling characteristics and, of course, its fuel consumption. In particular, landing with fuel tanks attached was a perilous occupation and David Irving cites the Hess aircraft (whilst in training) having to circle around the Augsburg airfield waiting for the fuel to be consumed, before a safe landing could be contemplated.[14] Firstly, some conclusions as expressed by others:

From the Franz Halder war diary, 15 May 1941: 'New facts discovered (Hess) – D. Planning of Technical preparations for flight (reserve fuel tanks).'
In *Double Standards* (1999): 'The specially fitted drop tanks contained an extra 1,800 litres of fuel, extending the range of the plane to a maximum of around 1,560 miles (2,600 kms).'
Wolf Hess (1986): 'With its two reserve fuel tanks, it had a range of 4,200 kilometres or 10 flying hours.'
Ilse Hess (1954): 'Messerschmitt … was tricked into fitting two auxiliary tanks of 700 litres each in the wings!'
James Leasor (1962): 'Messerschmitt technicians had fitted the aeroplane with a cigar-shaped auxiliary petrol tank …'
Derek Wood (1976): 'Off Holy Island he jettisoned his underwing fuel tanks.'
Len Deighton (2002): 'With a 900 litre tank under each wing …'
James Douglas-Hamilton and Roy Conyers Nesbit (1993): 'The machine did carry two drop tanks containing a total of 396 gallons of fuel (1,800 litres).'

By contrast, Dr Hugh Thomas claimed in 1979 that the Hess aircraft that flew (works number 3526) from Augsburg did not carry auxiliary fuel tanks and that a different aircraft crashed in Scotland (3869). Whilst the authors do not subscribe to Dr Thomas' theory, we do believe that it is quite possible that the Hess aircraft that took off did not have auxiliary fuel tanks, but that they were fitted en route. This possibility requires further analysis.

So there are two distinct lines of thought. Roy Conyers Nesbit's opinion is based on correspondence with Helmut Kaden (1910–82), the Messerschmitt test pilot, who became involved with the Hess mission in March 1941[15] when his predecessor, Willi Stör (1893–1977), was due to be posted to Japan in early May 1941.[16]

We believe that Rudolf Hess' subsequent actions make it obvious that one of his principal concerns was to preserve Luftwaffe secrets and consequently we take

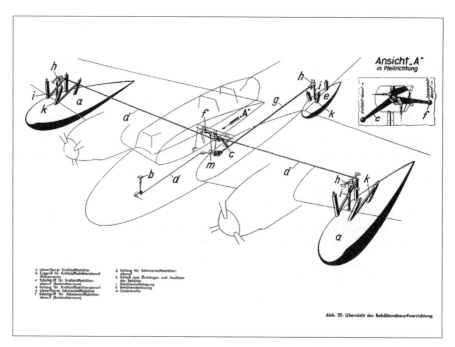

Auxiliary fuel tank system.

Kaden's later statements in the same light. We find it difficult to believe that Willi Messerschmitt, Willi Stör or Helmut Kaden did not have some idea as to the true nature of the Hess mission. It would surely be impossible not to wonder what Hess was up to, especially given the technical work that was being undertaken modifying his Bf 110.

Therefore, whilst we are quite content to assess the impact of all sizes of fuel tanks, we are not so ready to accept all that Helmut Kaden chose to tell Roy Conyers Nesbit. The reason for this caution will become apparent in due course. We are very much in the 'second camp' of thought – willing to believe, but certainly more evidence is required.

That additional evidence may be provided from some photographs of the crashed Bf 110 at Eaglesham. The remnants of the fuel supply lines hanging from the wings are clearly visible. We should state that we are quite sceptical of some of the 'crash photographs', as clearly they are not taken at Eaglesham at all, but at Carluke, days after the event. In this case, however, we are content that they are Eaglesham photographs.

The 'normal' 279-gallon (1,270-litre) fuel loading was sufficient to sustain a two-hour combat mission (typically at the higher engine rpms), or perhaps three hours at lower engine speeds, but a pilot will usually build in a contingency, as clearly it would be unwise to have just sufficient fuel to complete a flight.

The 900-litre auxiliary fuel tank.

The 75-litre fuselage oil tank.

(Aircrew today typically plan on a variable reserve of five per cent of total fuel, together with a fixed reserve sufficient to complete an additional five minutes' flight.) In 1941, whilst the concern would remain the same, the computation would be at the discretion of the pilot, mindful of the nature of the flight.

In researching the aircraft's specification, we have studied a number of illustrations of the various sizes of fuel tanks available:

Two of 48 gallons = 96 gallons (440 litres) (fitted under each wing, outboard of engine – jettisonable)
Two of 198 gallons = 396 gallons (1,800 litres) (fitted under each wing, outboard of engine – jettisonable)
Two of 88 gallons = 176 gallons (800 litres) (fitted under each wing, outboard of engine – jettisonable)
One of 110 gallons = 110 gallons (500 litres) (fitted under the fuselage, non-jettisonable)

At an engine speed of 1,600–2,000rpm, the extra tanks are more or less measurable in terms of additional hours' flying time. The 96-gallon (220-litre) combination would typically support an extra hour, the 176-gallon (800-litre) combination an extra two hours and the massive 396 gallons (1,800 litres) an extra four to five hours. The very fitting of the tanks would imply that combat flying was not the purpose of the flight and, therefore, lower fuel consumption could reasonably be assumed.

In extremis, with the two 198-gallon (900-litre) tanks fitted, the Bf 110 E-2/N would have sufficient fuel to support seven to eight hours' flight at between a 1,600–2,000rpm engine speed, with fuel consumption at 88 gallons (400 litres) per hour. The flight, as described by Rudolf Hess in 1942, apparently took five hours twenty-four minutes.[17] In other words, the flight as described in duration terms was quite possible, with auxiliary fuel tanks fitted.

Engine Oil Tanks and System

As well as the necessity for fuel, the DB 601N was a dry sump design requiring an efficient oil supply to ensure the engine was correctly lubricated. Each engine had an oil capacity of 7.5 gallons (35 litres), pumped at high-pressure by a Daimler Benz type *Doppelpumpe*, which had a capacity of 12 gallons (55 litres) per minute at 2,600rpm. This powerful pump was mounted between the inverted cylinder blocks. The actual oil consumption of the DB 601N was listed as being 1.1–2 gallons (5–9 litres) per hour, again dependent upon engine rpm.

An oil tank of 7.7 gallons (35 litres) was located behind each engine. The oil tanks from the Hess aircraft are currently in the RAF Museum reserve collection at Stafford. Each oil tank would be sufficient for just under a four-hour flight to one of up to seven hours' duration, again depending on the engine power settings.

For these longer flights, a 16.5-gallon (75-litre) *Schmierstoffbehalter* (oil tank) would be fitted underneath the fuselage. Typically, this would be fitted at the same time as wing drop tanks. This modification/configuration called *Rüstsatzes B1* (Field modification B1) would be carried out at the operational base, using factory-supplied parts.

However, in the case of the Hess aircraft there was no field modification. His Bf 110 came straight from the factory and the E2 designation gave it the available specification. It was already fitted to carry wing-mounted tanks for fuel and the additional oil tank under the fuselage.

With this tank fitted there would be ample oil for a five hour twenty-four minute flight. An additional 16.5 gallons would double the normal oil consumption. In their detailed and thorough analysis, Conyers Nesbit and Van Ackers assumed this tank was fitted and, indeed, made reference to it being rolled around the crash site by a Major Graham Donald of the Royal Observer Corps. The fitment of the tank was necessary if their description of the Augsburg to Eaglesham flight was accurate.

Eaglesham crash. Note the auxiliary fuel tank pipe fitment.

The Bf 110E manual gave explicit instructions. A hand-operated pump in the rear cockpit would be used to pump additional oil into the tanks in each wing. A three-way valve was fitted to direct the oil between the tanks as required. As the instruction manual stated, *Nach jeder Stunde Flugzeit sind je Behälter 7.5 Liter Schmierstoff nachzupumpen* ('After every hour of flight 7.5 litres of oil should be pumped in each tank'), a process that would require around two minutes of pumping. Once the reserve oil tank was empty, the pump would no longer work and the tank could be jettisoned by a release lever in the rear cockpit. The oil line from the tank to the handpump would be closed by a *Rückschlagventil* (non-return valve). Hess made a solo flight so the pump could not have been operated, given its normal placement.

The system was theoretically in place: there was certainly the ability in terms of fuel and oil for Hess to fly for five hours twenty-four minutes. But did he?

7. THE FUSELAGE AND OTHER PARTS

At the time of writing the fuselage of VJ+OQ is in temporary storage in Hangar 5 at the Imperial War Museum (IWM), Duxford, England. It is there simply because the main museum in Lambeth, London is currently undergoing refurbishment and the larger exhibits have been sent to Duxford for safekeeping.

In December 2012 the authors travelled to Hangar 5 to study the fuselage. We were keen to see the dinghy escape mechanism and the heating system vent that would prove the aircraft to be an E2. This would enable us to re-check and confirm the possible flight duration and fuel consumption figures.

Alongside the fuselage was one of the DB 601N engines from the Bf 110, with the type designator 'N' clearly marked in white paint on the crankcase. The authors requested permission to take close-up photographs, but were denied access on account of health and safety issues surrounding the exhibits.

Undeterred, we took what photographs we could and, in particular, we tried to ascertain if the 16.5-gallon (75-litre) reserve oil tank had been fitted under the fuselage. In order for such a flight as Hess undertook (according to him), the reserve oil tank would have to be fitted. Without it, there was a very real danger of an engine seizing during the long flight. A sensible pilot would not take such a risk.

We already knew the oil tank would present a mechanical challenge. We knew it was usually jettisoned from the observer/gunner's position of the *Beobachterraum* (observers' cabin) and that the handpump mechanism was usually operated from the rear cockpit. We had assumed that modifications would have been made to enable the pilot (Hess) to manually pump the oil from the tank and then jettison it when empty.[18] We were visiting Duxford largely to confirm what we already knew. We believed we were just being thorough.

The following week witnessed a dramatic increase in telephone traffic between Northamptonshire and Norfolk. The photographs that Richard Wilbourn had taken had cast serious doubt on whether a drop tank had ever been fitted. The jettison device was indeed present and apparently unused, but the seemingly undeniable evidence was that the hole that would accommodate the oil feed pipe had been blanked off. The non-return valve had been covered by a brass cap, complete with wired-on security seal. A reserve oil tank had not been fitted for the flight.

Practically, without such a tank the flight duration was limited to around four hours, especially if the parts of the flight demanded high engine rpm. On a flight lasting five hours twenty-four minutes, a rational decision would certainly be to fit such a tank. To not do so would be a gamble, especially given that the instruction manual instructs the pumping of 1.6 gallons (7.5 litres) of oil per engine per hour.

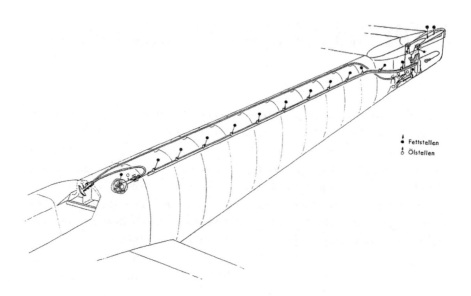

Lubrication points for dinghy release – Bf 110 E/2.

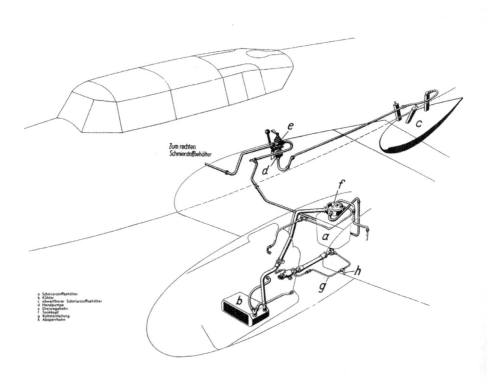

Oil tank pumping system.

The blanked-off and wired oil line.

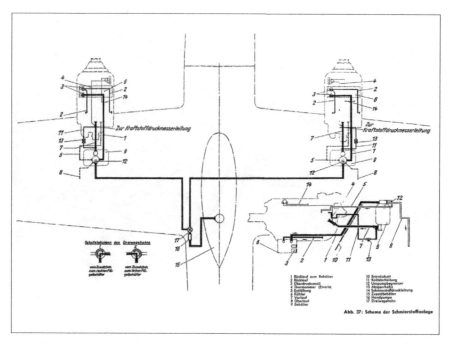

The oil handpump.

The fuselage at Duxford, showing the closed oil tank locking mechanism.

This has a fundamental impact on the flight, as it is agreed that the duration was five hours twenty-four minutes. It would make no sense to fit two 198-gallon (900-litre) auxiliary fuel tanks under the wings when the engines did not have sufficient oil to use the extra fuel.

Consequently, Richard arranged to obtain supervised access to the fuselage, thus circumventing the prevailing health and safety issues. This was done on 7 January 2013. His report was written the following day:

Richard Wilbourn: Report on Visit to Duxford – 07.01.2013
Visit made to Hangar 5 to carry out a visual examination and photograph the remains of the Hess Bf 110 fuselage, which had recently been moved from IWM Lambeth. This was a follow-up visit to one made 30.12.2013 when the exhibit was found to be confined behind a tape with the right-hand side out of sight. Permission was given by IWM Duxford staff to make a supervised inspection all around the item. The supervision and caution were due to health and safety concerns; this is a working hangar, and there is considered to be a possible asbestos risk from this item.

Overall:
The fuselage is still mounted on a black exhibition frame. The rear end of the item contains two rolls of a black foam material and is wrapped in a cling film which is further secured with brown parcel tape. Access to the public is generally good to the left side; it is close to the walkway and offers a good view into the front of the fuselage. One of the engines is placed directly behind the exhibit.

From the side out of view to the public, it is clear that the right-hand side of the plane is less complete, a large square hole had been cut, hacked out, where the side *Balkenkreuz* cross had been removed. [This is now displayed in the RAF Museum, Hendon.]

It was noticed that there is a number, painted in white, in an area under where the tail would have been. Cling film obscures some of it, but 869 is clear to see, with another digit before this being behind the covering and on a more damaged part of the plane. This corresponds partially with the supposed works number for the plane 3869. A request for permission to pull back some of the film covering was denied by IWM staff, because of the concerns of possible asbestos contamination.

Forward part of fuselage:
This second visit was largely undertaken to carry out a closer examination of details noticed during the earlier visit.

The first parts of the fuselage are the damaged partial section (*Rumpfteil*) 7 and the more complete section 8. This section 8 contains a number of inspection/access panels and, from the Messerschmitt Bf 110 *Handbücher Bedienungsvorschriften*, is where the auxiliary, jettisonable engine oil tank (*Rüstsatzes, B1*) would have been mounted. It also contains the large remnants of the Siemens K4ü rudder control mechanism.

Of particular interest was a mechanism on the inside floor of the section. This has been identified as the suspension/release system for an auxiliary oil tank (*Schloss zum Einhängen und Auslösen de Behälter*). Part of the mechanism protrudes through to the outside of the fuselage and can be seen as a tapered lever (*Hebel*) in a slotted hole.

A little further towards the rear of the plane is another hole through the floor, fitted with what appears to be a tapered 'rubber' grommet. This is where the suction pipe from the non-return valve (*Rückschlagventil*) would emerge and go down into the tank.

To the side of that opening is another which is fitted inside with a metal strip and shaped ferrule. This correlates with the positioning hole or guide (*Führungen*) for one of the tank struts (*Behälterabstutzung*).

To the front of the mechanism a cable attachment is showing. This cable is the release control which went forward into the crew compartment (*Seil zug für Schmierstoffbehälter abwurf*). From the arrangement of the parts of the mechanism, it appears that it is in the closed position; the lever under the plane is forward and close to the fuselage, and the hook part of the latch, which held the attachment (*Behälteraufhängung*) in the 'Schloss', is visible. There is no significant damage apparent and, other than a slight bend in the side plates behind it, the mechanism appears to be in good condition.

Behind this latch system, where the top of the non-return valve would attach to an oil line, is a blanking cap, which appears to be made of brass. There is no oil line (*Endstück der Schmierstoffleitung*) or remains of one present and the cap has the substantial remnants of a twisted wire security seal still in place.

Conclusion:

The aircraft had the fittings and mechanism to carry an engine oil drop tank.

This mechanism is still complete and in good condition. The mechanism and the area around it are largely undamaged and show no signs of any violent detachment such as may result from crashing.

The apparatus appears to be set in the closed position. This is a cable trip release mechanism and so could not have been re-set from the crew compartment.

The oil pipe connection was not in place and the fitting is covered by a sealed blanking cap.

This leads to the conclusion that no external oil tank was fitted for this flight.

We believe there is little or no doubt. The Hess aircraft did not have an auxiliary oil tank fitted. It is inconceivable that the British, post-10 May 1941, would have stripped the crashed aircraft and then fitted a sealed blanking cap to an auxiliary oil tank fitment.

This finding has profound implications, but the most notable being that the Hess Bf 110 could not have realistically flown for five hours twenty-four minutes. To precis the argument: each engine oil tank was emptying at a typical rate of 1.65 gallons (7.5 litres) per hour (more if the engines were operating at higher rpm settings); each tank held 7.7 gallons (35 litres); therefore, 7.7 gallons (35 litres) consumed at 1.65 gallons (7.5 litres) per hour would allow a flight of approximately four hours forty minutes' duration. Without the handpumping system and reserve tank the engines would run out of oil and seize. Rudolf Hess would have then crashed in the North Sea, or over the south of Scotland, depending on when the oil ran out. The Hess mystery would then have become an Amelia Earhart-type affair, rather than the far more important political mystery it has become.

Following this startling discovery, we were surprised to learn that there are further parts of the Hess aircraft still in official custody.[19] Consequently, in February 2013 we travelled to the RAF Museum reserve collection in Area 6 at Ministry of Defence (MoD) Stafford. We were welcomed by the very helpful Ian Alder, who showed us the 'Hess pallet' which comprised the following parts:

The pilot's roof and side panels of the Bf 110 cockpit frame, Ref. 408517.

Parts of the observer cockpit frame. This proved to us that there was only one person on board, as the whole of the observer cockpit frame was jettisonable. The fact that it was present would suggest that it crashed with the rear frame in place.

A leather or fabric tonneau cover, presumably from the rear of the observer's cockpit, Ref. 137480.

Two armoured plates to protect the pilot, Refs 137484 & 137485.

The retractable ladder that fitted to the fuselage by the trailing edge of the left wing, Ref. 174856.

In addition, there were two rubber-coated tanks, Refs 137482 & 137483, both embossed with the initials SB. These were described as 'fuel tanks', but we believe it far more likely that they were actually the 7.7-gallon oil tanks mounted behind each engine. The SB denotes *Schmierstoffbehälter*.

Consequently, at the time of writing, the following parts are available for public inspection:

The tank release mechanism (b) as shown in the Bf 110 manuals. This view shows the layout for a fuel tank application but the details are the same for oil except that no filling pipe (d) is used. Please note the non-return valve (e); on the Hess plane this is blanked off and without any following pipe (c).

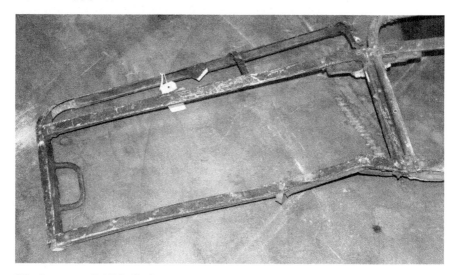

Pilots' canopy at RAF Stafford.

Nachdem das Dach (6i) der Schützenklappe (6k) mittels Scharnier (als Lagerbolzen sind Splintbolzen zu verwenden) angelenkt ist, wird unter gleichzeitiger Einführung des Deckelzapfens in die Führungsschiene (27m) am Windschutzaufbau-Rückteil die Lagerung der Schützenklappe hergestellt.

Stimmen die Löcher der Klappe mit den Löchern der Lagerböcke (26a) am Rückteil überein, so werden von innen nach außen die Bolzen (26b) durchgesteckt. Der Bolzen (26b) ist ohne Gewinde, jedoch mit einem Ansatz am Kopf ausgeführt. Zur Sicherung ist die mittels Senkschraube (26d) gehaltene Scheibe (26c) über den Bolzenansatz zu schieben.

WindschutzaufLau-Rückteil (Ausführung bei Verwendung der MG 15)

Der Verschlußhebel (27a) ist am Windschutzaufbau-Rückteil (27c) anzubringen. Der Hebel ist mit dem Sechskantbolzen (27d) unter Verwendung von zwei mit Führung versehenen Abstandsscheiben (27e) wie folgt zu lagern: Die Abstandsscheiben mit ihren Führungen in die Langlöcher der Konsolen (27g) stecken, Hebel (27a) zwischenschieben und den vorher mit großer Scheibe (27f) versehenen Bolzen (27d) durchschieben. Vor die Kronenmutter ist ebenfalls eine große Scheibe zu legen. Die Mutter darf nur handfest angezogen werden, da sonst der Hebel klemmt (Sicherung durch Splint).

An den hinteren Rahmen (27k) des Windschutzaufbau-Rückteiles (27c) ist oben das Führungsstück (27h) für den Zapfen der Schützenklappe anzuschrauben.

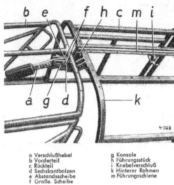

a Verschlußhebel	g Konsole
b Vorderteil	h Führungsstück
c Rückteil	i Knebelverschluß
d Sechskantbolzen	k Hinterer Rahmen
e Abstandsscheibe	m Führungsschiene
f Große Scheibe	

Abb. 27: Windschutzaufbau-Rückteil mit Knebelverschluß

Der kurze vordere Zugbügel (25c) ist mit einer Sechskantschraube am vorderen Anschlußbeschlag (25d) des Windschutzaufbau-Rückteiles zu befestigen. Der hintere Zugbügel (25b) wird von außen an den hinteren Rahmen der Klappe (6k) angeschraubt (Pertinaxauflage nach außen).

31

Rear canopy release mechanism.

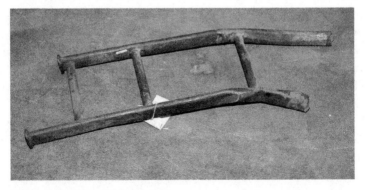

Retractable ladder at RAF Stafford.

Oil tank at RAF Stafford.

Imperial War Museum (IWM), Duxford: The fuselage and a DB 601N engine.

Museum of Flight, East Fortune, Scotland: A DB 601N engine and Royal Observer Corps map.

Lennoxlove House, Haddington, Scotland: Hess map(s) and aircraft compass.

MoD Stafford: List as above.

RAF Museum, Hendon: The *Balkenkreuz* from the side of the fuselage and an ROC map.

Durham County Hall: An ROC map of the approaches to North-East England.

Somewhat bizarrely, perhaps, the IWM in London also list further flight instruments from the aircraft, together with a pair of Hess' underpants. The authors make no claims as to the authenticity or otherwise of the latter items.

The authors also have no doubt that further parts exist in and around Eaglesham, Scotland, taken from the crash site on the night of 10 May 1941. There is also a British Pathé newsreel (canister UN1265D) which gives a passing view of the fuselage (complete with *Balkenkreuz* at that time).

While at MoD Stafford, we also enquired as to the provenance of some of the articles as a number were tagged 'Hess' and some 'alleged Hess'. The fact is that we do not consider there to be any particularly controversial evidence apart from the fuselage.

Apparently, the remains of the Bf 110 were initially taken to Carluke and dumped with other aircraft parts. The wreck was then taken to Carlisle to be re-assembled at an RAF maintenance unit (operated by Scottish Aviation Limited), prior to being loaded onto a 'Queen Mary' transport trailer and taken south, to be used for propaganda purposes. There are photographs of the trailer in Oxford.

From there we understand the engines were taken to RAF Biggin Hill for storage and eventually transferred to RAF Bicester, before final transfer to MoD Stafford. The rest of the Bf 110 stored at MoD Stafford came from the Newcastle-upon-Tyne Science Museum in 1977.

What is probably more important is what is not in MoD Stafford. We would like to have seen the cockpit, for the existence of the amended radio equipment and of a handpump for the reserve oil tank, or otherwise; and the wings, for evidence of auxiliary wing tanks. We would also like to see the mythical 'greased up' machine guns that were duly photographed at Carluke. Like Major Donald in his letter of 11 May 1941, we doubt any such guns were ever fitted.

It is unfortunate, but the fact remains that, besides the mechanism for the reserve oil tank, there are no parts remaining on display that give any clues as to how the aircraft was modified to facilitate a 'solo' peace mission. However, we now believe that the discovery concerning the 'blanked-off' oil pipe is one of the most significant in respect of the Hess flight for the past seventy years. Its implication is stark – Hess could not have flown for as long as he claimed; he may well have had enough fuel, but he did not have enough oil.

We now believe that Hess landed in Germany en route; basically, he had to. Presumably, to fit an oil-pumping system in the front cockpit was adjudged too cumbersome and Hess certainly had enough to do without the additional work, but more likely, he had calculated that by landing he did not need to have an auxiliary oil tank – the existing tanks could merely be refilled.

8. THE LENNOXLOVE MAP

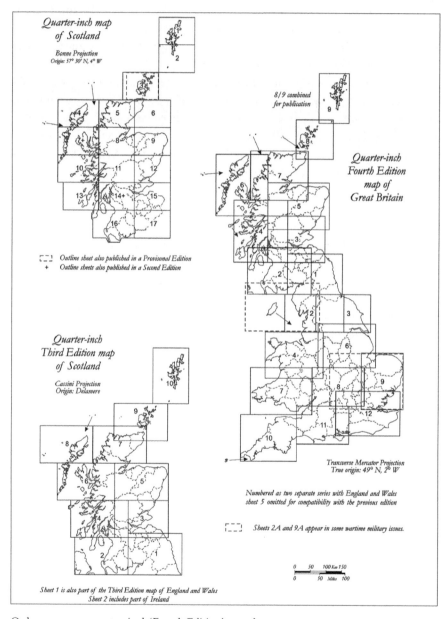

Ordnance survey quarter-inch 'Fourth Edition' note sheets.

The Lennoxlove Map, as we describe it, is so called because it currently hangs (framed under glass) in one of the rooms open to the public at Lennoxlove House, just outside Haddington, Scotland. The room also contains various items commemorating the many aeronautical exploits and military service of the 14th Duke of Hamilton and his three brothers. The authors first visited the house in 1996 and were fascinated by the map. Initially, in the time allowed, all we noticed was that Dungavel House was not even marked. Since that time, we have visited it on a number of occasions and slowly our understanding of the map has developed. However, our title, The Lennoxlove Map is actually not technically correct.

Firstly, it is actually two maps joined together, both with a scale of 1:250,000. In fact, they are British projections, originally of 4 miles to the inch, slightly expanded to the metric 1:250,000. This scale demonstrates that they were relatively recent maps, as the British Ordnance Survey (OS) had only recently commissioned the new 'Fourth Edition'. The 'Third Edition' had disclosed slightly different areas of Scotland, and far more of Northern Ireland. The differential between true north and magnetic north had been manually updated by Hess (presumably), noting that the information as being accurate at 1 January 1941. The original differential was marked as being at 1 January 1935, which date again ties in with the release of the 'Fourth Edition'. The Charles Close Society has kindly dated the release date of the new edition pertaining to Scotland as being between 1936 and 1938.

The maps are of German manufacture, but based on or directly copied from the British OS projection. This explains why certain oddities appear. Bizarrely, Prestwick airfield and Carlisle airfield maintenance units are both marked with circles, but as far as we can see, no other airfields are marked on either map. Consequently, we originally wondered if they were actually British maps, but they are British projections transposed and used by the Germans.

Creases and grime marks show where and how the maps were folded. Typically, in an operational squadron the relevant section of the map would have been folded and placed into a map folder, attached to the pilot's or navigator's leg. With Hess, this may not have been the case, on account of the uniform that he was wearing. Either way, the map was folded so as not to be an encumbrance in the already cramped cockpit of the Bf 110.

Secondly, the map was given to the Hamilton family very early on in the Hess affair. It was delivered to the 14th Duke of Hamilton on 22 May 1941, just twelve days after the actual flight. At that time, the Hamilton family resided at Dungavel House, near Strathaven. One could argue that it should more properly be called the 'Dungavel Map'.

Today, a letter from the Air Ministry sent in May 1941, which forwarded the maps, also resides in Lennoxlove House and is signed by R.H. Melville, the Under Secretary of State at the Air Ministry. With it came a camera and a compass.[20]

There is also the unresolved, but vitally important, issue of what precisely was given to the 14th Duke and why? Roy Conyers Nesbit, who provided the foreword to Lord James Douglas-Hamilton's book of 1993, writes that there was, in addition, 'A third map covering the area to the north is not on display.' By way of reference, Conyers Nesbit quotes a correspondence that passed between himself and Lennoxlove, dated October/November 1995. In fairness, he does not actually clearly state if he had seen all three maps.

The authors have written to Lennoxlove requesting permission to view the third map. The unexpected response came back that there is no third map.[21] We wrote again, this time pointing out that the Hamilton Palace website also mentioned the third map. The same reply came back, this time saying that Lennoxlove would ensure the website reference was removed.

Is there such a map? If it does indeed exist, why it is not displayed?

We can quite understand that the family must be heartily fed up with the Hess affair. As the 14th Duke is supposed to have said to Churchill: 'What do you do if a prostitute hangs herself around your neck?' The family has certainly found it difficult to escape the affair, but, equally, has also chosen not to when it suits. James Douglas-Hamilton has written two books on the subject and has appeared on television a number of times to discuss it. He has placed the research papers pertaining to the second of those books in the Scottish Record Office, Edinburgh. On requesting access to the papers, the authors were denied access in his lifetime. Requests for a meeting with James Douglas-Hamilton have been refused. (Alasdair Douglas-Hamilton has also recently written a biography of his father Malcolm, one of the 14th Duke's brothers.)

We repeat that we quite understand if James Douglas-Hamilton chooses to act in this manner; there are understandable reasons. But it is certainly not going to help in the search for what actually happened in the lead up to the May 1941 flight. His first book *Motive for a Mission*, makes no mention of the maps at all and only deals fleetingly with the flight. In his second book, he asked Roy Conyers Nesbit to provide the aeronautical detail, who did so in considerable depth, but again the book did not mention the fact that the author's family was in possession of the Hess flight map(s). The fact that the Hamilton family owned the land and company on which RAF Prestwick operated was also omitted.

On the subject of the Hamilton family, we pose the obvious question: if the Hess affair was really nothing to do with the family, why would the maps, camera and compass have been sent to them? Why were they not given to, say, the Lord Provost of Glasgow, or even Eaglesham Town Council?

On 22 May 1941, the Hamilton family was still living at Dungavel House, South Lanarkshire. For whatever reason, the 14th Duke purchased the Lennoxlove and Archerfield Estates in 1946, switching the main family residence from the west

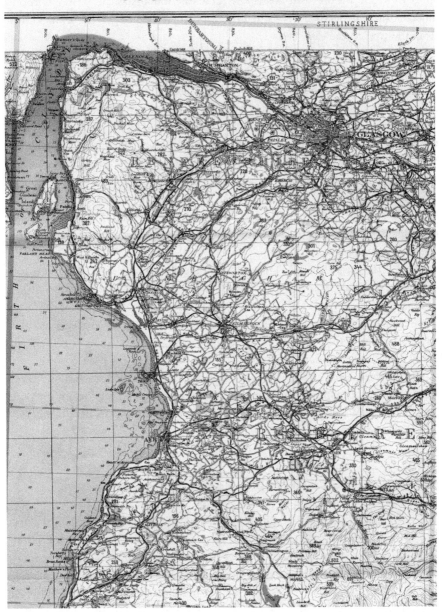

A contemporary Luftwaffe map of the Ayrshire coast.

coast of Scotland to the east coast after 400 years. Dungavel House was sold to the National Coal Board, despite the 13th Duke being buried in the garden. This move does require some explanation as most of the Hamilton lands and possessions were still on the west coast. The duke's nephew, Alasdair, writes, without explanation: 'He decided he wanted to move the centre of gravity of the family from the west to the east.'[22]

Finally, while it is obviously a map that was being used as part of a plan, there is no line drawn denoting the flight path, or indeed an intended flight path. Neither Dungavel House nor the airstrip is marked. On careful observation, it actually reveals a choice of approach to the intended landing site, which is not Dungavel House.

In previous chapters we have commented on the use of deceit or deception in the planning process. Unless a viewer of the map knew what had happened to Hess, it is very unlikely that he or she would be able to work out precisely where Hess was heading. As will be seen, an indicated route seems obvious by reason of the line of features carefully highlighted, but no specific target is marked. Hess knew there was a good chance that these papers would be scrutinised and so, once again, he would see it as his duty not to make the target obvious, following his military training.

What if the target was not Dungavel and the maps were marked up to reveal an operational RAF base? In that case we doubt very much that they would ever have seen the light of day. What if the maps also demonstrate the use of the latest German navigational systems? As it is, we wonder if the Air Ministry was too hasty in releasing the maps to the 14th Duke of Hamilton. In the map there are many clues as to the pilot's intentions.

The map is large. Consequently, it is not possible to reproduce an illustration of the complete map of sufficient scale to enable the reader to zoom into the relevant detail. We suspect that this is the prime reason its secrets have been concealed for such a long time.

A Strange Choice of Map

The two maps that have been joined together are British OS topographical maps, to 1:250,000 scale, though certainly not specific to aviation. The 'Fourth Edition' was updated in the 1930s, largely to cater for the growing interest in motor touring holidays. The railways have been overmarked and highlighted in heavy black pencil. On a non-aviation map they are not particularly distinct, being simply a heavy black line. Many of the hills have been height marked in metres, in blue crayon. An OS map has the heights marked in feet and so Hess had to convert the various heights to metres. Several high features are marked in red. Others features

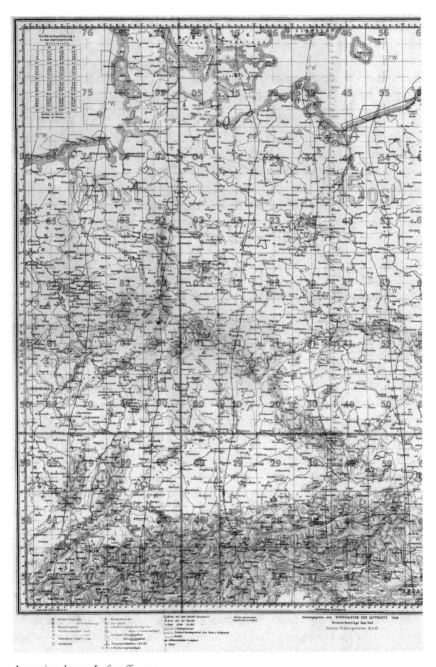

A restricted areas Luftwaffe map.

are pointed to by red arrows – such as Glengavel reservoir. The distribution of the markings is heavily concentrated within the limits of the fold marks and is heaviest along the path of the eventual flight.

We have acquired a 1936 Luftwaffe map of the area (Schottland Nr.2) and this is, of course, exactly the same projection and image, 4 miles to the inch, slightly expanded to 1:250,000. The heights have been marked in metres. The major difference between this and the Lennoxlove Map is simply that the Luftwaffe map has been overprinted with the German 'Gradnetz' grid system. Just like the Lennoxlove Map, the German map uses English place names and English symbols.

By way of further comparison, we have also acquired a British aeronautical map of the same area, dated 1942 (General Staff No. 3957 [Air]). This map uses more distinct colours: railways are clearly highlighted in black, lakes are a deep blue colour to aid recognition, and features such as viaducts and race courses (to be used in emergencies) are marked in red ink. The use of deep colour is advantageous in dark conditions. The point is that Hess had bought two or three large-scale road maps of Scotland, with English markings and a German border, and then marked it up so that, in essence, it has become the equivalent of the contemporary Luftwaffe map. He did not precisely convert feet to metres, the heights were typically rounded, but by doing so he eliminated any possibility that he might betray any Luftwaffe secrets. He basically hand-converted a road map into a fully functional aviation chart.

Needless to say, some have seen this as supporting the 'lone flyer theory', but the map has some further secrets to reveal. In fact, the Lennoxlove Map contains significantly more detail as to navigational systems than the then operational Luftwaffe equivalent. It is when these specific marks Hess made are analysed in detail that the map assumes a far greater importance than the Air Ministry perhaps realised in May 1941, when choosing to release it to the Hamilton family.

While describing the map in general terms, it is important to ascertain how the map was folded as it travelled across Scotland on 10 May 1941. When the map was being mounted in the frame, it appears to us that map Nr.1 was used in its entirety, whilst map Nr.2 was trimmed vertically along 3° 50' W longitude. In other words, we do not have both maps in their entirety. We have reproduced the OS diagram of the 'Fourth Edition' of the 'Quarter Inch' scale map, which shows the extent of each map and their potential overlap (p. 120).

There is a clear 'grime mark' where the map has been folded horizontally. This reveals actually quite a narrow 'corridor' visible to Hess. The northerly grime mark hits the Ayrshire coast between Saltcoats and West Kilbride, whereas the southerly grime mark is again horizontal, crossing the coast just to the north of Ballantrae.

We believe these marks to be very significant, as they must define the area that Hess was interested in. By inference, they also reveal those parts of Scotland that

Hess did not anticipate travelling over. Interestingly, we know from ROC records that Hess flew over the ROC post at West Kilbride — West Kilbride is certainly not on the 'exposed' part of the map.

Specific Marks of Interest

Firstly, there is a line of blue pencil triangles from Bamburgh Castle to the Solway Firth. It took us three visits to Lennoxlove House before we stumbled across the line of small blue triangles, pencil drawn, that start in the Solway Firth and stretch northeast towards Bamburgh/Farne Islands.

If one studies the map pertaining to the Ayr area, one finds two lines of different length dashes marked in pencil and extending out into the Firth of Clyde. Once again the concentration of effort is in two places: firstly, the east–west corridor from Bamburgh to Ayr and, secondly, the area around Dumfries and the Solway Firth.

Throughout the map, at seemingly random locations, Hess chose to mark, in black pencil, the number 450 and then (450) in brackets. There are a cluster of these markings actually in the North Sea, which made any speculation that they related to geographical features a nonsense. These symbols, if that is what they are, were certainly the most challenging aspect to decipher, achieved some seventeen years after we had first seen the map. These markings will also be described later in this book.

Finally, there are other numbers, seemingly not related to anything in particular, literally scattered across the map: 155, 145, 108 and 58 all appear and are marked in kilometres, in contrast to the height measurements that are all rounded to the nearest 10m. These figures appear to be very precise. We were intrigued as to what was being measured or represented.

Clearly, there is a lot more detail than at first glance. We will give further details of the important markings later, but believe it important to give first the details of the Pilot's Notes for the Hess flight that we have obtained and the German navigation systems Hess tried to utilise. Although hand marked, we now believe the Lennoxlove Map is actually a sophisticated German radio navigational chart, interspersed with a host of visual recognition markers. It gave Hess all the information he needed.

9. THE MYSTERY OF THE FLIGHT NOTES

While attempting to interpret the markings on the Lennoxlove Map, we were approached by Peter Padfield, the well-known and respected military historian, who had obtained what were claimed to be and described as the flight notes of Rudolf Hess. He and his son had tried to interpret them, but had struggled to make any sense of them. Initially we came to the same result.

We had pestered Peter as to the provenance of the notes and he told us that they had come from a Professor A.W.B. Simpson, a prominent human rights lawyer who had died in 2011 at the age of 80.

Professor Simpson had apparently obtained the notes from a David Oliver, who had served in the RAF. Copies of the notes had been made in the late 1950s and there were rumours that the notes had also been taken to *The Times* newspaper. 'David Oliver' had apparently served at the Central Navigation School, RAF Shawbury, Shropshire. Later we were to find out from Peter that Professor Simpson had referred to additional documents. We were told that the documents originally included:

1 Part of a railway map of Great Britain to a scale of 1:1,000,000, which was 'very indistinctly' marked with a number of courses across Northumberland and into southern Scotland.

2 A typed document covered with hand-written annotations and calculations showing details of legs and distances. This is our Flight Plan 1.

3 A sketch map of the area to the west of the Farne Islands marked with railways and hills.

4 A two-page document, which includes a set of calculations for the time taken to cover the distances of 290, 410 and 370km (in order as given) at speeds of 300 to 520kph at 10km intervals (as reproduced on the following page).

5 A hand-written document annotated with four calculations of the estimated time to be taken to complete the flight, or part of it. This is our Flight Plan 2.

Leg
Distance **km/h**

	300	310	320	330	340	350	360	370
290	58	56	54	53	51	50	48	47
410	82	79	77	75	72	70	68	66
370	74	72	69	67	65	63	62	60

	380	390	400	410	420	430	440	450
290	46	45	44	42	41	40	40	39
410	65	66	62	60	59	57	56	55
370	58	57	56	54	53	52	50	49

	460	470	480	490	500	510	520
290	38	37	36	36	35	34	33
410	53	52	51	50	49	48	47
370	48	47	46	45	44	44	43

Speed v. distance. Note the choice of distances specific to the plans.

It would have been very interesting and helpful to our research if we had sight of all the original documents. We only had the two flight plans and our re-creation of the speed/leg distances, Document 4. With that paucity of detail we began our research.

Firstly, John Harris contacted the Air Historical Branch but they did not recognise the notes. He then contacted RAF Shawbury, who referred us to the National Archives. They also denied all knowledge of the notes, as did the RAF Museum, Hendon. John then consulted the book *Man Is Not Lost* by Group Captain 'Dickie' Richardson for the history of RAF Shawbury.[23] Whilst much of the book deals with early aerial navigation and techniques (see later chapters), Richardson ended the war as Deputy Commandant and Director of Studies for the new Empire Air Navigation School, based at RAF Shawbury. As Richardson

says, 'We decided our first aim should be to create a central repository of navigation knowledge, covering every aspect of military aviation ... This prodigious
mini-empire drew upon the resources of ... specialised sections, namely radar,
signals and astro-nav aids, compasses, instruments, maps and charts, meteorology
... a museum and finally editorial.'

It therefore seems perfectly possible that the Hess flight notes (always assuming
they were rescued from the crashed Bf 110) had ended up at RAF Shawbury and
were copied when the navigational school closed in the late 1950s and moved to
RAF Manby in 1963. The explanation given to us still appeared plausible.

We then checked with David Oliver, the well-known aviation editor and
writer, but once again, he had not heard of or seen, the flight notes. We were
clearly looking for a different David Oliver. In short, we had drawn a blank.
It would then have been easy to dismiss the notes as 'mumbo jumbo', or a forgery,
and go no further. In some ways it would have been easier to have done so, except
for one remarkable fact. We now believe them to be a very poor transcript of the
original Hess pre-flight planning notes, probably transcribed by someone unfa-
miliar with air navigation and not a fluent German speaker. Some details remain
unclear, but we believe that we now largely understand the notes and their later,
terrible implications for Hess.

Of most relevance, there are references contained within the notes that directly
refer to and relate to the Lennoxlove Map and other navigational and operational
details that certainly stand up to very close scrutiny. In other words, we believe
that the Lennoxlove Map and the flight notes were drawn up at the same time.
References appear on both documents that relate to each other.

Peter Padfield's son, Guy, had transcribed the notes on to a word processor, and
the numbers and phrases appear to have become muddled; there seemed to be
little or no order to them. We reproduce the copies of the original notes we were
given by Peter exactly.

Our initial impression was that the two pages were different in their objective. The first page seems to be a chronological plan, with kilometres and other
instructions. The second a series of numbers, which appear to be details of times.

We also considered whether the notes were actually muddled up completely
and that some numbers were even on the wrong page. Slowly the flight notes
began to come together. We believe one sheet was a preferred route (Flight Plan 1);
the other gives four options to achieve the same goal, the flight to and across the
North Sea (Flight Plan 2).

We also believe that, in the end, Hess did not follow any of the options described
in the notes. We were mindful that they could still be complete 'bunkum', but
why would Hess bring notes with him that he had not used, and why would Peter
Padfield have become interested in them? We noticed that, if arranged carefully,

Flight plan 1, as given to the authors.

Strecke	Kurs	.km	Min. Koln No. 216.5
Au.-Bo	370		
Bo. - A	290		
A - B	410		
30 Min v.A	aufnehmen	O3e [Oje] I !	

B 1 290 km von A Peilung Oslo 76 z.K. (No186.5)

" Kalunbg. 117 " (" 16o)

B 410 " " " Peilung Oslo 86 z.K

B - C   170

nach 1o Min. Vollgaz(1.3 a) Automatik!

Kuhlung ! T-Abwurf! Hohe!

C nach 1o 1 12 Min. erreicht

C - Insele	40	Cheviot - I pei-
		len 255
Inselen See	100	(530/4000m:) 12'(500)
See - Du	58 /	(530) Do 4 -

Du - Westk		
Inseln - Westk.	220	
D (Irische See) - E Nordkurs 28 km		
E - Du	35 6475)	1.3 a (1000)

[Navigational calculations made out by R.Hess]

	II		i				
				a/ 55 [?] 55			
a	Rum [?] 3h 45		42 kuste A	42			
b	- 3h 30		35 B' //B 60				
a	b	31 Kuste	25				
60	verdun 60	5 Insele	5				
42	Kuste 42	137	187 56	B2/g/B1 [?] 77			
31	Kuste 25	Kuste 3h 17					
5	Insele 5	168	b//				
3h 15 //	3h 30	Rum [?] 2h 48	3h 07				
+ 15	+ 15						
3h 30	3h 45	Wind + 15	15				
		3.03	3h 22				
	+20						
1/2 J [?]	+20	Kuste IIa					

Flight plan 2, as given to the authors.

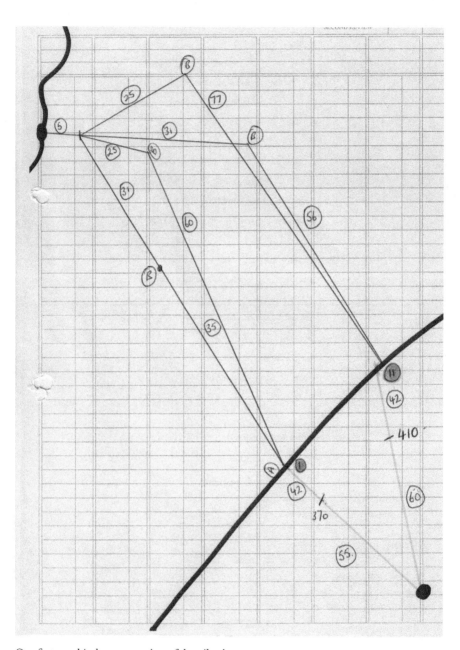

Our first graphical representation of the pilots' notes.

the jumble is actually a four-column table, which is almost arithmetically correct. This is reproduced below:

II			I		
a		b	a		b
60	VERDUN	60	55	?	55
42	KUSTE	42	42	KUSTE	42
56	B2/G/B1	77	35	B'//B	60
31	KUSTE	25	31	KUSTE	25
5	INSELE	5	5	INSELE	5
194		209	168		187
3h 15		3h 30	2h 48		3h 7
15	WIND	15	15	WIND	15
3h 30		3h 45	3h 03		3h 22

As you can see, the table gives four options. The flight times appear to range from just over three hours to three hours forty-five minutes. We were a little apprehensive to intepret the letter 'h' as denoting hour. What little German we had would expect us to have seen 's' for *stunde* (hour). Was this a British fake document after all? After a little work we discovered that lower case 'h' was also used by the Germans to denote hours. We carried on.

Moving on to the figures, each of the two columns marked I and II show similar results until after the line KUSTE, i.e, 60 & 42 and 55 & 42. Eventually, we deduced that what we were seeing was essentially two flight paths to the coast and then a variety of ways to approach the same point 'INSELE'. All four routes ended at the the same point, which was then five minutes away from the 'INSELE'.

We then drew the above diagram and suddenly much became clear. The table refers to four means of getting up the North Sea, presumably while being mindful of the intersecting beams (please see later chapter). The two points of entry to the North Sea appear to relate to Den Helder (A) and Borkum (B), both points shown by Hess on his 1941 flight plan. Given what we had discovered at Duxford – that there had been no reserve oil tank fitted – we were intrigued to see that the first leg of both options appeared to have a pause: column II after sixty minutes, column I after fifty-five minutes.

It became apparent that Hess was actually planning to land en route, a plan that we now believe was actually a necessity, not an option.

When writing the hardback version of this book we fear we had made a mistake in assuming that the starting point for the pilot's notes was Augsburg – the same as for Rudolf Hess. In 2018 Richard Wilbourn was working on the notes and had a moment of revelation. What if the notes started at the stopover airfield, not Augsburg? It all made sense very quickly. If the plane was to be refuelled (or even a different plane used to get Hess from Augsburg to the stopover airfield), there would be no need to consider subsequent options. The fuel usage would be the same from Augsburg to the airfield – wherever it was.

Harris then got in on the act too. We had long been mystified by the reference to 'Verdun' on the notes. Clearly this was unlikely to be Verdun in eastern France and we momentarily considered Voerden in northern Germany. However, after some searching, Harris discovered that Verdun was the name given to the newly opened army barracks in Giessen, just north of Frankfurt. The barracks had been opened in 1935. Had we at long last found the true stopover point?

In 2020 Harris then travelled to Giessen to establish the scale of the airfield. He was not disappointed. Post war, the occupying American forces used the base as a major distribution base for the entire US forces. In 1941 the base was certainly capable of dealing with Hess landing and either refuelling or swapping a transit Bf 110 from Augsburg for his ready-and-waiting werk nummer 3869.

We then were interested to note that there were further Hess connections with Giessen. His tutor from his days in Egypt, Alfred Kaufmann (1868–1946) lived there and had corresponded with the Deputy Führer. Kaufmann was also known to Karl Haushofer, both men being described as 'orientalists'.

However, did Giessen correspond with the pilot's notes?

If one accepts that Giessen is the starting point, then the next step as described is Giessen to Den Helder in sixty minutes and Giessen to Borkum in fifty-five minutes – two options as to where to cross the coast. But does it all fit?

Giessen to Borkum is 380km and Giessen to Den Helder is 360km.

Hess had deliberately chosen 370km as a leg distance (see p. 129). We now understood the pilot's notes – they had begun at Giessen. Not Augsburg.

The total time in minutes refer to the time in the air from Giessen. Not Augsburg. This is vital as it allows Hess to fly without the necessity of a hand oil pump.

This is a major finding in both our work and the Hess affair in general as it demonstrates connivance. With connivance comes knowledge, thus destroying the 'solo flight' theory once and for all.

The notes remain a mystery and their provenance is far from secure. How they got to Brian Simpson seems most odd. We do believe them to be wholly genuine, but almost wish we did not, given the lack of provenance. They do, however, link all the components together.

We will now move on to describe the German radio navigation systems available at the time. This is the key that provides the link between the Lennoxlove Map, the pilot's notes and what actually happened on the evening of 10 May 1941.

10. GERMAN NAVIGATION SYSTEMS

The Hess flight over the North Sea was clearly a challenge for any lone flier to navigate. The obvious difficulty of the task has led to various suggestions of, for example, additional crew in the Bf 110, accompanying aircraft and greeting flights to guide Hess along his course.[24] Some have suggested the use of radio bearings, fixed from Kalundborg, Denmark, and guidance beams, like Knickbein, as possible aids. Navigation over the sea was a crucial aspect of the flight. From what we know of Hess, this would not have been left to chance.

We now seek to analyse the various contemporary means of navigation available to Hess when planning his flight. Throughout this part of our research, we have received much help and assistance from the acknowledged experts in this field: Dr Phil Judkins in England, Colonel Michael (SES) Svjegaard in Denmark and, in particular, Arthur Bauer from Diemen, Holland. Arthur has granted permission for us to reproduce his 2004 treatise on the subject, which deals with the development of the systems in much greater detail and with deeper understanding than we currently possess. This forms Appendix 1 and the reader is recommended to study the section. With the appendix in mind, we have summarised the available navigational tools available to Hess and tried to assess what was of practical use to him.

Before maps or radio, there was the Mk I eyeball. Rudolf Hess trained as a pilot during the latter years of the First World War. While radio navigation systems were in existence by that time, the vast majority of flights were carried out by simple visual recognition and comparison to a map of the area. Roads, railways and canals provided recognition points, together with woods, lakes and streams. Viaducts were often specifically marked as they provided a cross-check between water and railways or roads, an early form of 'fix'. As we have seen, the Lennoxlove Map, at first glance, provides a textbook example of how to draw up a map for a visual flight, with all the features clearly marked.

Obviously, visual recognition becomes more difficult at night, or in cloud or fog. When sending the map to the Hamilton family in May 1941, the Air Ministry noted that it had been marked up in accordance with the practice of the last war.[25]

Mapping

At the time of the Hess flight, the standard Luftwaffe mapping system was the *Gradnetzmeldeverfahren*, abbreviated to 'Gradnetz', which had been in existence since before 1939 and, with a few modifications, was to last until 1943. The system enabled a common map-reading system over a number of different map sizes, scales and projections. The system broke the world down into grid squares of diminishing scale:

Zusatzzahlgebeit: based on the Greenwich Meridian, these sectors were bordered by every ten degrees of longitude and latitude. They were sub-divided into 100.

Grosstrapez: each of a degree of longitude and latitude and given numbers from 00 to 99. The numbering sequences were in a different order to the east or west of the Meridian. Each was separated into eight sectors of two wide and four squares tall.

Mitteltrapez: numbered from the top left corner one to eight. A further division follows into nine.

Kleintrapez: equal square divisions numbering from the top left corner. Until 1943 these were divided into four.

Meldetrapez: numbered one to four, which were again divided into four.

Arbeitstrapez: which, again until 1943, had the descriptors lo (*links oben* - top left), ro (*rechts oben* - top right), lu (*links unten* - bottom left) and ru (*rechts unten* - bottom right).

Further details of the 'Gradnetz' system can be found in the works of Andreas Brekken.

We have examined a Luftwaffe *Gnomischerkarte* (Gnomonic chart) using the 'Gradnetz' system at the British Library. The Gnomonic projection ingeniously allows lines of bearing to be drawn as straight lines, the projection adjusting for the curvature of the earth.

Not surprisingly perhaps, the German mapping industry had experienced somewhat of a renaissance after the immediate First World War decline. Staffing numbers at *Die Reichsamt fur Landesaufnahme*, the German topographic surveys department, had increased from 539 in 1935 to 1,325 in 1937.[26] So, in researching the equipment that Hess would have had at his disposal, we have purchased some original wartime maps, some of which were actually used on raids. We were impressed by the quality of the product, but surprised at the sheer number of variations produced. Whilst researching this book we have acquired:

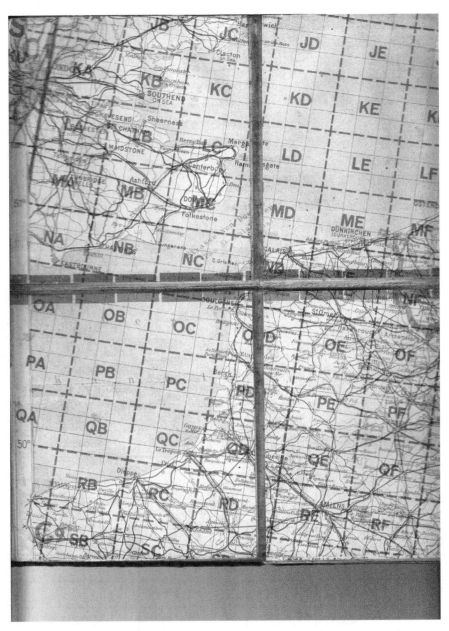

The 'flappable' gradnetz map book.

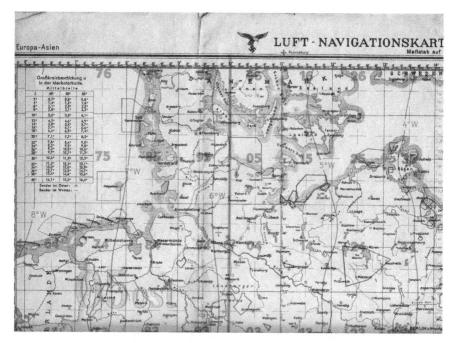

The Luftwaffe restricted area map.

LOCATION	SONNE OR ELEKTRA NO.	CO-ORDINATES OF LOCATION	BEARING OF NORMAL	MAST SPACING IN METRES	FREQUENCY KCS.	MAST SPACING IN L (λ)	FIRST HEARD	LAST HEARD	REMARKS.
HDR&ELKTRA	S ?	35°02'00"N. 25°43'38"E.	156.6°	1800 M.	481	2.89	May 1943		
BEAUVAIS	S19	49°25'49"N. 02°15'09"E.	324.75°	1875 M.	307	1.92	18.1.44.	13.8.44.	
STAVANGER	E 1	58°37'30"N. 05°37'48"E.	247°	2716 M.	319/297/319	2.89	May 1941		This Elektra first transmitted on 319 Kcs. and later changed to 297 Kcs. It was converted to a SONNE on 297 Kcs. but reverted to 319 Kcs.
HUSUM	E 2	55°21'53"N. 08°43'16"E.	269.5°	1792 M.	481	2.88	Aug. 1940		This site was to begin with E1 but later re-numbered E2, STAVANGER becoming E1.
BAYEUX	E 3	49°20'48"N. 00°42'35"U.	003°	2900 M.	297	2.95	Dec. 1940	Nov. 1941	Transmitted as SONNE on 306 Kcs. 25.8.43.
MORLAIX	E 4	48°32'48"N. 04°06'00"W.	325°	3230 M.	291	3.13	11.11.41	7.8.43	
QUIMPER	E ?	48°09'00"N. 04°13'35"W.	240°	2922 M.	316	3.17	Oct. 1942		
HDR&ELKTRA	E ?	35°02'00"N. 25°43'38"E.	156.6°	1800 M.	481	2.89	Aug. 1942		Converted to SONNE in May, 1943.

A table of Elektra/Sonne locations from history of RAF 80 Wing.

A 'Gradnetz' map of continental Europe, mounted on Perspex sheets, so as to allow easy 'flipping' of the pages from one area to that adjacent, vertical or horizontal.

A Luftwaffe map of Great Britain: this details all rivers, canals and estuaries. This is described as an *Ubersicht der Gewasser* (Survey of Waterways). This demonstrates the level of detail they were able to achieve.

A Luftwaffe map of Germany (*Navigationskarte in Merkatorprojection* – Navigation chart in Mercator projection) at a scale of 1:2,000,000 showing restricted air spaces. This too is a 'Gradnetz' map, and we have acquired a black and white copy for daytime flying and a coloured chart for the night. The restricted areas are around airfields, but there are other areas marked such as Peenemunde, to facilitate rocket testing.

Of particular interest is the fact that, on the German map, the Kalundborg radio station is marked in the margin as a *Rundfunksender* (radio transmitter) and the map reveals it to be virtually due north of Augsburg. Allowing Kalundborg to be marked (but certainly no other radio stations), the *Reichsamt für Landesaufnahme* was actually indicating that Kalundborg was not militarily important. In February 1940, the *Verordnung über die Veröffentlichung kartographischer Darstellung* (KartVeröffVO) was issued, stating that each map had to be assessed for its economic or military significance, and where appropriate, items 'should be omitted or falsified'. The fact that Kalundborg was allowed to remain presumably shows its low military value.

The Germans appeared to have a map for every purpose. Hess had no shortage, in theory at least, of maps to choose from. That is what made his eventual choice, based on British OS road maps, seem, at first glance, so odd. We now believe this was very clever indeed, as the maps were marked up for sophisticated radio-navigation direction-finding, but disguised as being the above. It certainly appears to have fooled the British Air Ministry in May 1941.

In theory, Hess could have used such mapping and dead-reckoning by time and compass to guide his way up the North Sea, but his course and timings would then be critical for success. To put the proposed flight into context, in 1927 Lindbergh had crossed the Atlantic Ocean on a solo flight, so such an undertaking was certainly not unprecedented, but that was not in wartime; though navigation had certainly improved in the pre-war years.[27] In 1941, Hess had to avoid detection by radar and interception or observation by patrolling ships or aircraft and arrive at his destination at the right time. His heading and distance to (if the commonly accepted flight plan is considered) his turning point towards Northumberland was key to his success. Would Hess have trusted to time-consuming calculation or would he have used other means, or both?

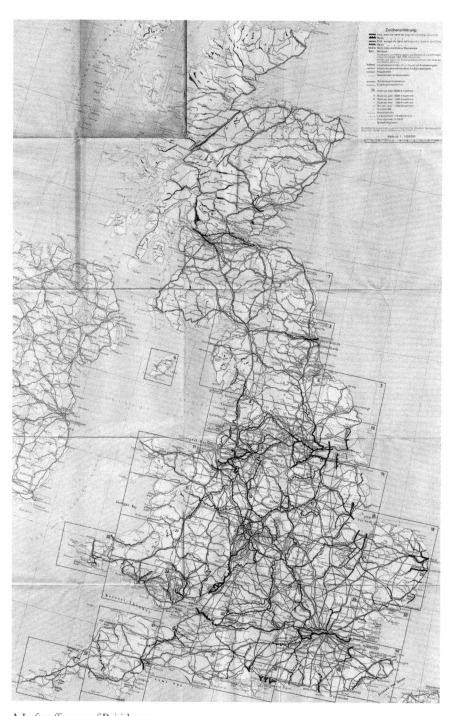

A Luftwaffe map of British waterways.

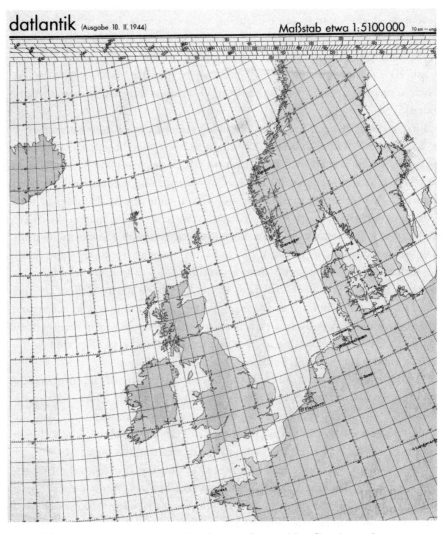

A rare Kriegsmarine gnonomic projection, showing German Navy listening stations.

Radio Navigation and Guidance

The pace of technical development in radio and radar at the time of the flight, driven by conflict, should not be understimated. The secret nature of much of this development does lead to some problems with the chronology of the advances and may have further prompted the need for covert planning and later denial or misleading responses. This is a complex field, but we are convinced that Hess would have planned the use of the technology to improve his chances of success. There is plenty of evidence to support this view, but which system would best fit his task?

First, radio bearings. Hess' story has many references to Radio Kalundborg[28] or Saarbruken.[29] These stations are thought to have played particular tunes as a form of message and acted as beacons from which positions and bearings could be taken. Elsewhere, alterations to Hess' on-board radio equipment have been reported.[30] We need to examine the use of radio as a beacon. In order to fix a bearing on a station, Hess would have had to tune in the equipment in the Bf 110 to find the 'null'[31] sectors and so set his position by azimuth, the clockwise position measured from true north. If he could not tune the fixed loop-type aerial, he would have had to align his aircraft with the radio source and read from his master compass. It is unlikely that Hess would have been able to turn an antenna to find a bearing, a shortage of space in the cockpit and time would have made that very difficult. A radio beacon was more commonly used for an aircraft to 'home in' on when returning to base, the information being displayed in the cockpit on the *Anzeigerät für Funknavigation*, AFN-(1/2).

The setting of his position by azimuth only gives part of the information required for navigation; he would need two bearings to get a clear idea of his position. Some have suggested that, once he had found Radio Kalundborg, he could fly due west from it to find his 'target' of Dungavel, which is said to be on the same latitude. Roy Conyers Nesbit makes mention of this possibility.

The Germans did employ various means of guiding aircraft to their target, including the Knickbein radio-beam system. These systems were known to the British and often misdirected by the 'Beam Benders'. Not only were they unreliable, due to British interference, they were specifically intended for multi-crewed aircraft leading bomber formations. Consequently, they needed some effort, skill, time, space and equipment to operate them. Additionally, and perhaps fatally for the Hess flight, they had to be switched on and directed at a target. If Hess' flight was really hidden from both sides, this would have demanded a lot of co-operation from the operators of the system and a general awareness of what was happening. Hess needed a simple to operate and low key navigation aid.

The Husum ELEKTRA station.

Secondly, Elektra and Sonne/Consol. In addition to the bombing systems that had been developed, there was also a Lorenz radio-guidance system, fully operational, called Elektra. This guidance system (*Leitstrahl*) was a development of the Lorenz blind-landing system, where the approaching aircraft would receive Morse signals to mark its position to the left or right of the approach to the runway. The landing system had been used successfully since the mid-1930s.

Dr Kramer at C.Lorenz AG (now Alcatel-SEL AG) had used the interaction of three transmitting antennas to throw out lobes of signal lines on fixed bearings, each with a sequence of Morse dots or dashes to one side or the other of each of the lobes or 'beams'. In this way, a pilot could keep to the continuous tone (equisignal) sector and fly along a known bearing. The Germans established several of these Elektra stations, which would mostly operate during the daytime; night conditions caused reduced accuracy from the signals. Stations included Elektra 1, Varhaug in Stavanger, Norway and Elektra 2 (originally E1 until Stavanger was given that designation) Poppenbüll near Husum, Germany. Elektra did not identify individual equisignal lines, other than by the known fixed bearing to the transmitter, and the navigator had to know approximately where they were as a starting point. Rather inconveniently for understanding the system, at the time of the Hess flight, improvements to the Elektra system were underway and the stations were undergoing conversion to a later development of the Elektra system known as Sonne.

Sonne used the same aerials and broadcast patterns as Elektra but, importantly, the signals could now carry navigational information. Instead of the dots and dashes to each side of the equisignal line, the stations now broadcast different numbers of dots and dashes between each line. The station continuously broadcast a two-minute signal sequence containing meticulous bearing and positional information.

The station broadcast an identifier call sign, then a short continuous tone to allow a bearing fix to be taken. The big difference from Elektra was that, after a short pause, a sixty-second transmission of numbers of dots and dashes was broadcast. These Morse characters always added up to sixty, but numbers of each character varied across the distance between the equisignal lines. In between the change from dot to dash, the keying merged into a short continuous tone before breaking out again into the next character. By counting the numbers of dots and dashes, the navigator could further refine his position between the equisignal lines. The difficulty in counting the characters as the sequence approached the change over from one to another could be overcome by timing the arrival of the short combined tone with a stopwatch; the sequence lasted for 60 seconds, so that every second was equivalent to one dot or dash. The whole transmission would repeat every two minutes and was repeated over all the equisignal lines in the pattern of dots into dashes or dashes into dots.

The extra information carried by Sonne became an important aid to navigation; the system was so useful that the Allies were to stop attempting to bend the signals, but rather to make use of if under the codename Consol. It was still in use from some stations, like Stavanger, into the early 1990s. This could explain why so little of the system has been mentioned in the Hess story to date; it was still very current technology.

In summary, the Germans had a passive radio net across the North Sea; it could have operated a beam flying system, Elektra, which gave only rudimentary navigational information or, in addition to that, the basis for a much more accurate positioning system, Sonne. Neither had to be 'directed' or switched on at a given time, but equally, both could be switched on and off as the need arose. Hess did not necessarily have to arrange for it to be active or wait until a Luftwaffe raid, and it was not being actively 'bent' by the British. Did Hess have the equipment training or time to use either system? If so, who would have trained him?

The practical operation of Elektra and Sonne only required basic equipment: a standard Luftwaffe radio, like the FuG 10EL[32] (as described later), a stopwatch and a map or conversion table. The only modification required to the radio was to put the radio receiver in the front cockpit, or make the set controllable by the pilot. Once set on a station, there would be little to do.

The original Elektra maps are very difficult to find[33] but the British Library does hold some slightly later German Sonne and British Consol charts. We obtained a copy of the British Consol chart, as it included the Stavanger station, and have seen the German Sonne chart, Nr. 2020 *Grossbritannien* (Great Britan), Sonne 5 Holland and Sonne 6 Quimper (Brittany, France). The Luftwaffe chart showing the Stavanger station is in the British Library, but has apparently been lost since 2009. The Luftwaffe map shows the Sonne equisignal lines and Morse sectors overlaid on a 1:200,000 *Schiefachsigergnomishernetzenwurf* (Gnomonic projection) 'Gradnetz' chart.

The practicality of Hess tuning the radio and counting and noting specific numbers of dots and dashes or time in seconds, or referring to a navigation chart, does not seem likely for his flight. He would be otherwise occupied.

There is, however, another more practical use of the radio beams. By employing them as waymarks, Hess could have maintained a compass bearing and then, by counting the number of equisignal lines as he approached and passed through them, fixed his position along his course. His turning point towards Britain could then be determined. If he were to lose his position, there was little in the circumstances that either Elektra or Sonne (or any beam system for that matter) could do for him without a lot of calculation or retracing his course. This far more simple use of the technology is exactly that which we believe he used, and is what the pilot's notes demonstrate he planned to use.

The Practicalities

A relation of one of the authors is a serving RAF officer with a background in navigation. We asked him some basic questions about navigation and how it was likely to have been achieved at the time of the Hess flight.

Our navigator explained the dynamic nature of the problem and how knowing where you are and where you are heading is as much a product of a combination of factors as it is relying on any one particular guide. The most basic form of navigation was and is still achieved by sight. Looking for features and comparing those with a chart or a mental map is the simplest way to navigate.

An on-board compass, if correctly calibrated, will give a heading for the aircraft, but varying wind speeds can allow a lot of error to creep in. The Bf 110 had a Siemens autopilot linked to the master compass that was mounted in the rear part of the fuselage. This can be factored in when planning a flight but, even as we saw on our short flight from Carlisle (see Chapter 16), the errors can quickly magnify.

The sun, the moon and the stars do offer known points and they have been used extensively as means of fixing a point (astro-navigation) almost for as long as man has travelled, though very good time-keeping is essential. Little help for Hess here, but the flight towards Britain was basically towards the setting sun. Accurate measurement of airspeed is important so that the flier can compare the arrival at any point with his original plan. There are references to Hess asking for the calibration of the aircraft's pitot tube, a device which measures airflow and drives an airspeed indicator.

So, we trust that we are now building the picture of how Hess was to achieve his challenging flight. He would have measured his progress along a compass bearing and from a known start point in terms of time to waypoints. In the absence of visual features over the sea, he would have used the beams emitted from a radio beacon, together with an expectation of duration obtained from his wristwatch. At a point following the crossing through a given number of beams, he would turn on to another known bearing and head toward the British coast.

As our RAF navigator colleague told us, and as we would probably have worked out for ourselves, the coast of Britain is a fairly easy target to find, the difficulty is finding the correct point of entry. To facilitate this, there is the principle of 'funnel features' and entry points. Once on a rough bearing to the coast, Hess needed some landmarks to fix his approach. There are several prominent features along the Northumberland coast, from islands to castles and lighthouses. Any of these features, or a combination, would have helped Hess to home in on his major navigational landmark, 'The Cheviot', the highest summit in the Cheviot Hills and close to the Scottish border.

This was his 'entry point' and the start of his flight over Scotland. From here on he could find his destination by following a general bearing and recognising landmarks, such as hills, lakes, waterways and, importantly, the railway lines along his way. Railway lines have always been a valuable landmark: they are permanent, they go from one known place to another, they are clearly not a natural feature and, with the polished surface of the rails, they are easily observable under a wide range of visibility conditions.

However, before moving on to the flight, we need to establish the precise position, frequencies and operation of the Elektra stations at Stavanger and Husum, for reasons that will become clear later in the book.

Stavanger and Husum Elektra Stations

By 1941 the various German radio-navigational systems were developing rapidly and Elektra/Sonne had made pinpoint accuracy a possibility, if the operator had the need, the time and the available space. The RAF was still mainly relying on the 'traditional' astro-navigation and dead-reckoning methods. In 1941, the Butt Report made the case that RAF bombing accuracy (and hence by inference, navigation) was at that time quite inadequate. Eventually, the RAF would develop the 'Gee', 'Oboe' and 'H2S' systems by way of response.[34]

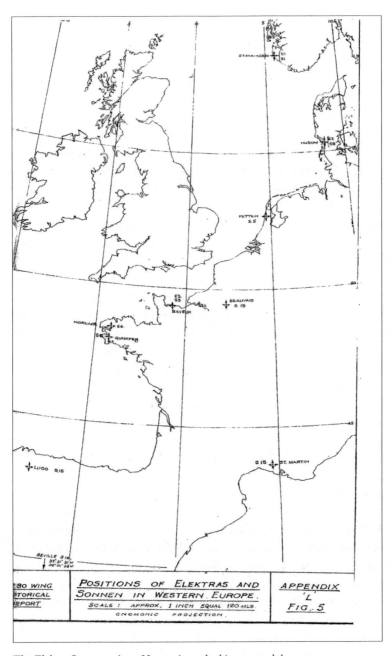

The Elektra Sonne stations. Husum is marked inaccurately!

This should not be too much of a surprise, as by early 1941 the British, when compared to the Germans, had not completed very much bombing.

The story of the 'Battle of the Beams' in 1940/1941 is reasonably well known and the R.V. Jones autobiography is an excellent telling of the story and the British response to the threat posed by German navigational systems.

As already debated, the authors have significant reason to believe that Hess did not use the Knickbein system, as a solo pilot would have found it too difficult to operate. Instead, we are content that he attempted to use the older and somewhat simpler system, designated Elektra. Further clues to its use can be taken from the many references made about the radio equipment in the Hess aircraft. In particular, in Helmut Kaden's lecture to the Hess Society in 1989, he reports the details of dots, dashes and continuous tones being heard in the headphones, which we know are the signals from the Elektra system. Furthermore, when Hess had complained to Josef Blümel, a radio technician,[35] about the radio not working, he had been told to fly farther north. Owing to the pattern of the beams produced by the transmitter, Hess would have found no useable Elektra beams from Husum until he had almost reached the German coast, and none from Stavanger until he was some way out over the North Sea.

As Arthur Bauer has described (see Appendix 1), the Elektra system consisted of three fixed masts, the largest in the middle. The distance from the middle mast to the outer masts effectively fixed the wavelength of the station.

Again we are grateful to Colonel Michaël (SES) Svejgaard from Denmark and Dr Phil Judkins for forwarding some photographs of various key components.

The British were clearly very interested in the system and PRO file AVIA 6/12437, gives further details as to its operation. These details come from a history of No. 80 Signals Wing RAF, which was detailed to monitor the transmissions. It should be noted that the files and photo-reconnaissance were typically dated 1943–44, by which time the Elektra system had developed into Sonne.

The important points to grasp as regarding the Hess case is that the first two Elektra stations, E1 Stavanger and E2 Husum, were the two stations that covered the area that Hess flew through. There were others, as the diagram shows, but they were not positioned to influence the Hess flight. Both covered the North Sea and both covered Lowland Scotland. The system was quite capable of reaching the farthest extremities of the Hess flight.

The Elektra system did not remain in service for too long, as it was deemed too easy to 'jam', usually by a process that was called 'meaconing', whereby the radio waves were distorted (bent) by the British. Eventually, it was then developed into the Sonne system, which lasted throughout and beyond the war. As Mr Bauer notes, the name was somewhat ironical: Sonne is German for sun, and at night the system was known to be less reliable in terms of accuracy. Eventually the system spread throughout Europe, as shown on the attached map. Consequently, it was certainly in place and operational for Hess to use.

The Stavanger Elektra site was actually on the outskirts of Varhaug, a small village some 25 miles south-west of Stavanger, Norway. An RAF air-reconnaissance report dated 21 October 1941 describes the site as being at Husvegg, which is adjacent to Varhaug and gives the co-ordinates of the site as being:

58° 36' 10" North
05° 38' 53" East

We have so far, been unable to locate an original Elektra chart for Husum or Stavanger. This is a little surprising, given the numbers that must have been produced at the time. But we have been able to locate a later Consol chart, which, as described, is a development of the earlier system. This map came from the instruction book of a nautical radio-navigation system of the 1970s. However, it does show how the system worked and, importantly for us, uses the same bearings and headings of the earlier system.

The Husum Elektra station was photographed by the RAF on Christmas Day 1944 and the following information obtained:

54° 21' 50" North (not 55° as per the 80 Signals Wing report)
08° 43' 14" East

In a similar manner to Stavanger, the Husum station was actually near Poppenbüll, on reclaimed *koog* (polder) some 15 miles south of the town of Husum.

Stavanger and Husum were the first two Elektra stations, E1 and E2. Consequently, they were located near to areas of intense Luftwaffe activity. After the invasion of Norway in 1940, the Stavanger airfield soon became a 'hub' and regularly drew the attention of the RAF. Husum was ideally located to provide cover for the Wadden See airfields and the major Luftwaffe base at Westerland on the Isle of Sylt. Elektra was also used by the Kriegsmarine (German Navy) and so its proximity to the port of Kiel would have been a consideration when positioning the sites. Both stations were at virtual sea level.

Each station accommodated sixteen men, with four being on duty at any time. There were eight-hour shifts and adjustments to the outer masts were achieved by pedalling. The staff slept on the site, and food was obtained from the local farms. It was noted that, 'everything was in a rather dirty state and the German personnel somewhat slovenly'.

The photograph illustrates position of the FuG10 (Funk Gerat 10) system directly behind the pilot of the Bf 110. Note the EL component directly in front of the 'Bordfunker'.

The Eaglesham crash site. Note the loop aerial beneath the Balkenkreuz.

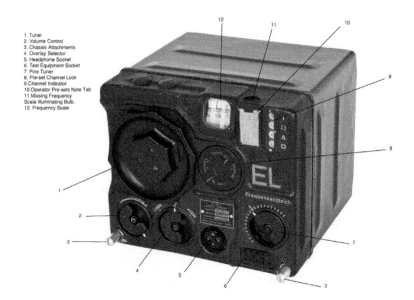

1. Tuner
2. Volume Control
3. Chassis Attachments
4. Overlay Selector
5. Headphone Socket
6. Test Equipment Socket
7. Fine Tuner
8. Pre-set Channel Lock
9. Channel Indicator
10. Operator Pre-sets Note Tab
11. Missing Frequency Scale Illuminating Bulb.
12. Frequency Scale

The Fug 10EL.

The Lorenz FuG 10EL and Loop Aerial System

By the outbreak of the Second World War, the FuG 10 (later FuG X) was a standard fitment to all Luftwaffe heavy aircraft, where it served for both radio and crew communication. The installation was made up of modules which could be easily removed for repair or upgrade. The major components of the system were the transmitters, *Senderkurzwelle* (Shortwave – SK), and the *Senderlangwelle* (Longwave – SL), each paired with a corresponding *Emfanger* (receiver), EK and EL respectively.

The FuG 10EL receiver covered frequencies around 300–600kHz and would have been used by Hess to receive signals from the Elektra transmitters at Stavanger, which was operating on 297kHz and 319kHz; Husum was operating at 481kHz.[36] Both stations were well within the FuG 10EL frequency range. 'Sonne and Elektra were so-called medium wave, some say long-wave, systems operating between say approximately 300–450kHz. The only radio necessary was thus one that covered this wave band. The Germans used then a 10EL or equivalent types.' (Arthur Bauer)

The equipment was manufactured by Lorenz AG and the radio waves were received by the aircraft by way of a fixed loop-type aerial, which was attached to the underside of the fuselage of the Bf 110. Initially, the fixed aerial would have been aligned with the central line of the aircraft fuselage.

The often reproduced photograph of the Eaglesham crash site certainly shows a loop aerial just to the left of the *Balkenkreuz* on the remains of the fuselage. When we visited IWM Duxford, it was obvious that the loop aerial had been fitted and then taken out of the fuselage, together with the master compass and oxygen bottle mechanisms. These items have yet to resurface from 1941. We suspect, but do not yet know, that they were rushed to RAE Farnborough for examination.

When an observer/gunner was flying in the rear cockpit (usual on operations), the loop aerial may have been fitted with a mechanism to allow it to be rotated, so as to locate a particular bearing. As far as the Hess flight was concerned, this requirement would have necessitated yet more equipment to be transferred into the front cockpit and, therefore, we consider it highly unlikely that Hess had arranged for the rotating mechanism to be fitted. Given what we have learned about the Elektra system, this was not a requirement.

As part of our research we acquired a working FuG 10EL transceiver, together with a copy of the original manual from Archiv-Hafner. We wanted to ascertain if there were further clues to be obtained from the equipment, possibly by linking it back to the pilot's notes, or even the Lennoxlove Map, or, as events turned out, both.

We were not to be disappointed. One of the features of the FuG 10EL allows it to be pre-set with four frequencies, designated I, II, Δ and □. This allows the operator to readily change between radio stations without the need for manual re-tuning; a white panel is provided next to the illuminated channel indicator for these settings to be noted in pencil. Straight away, we noticed that these symbols correlated to the pilot's notes and the Lennoxlove Map – the line of blue triangles. Note the top right-hand corner of the receiver.

There was one further link that Richard discovered. The pilot's notes (of unknown provenance) give the instruction: '30min v.A *aufnehmen* [receive] 03e1'. This we now believe should be translated as: '30 minutes from point A (von A) – switch on machine (FuG 10EL) to setting 0 (*Frequenzangleich* – Fine tuning), 3 (pre-set frequency Δ) – ELEKTRA STATION 1 – E1 (Stavanger).' '0' was the 'default' start position setting on the machine – the *überlagerungswahlschalter* (override selector switch).[37]

In his headphones, Hess could now listen for the dots, dashes and continuous tones of the Elektra system to guide his flight across the sea.

Consequently, it now appears to us that the FuG 10 system was also part of the planning process that was carried out at the same time as the pilot's notes and Lennoxlove Map were being prepared and marked up. There have been a number of accounts of alterations and amendments to the radio equipment, to facilitate its operation from the pilot's seat in the Bf 110.

We are not alone in this supposition. David Irving, in his narrative from the *Reichssicherheitshauptamt* (Reich Main Security Office – RSHA) interrogations, also makes mention of Elektra; he does not make any further reference to the system other than report that: 'Pintsch phoned the air ministry and asked them to switch on a certain beacon …' The name of the beacon does concur with the request to switch on the system; Elektra was probably operated as required, Sonne was constantly operational. Other than by David Irving, there has been little discussion as to how Hess achieved his flight. This aspect is fundamental because it could also explain what went wrong and caused Hess to act as he did.

On 12 February 1950, Hess wrote from Spandau to his wife, Ilse: 'Everything turned out quite otherwise than I had expected; the compass point to give me the right bearings, which I needed so badly at the decisive moment, was just the one thing missing … Before taking off I had lived in a world of … radio bearings (which afterwards failed to function) …'

11. THE BRITISH AIR DEFENCE SYSTEM

Hess was not knowingly assisted in any way to travel through British airspace in his attempt to land in western Scotland. This is for the simple reason that he did not need to be.

Way back in 1991, John Costello [38] made the allegation that the RAF effectively lent a 'blind eye' to the Hess aircraft and allowed him to fly through British airspace unhindered. John, who we met prior to his untimely death, [39] was a professional historian who depended on his writing to earn his living. Hence, there was always perhaps the temptation to chase the headline and, whilst his conclusion was incorrect, his research did at least make an attempt to describe the air defence structure that was in place.

James Douglas-Hamilton was able to call on Roy Conyers Nesbit in his 1993 work to refute Costello's conclusion. [40] The main issues revolved around the control of the airspace; we now give our interpretation.

While most Hess authors take account of the extent of the 'Chain Home' radar system, the RAF Coastal Command mounted patrols ranging much farther across the North Sea than its electronic counterpart. While aimed at anti-U-boat operations and shipping protection, it also played a part in reporting and sometimes intercepting incoming German air raids. This was the first obstacle that Hess would have to avoid.

We reproduce the extent of the Coastal Command patrols in late 1940. As can be ascertained from the diagram, regular patrols were being operated from RAF Leuchars, Thornaby and Bircham Newton. It was one of these patrols that produced the first British engagement with the Luftwaffe, when on 4 September 1939 a Lockheed Hudson from Leuchars intercepted a Dornier Do 18 flying boat.

The next hurdle to overcome was 'Chain Home' radar. RAF Fighter Command was based at Bentley Priory, Stanmore, north of London. This non-flying station controlled the air defence of Great Britain from 1936, when the former mansion was acquired as the centre of operations for both Fighter Command and the ROC. Air Chief Marshal Sir Hugh 'Stuffy' Dowding had developed the eponymous 'Dowding System' in the immediate years before the Second World War, which comprised four elements:

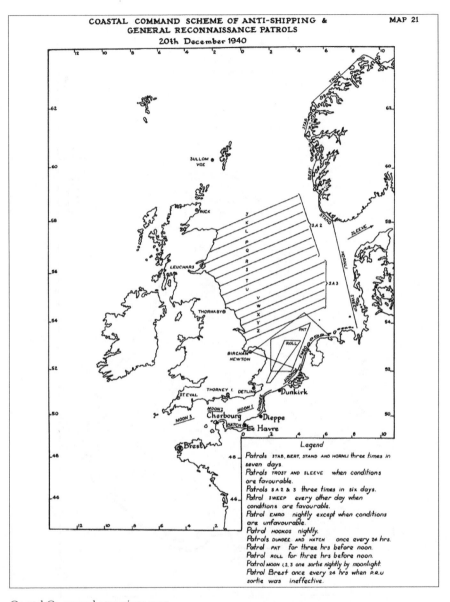

Coastal Command operations map.

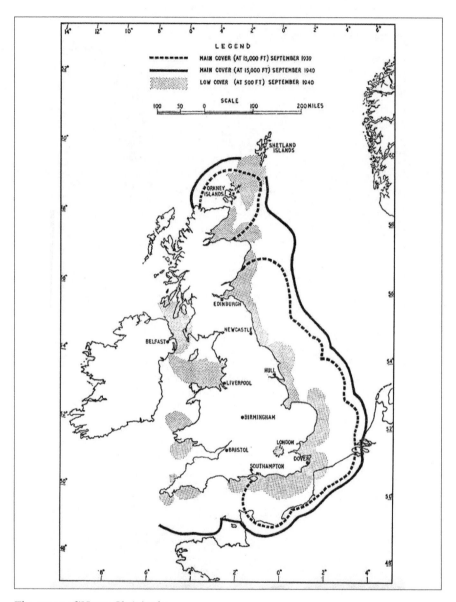

The extent of 'Home Chain' radar.

I: Radar observation until the coast
II: ROC observation once over land
III: Plotting
IV: Radio to vector fighters to their target.

The Hess flight was tracked under this system and we are quite content that at least parts I to III were carried out 100 per cent in accordance with the 'Dowding System', which at that time was the most comprehensive air defence system in the world.

Roy Conyers Nesbit covers the radar observation part of the flight very comprehensively and interviewed Felicity Ashbee,[41] the Women's Auxiliary Air Force (WAAF) operator on duty at Bentley Priory on the night of 10 May 1941. It was her job to track incoming aircraft from the radar reports being received by way of plots and relay them to the operations room by telephone. At that stage of the war, the information on the approaching contact was very basic and needed to be interpreted by Filter Officers, who relied on their judgement and experience to 'read' what was happening; the first stage was to telephone the local bases to see if they had any aircraft flying. Naturally, they would have been looking for the contact to behave in a typical manner and would have calculated their interception plans accordingly.

Ashbee, we have no doubt, did her job as instructed and noted the incoming aircraft from the reported plots. The 'Chain Home' system at that time had a range of some 120 miles into the North Sea, and so with the Hess aircraft travelling at 240–280mph, she would have approximately twenty to thirty minutes to 'tell' (indentify) the aircraft before it passed to the responsibility of the ROC for continued tracking.

In the aviation magazine *Aeroplane Monthly* in 1987, Felicity Ashbee wrote: 'It appeared 90 miles east of Amble, flying west, this is how Raid 42 was logged on the main plot at 2208hrs according to the 10 May 1941 Fighter Command Headquarters War Diary.' It appears to us that the system worked perfectly. Felicity also told John Costello that she waited for ten minutes to inform the operations room because the original report had come from Ottercops Moss 'Chain Home' station in Northumberland, which did not have a good reputation for reliability at that time.[43] Once confirmed by Bamburgh it became 'Raid 42'.[42]

During the ten minutes that Ashbee waited for confirmation, the aircraft would have travelled some 45 miles. Therefore, at 2218hrs, Hess would be no more than 45 miles out to sea, travelling at 5–6 miles a minute. This timing is confirmed by ROC post Embleton, Northumberland, reporting the aircraft as crossing the coast at 2223hrs. Bentley Priory must have then decided to act, for at 2220hrs (a mere two minutes later) Sergeant Maurice Pocock was scrambled from RAF Acklington in a Supermarine Spitfire of No. 72 Squadron. We have no doubt that Pocock would have shot down the Bf 110. The scrambling of the aircraft seems wholly consistent with the 'Dowding System'. Pocock was in the air, as were three Hawker Hurricanes of No. 317 Polish Squadron based at RAF Ouston. There were now four fighter aircraft in the sky capable of attacking the Bf 110. The 'Dowding System' was working effectively – so far.

We are now doubtful that Part IV was carried out as efficiently as the preceding three parts. If one chooses to believe John Costello, who interviewed Cecil Bryant DFM (Distinguished Flying Medal), then a 20-year-old radio telephone operator, an order was given not to attack the aircraft, or use anti-aircraft fire against it.[44] This contradicts the Pocock evidence. If no vectoring instructions were given, the fighters in the air would be searching for a very small target in almost total darkness. If one chooses to disregard the Costello evidence as the musings of a conspiracy theorist, the laws of probability prevail. Roy Conyers Nesbit quotes the statistic that, in May 1941, a total of 3,280 sorties were flown by RAF nightfighters, with a success rate of approximately 3 per cent, given that ninety-six enemy aircraft were destroyed. Therefore, statistically, Hess stood a 97:3 chance of avoiding being shot down. And the specifics of the situation must surely have widened those odds further.

With or without vector radio, which in the early days could be indistinct, we believe that Bentley Priory had achieved their task and put Pocock in a position to intercept, or perhaps at least see the Bf 110. However, Pocock, according to Conyers Nesbit climbed to 15,000ft, which would have taken between four and five minutes.[45] At 2225hrs, he was approaching this altitude over the coast of Northumberland. Conyers Nesbit quotes Maurice Pocock as having been vectored on to the flight path and that may well be the case, but he was far, far too high. According to the ROC Hess was nearly at sea level, 15,000ft beneath Pocock. The fact that Hess did not act 'typically' allowed him to avoid 'Chain Home' detection and interception.

Hess was reported by the ROC at Embleton as having already crossed the coast at 2223hrs. Therefore, we suspect that, unless Pocock was lucky enough to spot the Bf 110 while climbing away from the coast, it was then too late once he was at his patrolling altitude. Hess was already away to the west, travelling at a similar speed to Pocock's Spitfire, and desperately trying to locate 'The Cheviot'.

There were also the Hurricanes from No. 317 Polish Squadron already in the air. According to Conyers Nesbit, these aircraft were not instructed to intercept as 'they were not considered capable of operating at night and were not in a good position to make an interception'.[46] But if the fighters were 'not capable of operating at night' then what were they doing in the air at 2220hrs? Why were they not in a good position? If they were indeed the plot marked on the ROC Durham map, the fighters were actually patrolling down the Northumberland coast.

No. 13 Group, based at Usworth, near Newcastle, controlled the North of England and Scotland. The subsidiary sector stations were at RAF Acklington, Turnhouse, Dyce and Wick. So, all the information collected from the ROC and radar stations went to Usworth in the first instance, and then was collated and passed to the various sector stations. In turn, where appropriate, the sector stations would instruct the individual airfields under their command.

The whole of the Hess flight was covered by just two sector stations: Acklington and Turnhouse. Presumably because Ayr had only been operational for less than a month, it came under the direct control of Turnhouse (as did RAF Drem). Therefore, Douglas Douglas-Hamilton, 14th Duke of Hamilton, was very much in control of events once Hess had passed into western Scottish airspace, even if only on a theoretical basis. He was on duty that evening.

As for the eastern part of flight: from February 1941, RAF Acklington had a new commanding officer. His name was John Oliver Andrews and, at first sight, his appointment seems an anomaly in his career progression. Air Vice-Marshal J.O. Andrews, born in 1896, was the son of a Manchester brewer and had joined the Royal Flying Corps (RFC) in 1914 after initially enlisting as an army officer in the Royal Scots, Lothian Regiment. He was decorated as a fighter pilot and at the end of the First World War had received the Military Cross (MC) and bar, and also the Distinguished Service Order (DSO). During the 1920s, Andrews was obviously being 'groomed' for high office, spending time at Cambridge University and in Germany as a member of the Aeronautical Committee of Guarantee.

In the early 1930s, Andrews was in charge of seaplanes and, from 1932 to 1934, was in charge at RAF Mount Batten, a flying-boat station in Plymouth Sound, Devon. However, the rest of the decade saw him essentially training for higher rank. His postings:

December 1932:	Officer Commanding, RAF Mount Batten.
April 1934:	Staff, Directorate of Operations and Intelligence.
November 1936:	Re-qualified as German Interpreter, 1st class.
January 1937:	Attended Imperial Defence College.
December 1937:	Supernumerary, No. 1 RAF Depot.
February 1938:	Senior Air Staff Officer, HQ RAF Far East.
February/March 1940:	Director of Armament Development.
November 1940:	Assistant Chief of the Air Staff (Operational Requirements and Tactics)

Note the November 1936 appointment. In January 1941, he was made a temporary air vice-marshal, an appointment that was confirmed in April 1942. We assume the appointment was made prior to his posting to No. 13 Group in the

February of 1941, as it is traditional in the RAF that group commanders hold the rank of air vice-marshal.

What we find a little strange is that J.O. Andrews seems to be overqualified. He had a brilliant service record and was an academic. For instance, in 1932 he had won the Royal United Service Institute essay award. The 1930s appointments appear to be preparing him for high command, not an operational posting.

We now wonder if his appointment was more to do with his proficiency in German and intelligence matters, should an unexpected visitor arrive. By way of comparison, we looked at the record of Air Chief Marshal Trafford Leigh-Mallory who was placed in charge of No. 12 Group in 1937. His operational fighting record was much shorter than Andrews, yet he took the more prestigious appointment. Andrews took over at No. 12 Group in late 1942, following his time with No. 13 Group. It could just simply be that Andrews was passed over in favour of the more ambitious Leigh-Mallory, Park and Dowding.

The authors wholly accept that the above interpretation can be seen as stretching facts to fit theories, were it not for our meeting with Dougal McIntyre and his wife at their Prestwick home. Dougal, it will be remembered, is the son of David F. McIntyre, the joint founder of Prestwick Aerodrome and Scottish Aviation Limited. On the night of 10 May 1941, we know he was at Prestwick.

We went to the meeting with a list of questions, including a list of names of individuals that we wanted to know if his father knew. The name of J.O. Andrews drew the response: 'I can't add anything other than the name.'[47] We took that to mean that his father knew Andrews, which should not come as too much of a surprise, given that McIntyre was in charge of an aerodrome in No. 13 Group airspace.

Consequently, all we can say for certain in respect of the RAF command in Scotland that evening is that the commanding officer of No. 13 Group was a German expert, the Duke of Hamilton in the Turnhouse sector had some significant links with Germany, and that the base commander at RAF Prestwick/Ayr was an extremely close friend of the Duke of Hamilton and the Duke of Kent, the brother of King George VI.

Once Hess had avoided interception over the Northumberland coast, realistically he was unlikely to encounter any further problems (given that he would be flying in failing light over a very sparsely populated area) until he reached the West Coast of Scotland. This is exactly what happened, and will be described later.

If there was a British conspiracy at work that day, all they needed was oversight. Full control would require more people to be involved and therefore be much more difficult to manage, disguise or deny. We believe that less than ten people needed to know what was happening.

Though the air defence system was fully operational, Hess' flight plan did get him through; his plan was designed to evade the defences and exploit any weaknesses, and it largely worked. It has to be said that his planning, once over Scotland, would have benefitted hugely from some local knowledge. Our 2012 recreation of the flight demonstrated that, given the right landmarks, the navigation was quite possible to conduct visually.

In summary, the defences worked as they should, but they failed to bring down Hess. As it was, earlier events in the cockpit of the Bf 110 meant that no such interception was necessary.

12. GLASGOW AND THE NORTH AYRSHIRE COAST

The full moons in the first five months of 1941 were as follows: Monday, 13 January; Wednesday, 12 February; Thursday, 13 March; Friday, 11 April; Sunday, 11 May. These corresponded with the following major German aerial attacks on the British mainland: 2 January – Bristol and Cardiff; 7 January – Swansea; 19 February – Swansea; 13 and 14 March – Clydeside; 18 March – Hull (378 aircraft); 15 April – Belfast; 6 and 7 May – Greenock; 8 May – Hull; 10 May – London.

According to Walther Wewel, the pre-war head of the Luftwaffe, the objectives of strategic bombing were: to destroy the enemy air force by bombing its bases and aircraft factories, and defeating enemy air forces attacking German targets; to prevent the movement of large enemy ground forces to the decisive areas by destroying railways and roads, particularly bridges and tunnels, which are indispensable for the movement and supply of forces; to support the operations of the army formations, independent of railways, i.e., armoured forces and motorised forces, by impeding the enemy advance and participating directly in ground operations; to support naval operations by attacking naval bases, protecting Germany's naval bases and participating directly in naval battles; to paralyse the enemy armed forces by stopping production in the armaments factories.

These appear all very laudable in military terms. However, once the Battle of Britain had effectively been lost in the late summer of 1940, the German command switched their tactics to that of 'Blitz'. Whilst no doubt mindful of the above aims and objectives, in truth the Germans were trying to bomb the British to the negotiating table.

In early 1941, Glasgow and its hinterland were internationally famous for heavy industry. The John Brown shipyard on the Clyde had built some of the most famous ships of the time, including HMS *Hood*, RMS *Queen Mary* and RMS *Queen Elizabeth*. The re-armament programme had helped bring the city out of the depression. Typically, the workers would live close to their place of work, so from 10,000 feet there was little possible by way of discrimination between industry and residence.

The Luftwaffe had sent a reconnaissance unit to photograph the city and other local points of interest in February 1941. The authors have copies of some of the aerial photographs and thank the Royal Commission on the Ancient & Historical Monuments of Scotland (RCAHMS) for their co-operation in this matter.

[DUPLICATE FOR THE FILE.]

No. 18652.

Certificate of Incorporation.

I hereby Certify that

"Scottish College of Aviation Limited"

is this day incorporated under the Companies Act, 1929, and that this Company is **Limited**.

SIGNED by me at Edinburgh, this ninth day of August

One Thousand Nine Hundred and thirty-five.

John A. Inglis

Registrar of Companies,

Certificate of Incorporation of Scottish Aviation Limited, based at Prestwick.

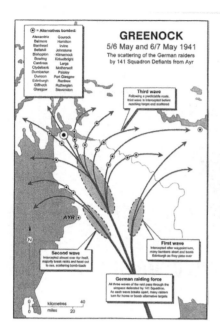
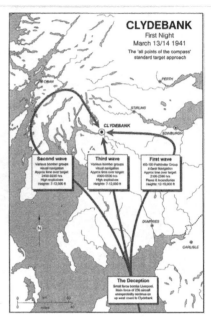

The 1941 Glasgow raids.

This 'sortie' was in confirmation of the earlier photographs taken between 1938 and 1939, typically from commercial aircraft operated by Lufthansa.

A month later, on 13 March, the Luftwaffe sent some 260 bombers to attack Glasgow, just after 2100hrs, dropping incendiary and high-explosive bombs. They left at approximately 0620hrs the following morning.[48] The following night the Germans returned with a force of 200 bombers at 2035hrs, leaving at 0227hrs.

Officially, the memorial records 528 dead and 1,000 injured, but barely a house in Clydebank had not been damaged.[49] Early in the war, a programme of evacuation had been implemented, but with so little 'action' in 1940, many of the populace had returned. A figure of 90 per cent occupancy has been quoted for the night of 13/14 March.

The *Glasgow Herald* newspaper posted the following tribute: 'The cool, unwavering courage of the people is evident, and when the full story of their heroism in the face of the Luftwaffe is told, they will take their place alongside the citizens of London and Coventry.' The phrase 'when the full story is told' is interesting. Newspaper reporting was strictly censored and nationally only an attack on a 'central Scottish town' was duly reported. There was little reference to the injured.

Glasgow was to suffer again when on 6 and 7 May (the Tuesday and Wednesday before the Hess flight ended on Saturday) Greenock was attacked in particular, again with incendiaries and high explosives. Notoriously, the local distillery in

Ingleston Street was hit and erupted in flames, providing a target for the following bombers. There are many stories of individual and collective heroism that are still fresh in the minds of local people today. (For a detailed account of the raids we recommend the excellent *Luftwaffe over Scotland* by Les Taylor.)[50]

These events are described to demonstrate that, while certain parts of the Hess flight passed over relatively undefended territory, when reaching its final miles, the relevant area was already on a high state of alert, with a bloody, torrid experience only a few days old. Unexpected visitors were unlikely to be welcomed.

In 2013, the North Ayrshire coast is quite rightly marketed as an area of outstanding natural beauty. The Firth of Clyde provides a scenic foreground for the more southerly western isles, such as Arran and the Cumbrae Islands. The sleepy coastal towns of Troon and Prestwick are now better known internationally for golf; Ardrossan and Largs to the north as ferry terminals for Arran and Cumbrae. Greenock (Gourock) also provides a route over the Firth to Dunoon operated by Western Ferries (Clyde) Limited.

In 1941, the picture really could not be more different and the resultant change is perhaps, for once, a positive reflection of man's progress in matters scientific.

Prestwick

Geographically its location is 55°30' North and 04° 37' West, and is 20 miles from Dungavel House and 21 miles from Eaglesham. It is on the Ayrshire coast and is located between Troon and Wallacetown. It is 32 miles south-west of Glasgow. When travelling at 200–300mph in a Bf 110, clearly these distances can be covered in minutes. At 300mph an aircraft will cover a mile in twelve seconds, at 200mph in eighteen seconds.

Today Prestwick is well known as an international airport, the only place that Elvis Presley has put foot on British soil and for its proximity to the famous golfing resorts of Ayrshire. However, seventy-nine years ago in 1934, one David McIntyre was simply looking for a site to build an aerodrome.

McIntyre was born in Glasgow in 1905 into a Clyde shipbuilding family. Like many boys and young men at that time, he was drawn to aviation and, in 1927, joined No. 602 Squadron of the RAF, at that time based at Renfrew, just south of Glasgow.

Importantly for this story, chronologically, the next pilot to join the squadron was Douglas Douglas-Hamilton, the then Marquis of Clydesdale. The two men were to become lifelong friends. As McIntyre's son Dougal writes, 'They were men from widely differing backgrounds whose mutual love of flying brought them together at a formative time both for aviation and the Auxiliary Squadron movement.'[51]

They were best man at each other's weddings.[52] The period from 1927 to 1933 appears to have seen the two men having a lot of fun flying various types of aircraft, from the DeHavilland Gypsy Moth to the Hawker Hart fighter.[53] A flight to Australia was even proposed.[54]

In 1933 the two men took part in the Houston Mount Everest Expedition, becoming two of the first to fly over the world's highest mountain. The impact of this achievement was great, combining aviation, very much the 'spirit' of the age, with the allure of Everest. On their return they were feted, wrote a book together,[55] and their consequent fame made many demands on their time. McIntyre was also working on plans for a round-the-world flight.[56]

The Conference for the Reduction and Limitation of Armaments of 1932–34 was an effort by member states of the League of Nations to prevent a post-1919 escalation of armaments. It failed when Hitler withdrew Germany from both the conference and the League of Nations in October 1933. The failure is the reason that Dougal McIntyre cites for his father's decision to try and make money from what he saw as the national need to re-arm. He cleverly anticipated trouble ahead and, consequently, came up with the idea of a pilots' training school: somewhere the RAF could send their future pilots and navigators.

David McIntyre approached the then Marquis of Clydesdale and his brother, 'Geordie' Douglas-Hamilton. On account of a previous Duke of Hamilton having over-mortgaged the estate, the remaining equity had been placed into a trust. So it was that the trustees of the Hamilton Estates became the owners and landlord of the 348 acres adjacent to Orangefield House, Prestwick, Ayrshire. A limited liability company was duly incorporated on 9 August 1935 called 'The Scottish College of Aviation Limited'.[57] Subsequently, the name changed to 'Scottish Aviation Limited', once the ownership of the original name had been acquired.[58] The original share capital of the company was:

Marquis of Clydesdale	43,545
Geordie Douglas Hamilton	30,045
David McIntyre	25,910
Company	500[59]

As the Marquis of Clydesdale was then an MP, his brother 'Geordie' assumed control of the shares, as well as being a director of the company. Clydesdale was not allowed to be a serving director of a company whilst engaged in government contracts. The private nature of the shareholdings was to cause various issues to arise when the airfield was expanded using government funding during the course of the war.

The period from 1936 to 1939 was one of rapid expansion for the 348 acres of Scottish pasture. The expansion was helped by the connections of the Marquis of Clydesdale. DeHavilland took shares in the new company in lieu of payment for DeHavilland Gypsy Moth training aircraft.[60] He persuaded R.L. Angus[61] to become a director of the newly formed company and, interestingly, would choose to fly from Dungavel House, where he lived (just 20 miles inland from Prestwick) whenever possible.[62] Things progressed:

December 1935 – Aircraft arrive.

February 1936 – First 34 students enroll.

1936 – Building work, hangars, offices, accommodation.

1937 – School expands to take on training of RAF volunteer reservists.

Hawker Hart aircraft arrive for pilot training.

1938 – Navigation training commences

Avro Ansons arrive for pilot training.

Further hangars and offices built.

1939 – Factory built to maintain Vickers Wellington bombers.

A second airfield at Grangemouth starts to be developed.

The effort required to achieve all this meant that, by 1939, neither Clydesdale nor McIntyre was in command of No. 602 Squadron. They did not have the time. David McIntyre was appointed to head Scottish Aviation Limited. Effectively, he was in day-to-day control of Prestwick airfield. This extended to the seaplane base at Largs and the maintenance unit at Carlisle. Clydesdale was also a serving MP.

The Marquis of Clydesdale's standing in the pre-war aeronautical circles was significant. He was internationally famous after the Everest flight, he was a serving RAF officer, he had privately owned a number of aircraft, owned his landing strip and now his family had gained control of what was to become the foremost aviation company in Scotland. Similarly, David McIntyre, while never as famous as the Hamiltons, was also a very impressive figure: RAF officer, Everest flight member and now head of a fast expanding aviation company. When Clydesdale and McIntyre took part in the Everest flight in 1933, they chose to fly the aircraft to Nepal and back.

Later in the 1930s, they both flew their relatively small and unrefined DeHavilland machines all around Europe. Flights to Switzerland, Austria, Germany[63] and France are well documented, and some authors have speculated that Clydesdale and McIntyre were being used as semi-official intelligence agents. Clydesdale was not the only member of the family being used in this way; 'Geordie' Douglas-Hamilton was to become the Chief of Air Intelligence, Fighter Command and his brother, David, also a serving RAF officer, was fluent in German. Dougal McIntyre's book shows pictures of his father in various European locations throughout the 1930s, and we should not be surprised by this, given both men's standing at that time and the general fascination with all things aeronautical. It was also potentially lucrative from a business perspective.

'Geordie' Douglas-Hamilton lived at Eldo House, adjacent to the Orangefield House, a lovely mansion dating back to 1723, which had become the control tower of the airfield by the simple expedient of removing its ancient roof and replacing it with the traditional aerodrome-type glass canopy. When the war began, the usefulness of the airfield became immediately apparent and the Supermarine Spitfires of No. 603 Squadron moved in during December 1939.[64] Thereafter, Nos 615, 610, 253, 141 Squadrons and No. 1 Squadron RCAF all occupied the base before No. 602 Squadron (The old 'City of Glasgow' to which both Clydesdale and McIntyre belonged) vacated on 15 April 1941. As has already been alluded to, the airfield was then transferred to the Atlantic Ferry Organisation (ATFERO) in early 1941.[65]

Therefore, on Saturday 10 May 1941, the airfield had no serving RAF Squadron. We also doubt the training school would be at its busiest at that time of the week, the students more likely to be enjoying the local hostelries than learning air navigation. PRO file AIR 28/653 records that, on 9 May 1941, students of No. 3 Radio School Training Squadron had moved to the airfield and billeted in a complex of huts. They had previously been billeted in the town.

We know that General Sikorski landed on the following morning and that a number of aircraft flew in on 15 May, but the airfield was relatively empty. It had been busy up to the departure of the last RAF Squadron in April 1941 and was to become incredibly busy from mid-1941 onwards, but 10 May 1941 would have seen it unusually quiet.

James Douglas-Hamilton makes no mention of his father's, uncle's, family's and trustee's role in the formative years of Prestwick airfield. Why might that be? His book is quite understandably full of the many other aeronautical achievements of his family. This omission has been rectified in the 2013 *Patriotic Duke* by Mark Peel.

There has been some confusion over the years as to the relationship with RAF Ayr. We know from the 'Hess archive' that, on 10 May 1941, a Boulton Paul Defiant was sent up at 2234hrs to intercept, piloted by Pilot Officer Cuddie and crewed by Sergeant Hodge.[66] In May 1941, RAF Ayr hosted No. 141 Squadron, which was equipped with the Defiant Mk.I night fighter. Their commander was Squadron Leader Loel Guinness, who worked from nearby Rosemount House, a large building that overlooked the airfield, which also doubled up as the command base for Prestwick aerodrome.[67]

Somewhat confusingly perhaps, RAF Ayr and Prestwick were literally adjacent; RAF Ayr being known locally as Heathfield. After the war, part of RAF Ayr was built on, while another part was taken over by the RNAS (Royal Naval Air Service) and became HMS Wagtail. On 10 May there was actually no distinction in terms of command structure, both being controlled from a command and a single commander who took his instruction directly from No. 13 Group, which in practice meant RAF Turnhouse.

RAF Ayr had only become operational on 7 April 1941, with three long concrete runways, 4,100ft, 4,500ft and 4,700ft. Being adjacent to Prestwick, which had only just started to receive the larger types of US bomber, a combined circuit was arranged for landing traffic. Therefore, the two airfields in name were essentially one operationally, with a joint commander. In terms of personnel, Squadron Leader Loel Guinness (a close friend of the Duke of Kent) and David McIntyre (a very close friend and business partner of the Duke of Hamilton) were in charge of RAF Ayr and Prestwick, whilst their immediate commanding officer was the Duke of Hamilton, in his capacity of commanding RAF Turnhouse.

ICI Ardeer viewed from the south.

ICI, Ardeer

In May 1941, the Imperial Chemical Industries (ICI) factory at Ardeer was, according to size, the most heavily defended area in the United Kingdom.

Constructed on a 100-acre site on the Ardeer peninsula, Alfred Nobel had chosen the site as his UK explosives base in 1871 for two main reasons: firstly, remoteness, and secondly because of the sand dunes. The dunes provided excellent natural protection from any accidental explosion. In 1926, the Nobel Company had been taken over by ICI and, in 1941, the site was extremely heavily protected. To both the north and south there were heavy anti-aircraft positions:

Stevenston: Longitude 04° 45' 12" North; Latitude 55° 38' 22" West
Irvine: Longitude 04° 39' 18" North; Latitude 55° 37' 09" West

These were not new. PRO file WO192/103 gives details of the guns provided during the 1914–18 war. In addition, there were twenty-four barrage balloons sited at Ardeer.[68] They detail the following distribution of Scottish balloons on 1 October 1940. Flying strengths during first year:

GLASGOW – 79
FORTH – 48 (October 1939)
LOCH ALSH – 16 (September 1940)
SCAPA – 35 (February 1940)
ARDEER – 24 (September 1940)
BELFAST – 16 (September 1940)

No. 18 Balloon Centre, Bishopbriggs, Glasgow
No. 929 Squadron: 24 balloons at South Queensferry (7 waterborne)
No. 945: 40 balloons at Glasgow
No. 946: 48 balloon at Renfrew
No. 947: 32 balloons at Glasgow
No. 948: 24 balloons at Rosyth
No. 967: 48 balloons at Ardrossan
No. 968: 16 balloons forming at Bishopbriggs; moved to Belfast, 12 September 1940 (8 waterborne)

PRO File AIR16 /395 provides further detail. On 2 April 1941, the file records the desire to increase the current 24 balloons to '32 LZ balloons and 8 Mk.VI balloons … The present 24 operational balloons are a thin protection'.

So a number of barrage balloons protected an impressive industrial complex, its location signalled by the large chimneys necessary for the various processes. At its peak, over 13,000 people were employed at the site, being transported in from the local towns by its own railway. Production lasted just into the new millennium, before closure. However, in May 1941, its importance, both on a local and national scale, cannot be underestimated. At its height it was producing 540 tons of cordite per week. The fact that its existence is not better known is a testament to the secrecy under which it operated for much of its life. We believe that its very existence played a major part in explaining precisely when and where Hess flew on 10 May 1941. The Luftwaffe was certainly aware of it and we reproduce a later (1947) picture of the site.

AA Command by Colin Dobinson[69] considers in detail the race to provide adequate air defences for the UK once war appeared to be inevitable. Appendix 2 usefully records the disposition of the available heavy anti-aircraft (AA) artillery. Typically, these were 3.7 or 4.5-inch guns. In June 1940, Ardeer received four, 3.7-inch mobile guns, followed by a further four the following month. In January/February 1941, the eight mobile guns became permanent fixtures at the two sites. In May 1939, each potentially vulnerable site was assessed as to how many AA artillery guns were ideally necessary for defence. Glasgow was deemed to require eighty AA guns. By May 1941, seventy-five guns were in place and another eight were positioned at Ardeer. This information was deemed so sensitive that, originally, the files containing it were embargoed until 2042.

Close to Ardeer was Ardrossan to the north, the site of a Shell Oil Company refinery, specialising in the production of bitumen. As already mentioned, the town was home to the No. 967 Barrage Balloon Squadron, equipped with forty-eight balloons. Largs was home to a flying boat/seaplane maintenance yard, operated by Scottish Aviation Limited. Fairlie is a few miles south of Largs and the location of a small dockyard. In November 1940, the Royal Navy moved the ASDIC (anti-submarine radar) research centre from Portland, Dorset, to the site.

We hope it can be seen that, from Turnberry to Greenock there was very little of the coast that did not present some form of peril to the uninitiated pilot. It was a very dangerous place to be flying: Ayr and Prestwick, both operational RAF airfields with day and night fighters; Ardeer, an ordnance factory heavily defended with barrage balloons and heavy anti-aircraft artillery; and Ardrossan, an oil refinery defended with barrage balloons

It is therefore difficult to understand why Hess would choose to target this part of the north Ayrshire coast. He actually seemed to be making for Ardeer,[70] probably the most heavily defended area in the UK. We do not believe that this part of the story has been adequately explored previously. In the later chapters we will show how an understanding of the features listed above dramatically influenced Hess' thought processes and actions on the night of 10 May 1941.

13. TIME, SUN AND MOON

When writing to his wife between 1941 and 1947, Rudolf Hess makes specific mention of the prevailing light conditions whilst making his flight: 'The North Sea was illuminated by an evening light of unearthly loveliness …'; 'I crossed the East Coast at about 10.00pm and after sunset … at this level the visibility was surprisingly good'; 'On I went over level ground, skimming merrily over house tops and trees and waving greetings to men working in the fields'; 'The smooth sea lay beneath me as calm as a mirror, lit by the rising moon'; 'So there I was … the mist barely illuminated by a full moon.'

To check that the descriptions could be true, we travelled to the west coast of Scotland on 2/3 May 2009, specifically to check the prevailing light conditions at 2300hrs. We arrived at Prestwick in the early evening and waited.

In 1941, the UK had operated 'double summer time', which is Greenwich Mean Time (GMT), plus 2 hours. This action was a counter reaction to increased traffic accidents, partly as a result of the wartime requirement to shroud vehicle headlights. This policy had been implemented as recently as 4 May 1941.

German time is usually 1 hour ahead of GMT, by reason of longitude. On 1 April 1940, it had adopted *Mitteleuropäische Sommerzeit*, which had the effect of adding another hour. So 11.09 p.m. in Germany was the same as in Scotland. Apparently Hess knew this. In the 1947 work *The Case of Rudolf Hess* by J.R. Rees, a map is reproduced that purports to have been drawn by Hess and is annotated with the various times at various points: 5.45 p.m. (1745hrs) and 11.09 p.m. (2309hrs) are shown as the start and conclusion of the flight.

Clearly, speed is a function of time and distance, and is vital in understanding the flight. Some authors have spoken of 'the missing hour', which we will analyse later, but a simple explanation of the 'missing hour' could just be a differential between the German and UK basis of time measurement. Hence, his need to be absolutely certain.

We needed to be in the same area as Hess as there is also a differential between the 'lighting up time' in London and Glasgow, some 400 miles to the north. We travelled to Prestwick. At the equivalent time to 2309hrs, on 10 May 1941 we made our observation. It was dark, very dark. So dark that it would not be possible to attempt to safely land an aircraft without some form of runway lighting. However, on 2 May 2009 we were seven days away from the full moon and, therefore, the prevailing light conditions as described above were without any moonlight. PRO File AIR 28/40 makes the point that there was cloud cover over Prestwick in the ratio of 3:10 on 10 May 1941, and that fact should also be factored into any assessment of light conditions. Any light that there was from the moon, low in the sky, was partially obscured by clouds.

It is possible to ascertain the sun and moon positions at any time and, from this, to gauge the condition of twilight. Though light levels vary from day to day depending on the amount of sunshine reflected in the atmosphere, this is sufficient for us to get a good idea of the flying conditions that Hess faced.

From: http://planetcalc.com/874/ Using the co-ordinates from Google Earth and all times at GMT +2 (BDST), the sunset times were:

Dunstanburgh Castle,	55° 29' 05"N, 01° 35' 26"W	22.00.11hrs
Dungavel,	55° 35' 56"N, 04° 07' 02"W	22.10.41hrs
Kilmarnock,	55° 36' 45"N, 04° 26' 55"W	22.12.15hrs
West Kilbride,	55° 42' 01"N, 04° 51' 27"W	22.14.06hrs
Eaglesham ROC,	55° 44' 38"N, 04° 17' 37"W	22.12.04hrs

At Glasgow on the day, the sunset time was 22:12:45hrs GMT+2, civil twilight ended there at 23:00:03hrs, with nautical twilight ending at 00:10:19hrs. This introduces a time for twilight, which has an accepted description of the prevailing light conditions. The sunset azimuth, the bearing clockwise as taken from true North, was that day around 304° and it would have moved around from 289° at an elevation of nearly 8° at 2100hrs. It would have been to the north of his course and set for all of his flight over Scotland.

The same calculators can set the state of twilight for each position along the flight. Civil twilight starts at sunset, sun elevation 0°, and ends at -6°. For this exercise we can consider the end of civil twilight to mean dark.

	Sunset Time	Time of Hess Pass	Sun Elevation
Dunstanburgh Castle	2200hrs	2228hrs	– 4.2°
Dungavel	2210hrs	2245hrs	– 4.9°
West Kilbride	2214hrs	2250hrs	– 5.0°
Kilmarnock	2212hrs	2300hrs	– 6.2°
Eaglesham	2212hrs	2309hrs	– 7.1°

Considering that Hess' altitude would have altered the timings and light conditions, this was also calculated. The time of sunset is one minute later for every 55ft of altitude, so about one minute for Hess at 5,000ft.

We can put the moonrise time, when it can first be seen over an ideal (flat) horizon, at Glasgow as 21:13:32hrs at an azimuth of 113.35°. This was to be a 99.02 per cent illuminated full moon, so potentially bright. In the area around Dungavel the approximate position of the moon would be:

Time (GMT+2)	Altitude	Azimuth
2111hrs	0°	113° (Approximate Moonrise)
2230hrs	08.14°	129°
2245hrs	09.44°	132°
2250hrs	10.13°	133°
2255hrs	10.42°	134°
2300hrs	11.10°	135°

So we have a bright full moon, but very low during the time of the flight and 'veering' from SEE to SE. At that time, while it was still twilight, and with the moon at a low angle of elevation, it is doubtful that it would have been much help with visual feature recognition navigation. However, the true effect on illumination and visibility is very difficult to ascertain or appreciate.

We can probably work on Hess having around thirty to forty minutes of useable light after sunset. It is interesting that his approach and over flight are all in a narrow time band in relation to the sunset as it progressed from east to west; was he intending to make the flight so late in the day?

He would have already been well into civil twilight as he reached Dungavel at 2245hrs. Going to the coast for bearings would have put him in what was effectively darkness on his return. Would he really have been able to find Dungavel by sight? The inescapable fact is that, when over Scotland, Hess was desperately chasing the light, without a realistic chance of success.

As the calculations have shown, sunset at Dunstanburgh (on the east coast of England, near to ROC Embleton) was at 2200hrs. Hess crossed the coast around twenty minutes later, technically towards the end of 'civilian twilight'. Already it was becoming far too dark to land a sophisticated aircraft such as the Bf 110. He was already in trouble.

By the time Hess arrived over Dungavel House at 2240 to 2245hrs., sunset had been some thirty-five minutes before. Hess was now technically verging towards nautical twilight, whereby no difference between the coast and the sky could be discerned. By this time his only light source was coming from the moon, which, while bright, was low in the sky. This presumably must have been sufficient to allow the various ROC stations to make a positive identification of the silhouette of the Bf 110. However, surely a controlled landing was no longer a viable option. It is questionable whether any form of unlit landing was now an option. We believe that, by this time, the flight had completely unravelled. Parachuting may now have featured in his thinking for the first time, as the only option.

Why does Hess, in retrospect, describe a situation in which he is wholly in control? The reality was that he was now reacting to events, he was no longer in control of them. The opening quotes to this chapter cannot stand scrutiny by reference to the facts and, once again, must be seen as devices to mislead.

Finally, we must consider the aeronautical implications of the position in which Hess had now found himself. The best way to ascertain the situation is to reproduce some current pilot training notes. Some of the comments are extremely pertinent. We should also add that there is no evidence that Hess actually had any prior experience of night flying. The following information is a precis of fuller notes kindly provided by a modern-day expert who wished to remain anonymous. It may be of interest that the anonymous contributor's mother shot down six German aircraft during the war!

Night Flight

Night poses a risk for all pilots regardless of experience, but the inexperienced pilot is especially at risk. Some 72 per cent of our flying information comes through the eye, and the eye is easily fooled at night. The inexperienced pilot has from twenty seconds to three minutes before losing control after the onset of spatial disorientation.

Once the eye lacks required information, the brain seeks information from the inner ear sensors and the proprioceptive system of our flesh and bones. When there is nothing for the eye to focus on it defaults to about 4ft. We will not see at a distance unless the eye is made to look into the distance. It is possible for an aircraft to turn so slowly that the body senses will not recognise it.

Night flying has a higher accident rate than identical day flying. Always have aircraft and flight kit prepared for unplanned night flight. Night causes usual visual flight aids to become non-existent. Night visual and sensory illusions are unique to the conditions. Do not look directly toward the area where you expect to see best; look slightly to one side or the other. This visual outlook applies to the landing flare as well as every other situation. The special skills of night flying can only be acquired and maintained by frequent night flights.

For night flying you must evaluate the relative risks of such a flight. A planned night flight is far less likely to make its planned departure time and arrival time. If schedule is going to be important, do not fly at night. Change either the flight or the schedule.

Being lost at night is more critical than in the daytime, just as will be an engine failure. Ten times as many accidents occur on dark nights and nearly 30 per cent of the fatalities, and an additional 15 per cent of the non-fatal accidents, occur at night when not quite 5 per cent of the flying takes place.

Some 19 per cent of total fatal accidents occur at night because of power related forced landings. Around 14 per cent occur during the day in similar power related fatal accidents. The disparity in these figures (they lie) is that only 4 per cent of flying is at night.

Flying at Night is Not …

just like flying in daytime … The hazards of night flying are directly related to the physiological limitations of the human body, not the aircraft. Humans do not perform well at night. Night flying will be different. Night flight is more stressful than day flying and very near to Instrument Flight Rules (IFR) flight without the required training. It should be. A moderate amount of stress will improve performance, keep the pilot awake and motivated. However, subtle events occur at night that would be easily detectable in daylight. The solo pilot at night is at greater risk than when flying with an attentive passenger. Night flight requires the pilot to be very familiar with the area and have special knowledge that can be acquired only through experience.

Night flight is so completely different from day that it requires careful introduction. Any pilot deficiencies become magnified at night. The night horizon is less visible and more indistinct. Night flight is semi-IFR with considerable reliance on the instruments. Clouds and terrain are from difficult to impossible to see. There can be a gradual loss of visual clues when flying into darker terrain. This leads to disorientation and loss of control.

Night flight adds to the risk of single-engine flying. Emergency options are reduced. You will be much more able to cope if you maintain radio contact with Air Traffic Control (ATC) and have a readily available frequency list. I avoid night training flights that have less than a quarter moon. It is recommended to have supplemental oxygen at 5,000ft at night and at 10,000ft daytime.

Flying a consistent profile is essential to safe night Visual Flight Rules. Be so aware that you do not descend below 1,500 above ground level until you are within engine out distance of the destination. Plan to make a standard $45°$ entry so that you will reach pattern altitude when turning downwind. If ATC gives you a straight in, maintain pattern altitude until you are on 2-mile final. Fly a Visual Approach Slope Indicator or Precision Approach Path Indicator if available. If you know your ground speed, multiply it by five to get a $3°$ descent path.

The absence of a horizon can cause loss of control. Both situational and geographic disorientation is more likely.

Our ability to make a truthful prediction of our next night flight is of extreme value. When night flying pilots flounder in hesitancy and indecision, we find that the successful outcome of any flight depends more on pilot confidence in his competence. Confidence is a by-product of competence.

Every night flight, or breath for that matter, involves a risk on some level. What we do can be evaluated and delineated as to the mathematical risk factor it presents to us. Every night flight decision we make holds consequences. Not making decisions also holds consequences. The ideal would be that we have the foresight to see living and night flying in terms of future consequences. We cannot, so we do what we can to face the risks.

A pilot must accept the presence of risk and the existence of fear. Both are present and accepted as part of the process. Being afraid makes you more careful. Your fears are insurance policies.

We use risk analysis to evaluate the consequences of starting the engine, taking off, flight altitude, direction, and landing. To do otherwise is to be oblivious of probability as it can and does affect all our lives. Do not say that you do not gamble, take chances, and challenge probability. You do and it makes your life more worth living because certainty will destroy incentive, interest and curiosity.

Some 40 per cent of all night take-off accidents have non-instrument pilots. Of all night accidents, the darkness of the night was listed as a factor in 54 per cent. Some 26 per cent were judged to be caused by spatial disorientation. Most of the take-off accidents occurred within 3 miles and one minute of take-off. The darker the night the more important instrument flight capability is.

Night landings are acts of faith. You must believe that the lighting and surface delineate the airport and a safe place to touch the earth. Oddly, taxiing at night is a very difficult process. Many aircraft lights do not light your way.

Physiology of Night

Over the age of 40 years, fatigue and smoking affect visual acuity and adaptation to darkness. Do not look directly at an object at night because the optic nerve location may not let you see it. The decrease in oxygen above 4,000ft decreases visual efficiency. The air force requires full oxygen from the surface at night. The light smoker is physiologically at 3,000ft before he gets into the aircraft. Above 8,000ft at night, it is a good idea to have oxygen. Since we do not see as well as might be desired at night, we must compensate using experience (brains) and technology.

Slow Down

The worst flying risk is the needless risk. The needless risk is most likely to occur when you are 'hurried' to do something.

Pilots must learn not to chase minutes by hurrying, because your limits of experience are being exceeded. If this should happen to you, speak up, slow down and join those pilots who stress being good over being lucky.

Richard Deacon, in his book *British Secret Service*,[71] devotes a whole chapter to the fact that, on 10 May 1941, six planets in the sign of Taurus coincided with the full moon. Consequently, in theory this made flying due west that much easier as the planets had aligned in a westerly direction. Deacon attributes this to all sorts of occult influences, but we believe that Hess would have been able to utilise them in the growing dark – nothing more 'occult' than that.

In conclusion, this is why the Hess mission completely unravelled. By the time he got to Scotland, the sun had set twenty-three minutes earlier and, thereafter, the flight was always going to be a race against time and the darkness. As we now know, the darkness won.

14. DUNGAVEL HOUSE – THE TARGET?

The book *Rudolf Hess: The British Illusion of Peace* was the first to question whether Dungavel House was the intended target of Rudolf Hess on 10 May 1941. It appears to the authors that it is a convenient target, if one were looking for a target to support a lone flyer theory; an airstrip, a reasonably relevant contact, no evidence of connivance. However, apart from the above, Dungavel House actually has little to commend it from an aviation viewpoint.

A flight to an English airfield could not guarantee that Hess would be met by an individual who was 'in on' the plan. Moreover, with the concentrated air defences it would be much more likely the aircraft would be intercepted and shot down.

A flight to England would actually be a pointless exercise. It would be a wasted effort as far as Hess was concerned and the likely outcome would be exactly as actually happened. Hess would be captured by those who followed their orders; some might recognise him, but most would not. Eventually he would come under the control of those who wielded power and we are quite convinced the eventual outcome would have been broadly similar to the events that unfolded in Lowland Scotland in May 1941. Peter Fleming's book, *The Flying Visit*, would have been seen to be even more prescient.[72]

No, the reason that Hess flew to Scotland was that he believed that he was flying to people who were (a) sympathetic to his cause and (b) would help him achieve his goal as outlined in the previous chapters.

We have visited Dungavel on four occasions (three by road, one by air), on the first of which John Harris was arrested and taken to explain why he was taking photographs of the location to the Governor of HM Prison Dungavel. Dungavel is a strange target and that is why we do not think it was any such thing. However, for all those looking to support the 'lone flyer theory' it is ideal. Hess would have had to be either mad or suicidal (just as they believe) to attempt a landing.

The Dukes of Hamilton ancestral home was really Hamilton Palace and not Dungavel.[73] Hamilton Palace had been the largest non-royal palace in the UK, though it had fallen into disrepair after being used in the First World War as a hospital. Ironically, due to the coal mining activity which in part had provided the family with their wealth, subsidence had claimed the palace, which was eventually demolished in 1921. From that time the family moved to Dungavel House, their former shooting lodge, near Strathaven, but they also had the use of other houses throughout England and Scotland, such as Ferne House in Wiltshire. The Duke of Hamilton involved in the Hess affair was the 14th Duke. However, his father, Alfred, the 13th Duke, had died only in 1940.[74] He was buried in the grounds of Dungavel. Therefore, it was as the Marquis of Clydesdale that Douglas Douglas-Hamilton had been previously known and it was as the Marquis of Clydesdale that he lived at Dungavel House, until March 1940 when he succeeded to the title.

Dungavel House was built as a shooting lodge, not a 'replacement palace'. Dungavel was obviously larger and grander than the normal lodge, which tends to be built in more remote locations. As mentioned, the family fortunes were somewhat reduced as an earlier duke had heavily mortgaged the estate.

Dungavel House is certainly remote. So, what is the attraction of a remote location? If a clandestine meeting is required then it makes sense, but being in the west of Scotland meant that (a) secrecy was potentially less likely, as the aircraft would have to cover a far greater time in the air over enemy territory and (b) finding the place would be potentially that much more difficult. There is also the obvious difficulty of flying across Lowland Scotland from the east coast to the west coast. It was never going to be easy, particularly in 1941 with enemy aircraft potentially to contend with and rudimentary navigational techniques as a guide.

Within a few miles inland of the east coast of northern England/southern Scotland, the hills rise, for example, to 'The Cheviot' at 2,700ft. Thereafter the contours rise and fall until the west coast is reached. Aeronautically it is difficult territory, particularly if one wishes to land in the middle of nowhere. Once far inland, away from the east coast, life becomes even more difficult as events bore out.

There has been confusion over the years as to the precise location of the airstrip. Consequently, we were pleased to see that Roy Conyers Nesbit, in the paperback edition of *Rudolf Hess: Myths and Reality*, has reproduced a plan of the extent of the airstrip, obtained from the Hamilton family.

The airstrip shown on the plan was much smaller than we had originally contemplated, being between the house known as 'The Kennels' and the A743 road. Since the Hamilton's left in 1946/47, there appears to have been some coniferous planting on part of what had been the airstrip and the old playing field for the prison, which took up most of the area. On an old OS map, the airstrip is shown as a separate enclosed area, probably no more than 2–3 acres. Until we saw the plan, we had imagined that the airstrip had extended to the B745 road, but this was not the case. The strip was enclosed (in 1941) and it appears that, for its construction, a small stream had to be diverted.

On subsequent inspection, we now doubt if it extended to much more than 150 yards. The landing run for a DeHavilland Gipsy Moth was around 100 yards. In other words, it was adequate, but only just, for these early types of aircraft.

Even if Hess had thought (as we had) that the airstrip also included the adjacent field, a visual survey of that field shows that it is approximately 500 yards long and boggy. It is not flat. It has a slight gradient as it follows the contours of the hill that continues behind the prison on the other side of the road.[75] From the air there is only one practical line of approach; Hess would have to fly past the house on his east/west path and then turn to try to land travelling uphill onto the strip. It would have been impossible to land downhill without catastrophe. The prevailing wind direction is from the south-west, as evidenced by the many wind-bent trees in the area. To land uphill would also require landing with a tailwind, instead of landing into the wind. To avert disaster, gravity and friction would have to combine and be victorious over wind speed.

On our last visit, the old airstrip and the adjacent field were occupied with quietly grazing sheep. There were large patches of sedge, a sure agricultural sign of a wet field. We obtained the weather records for Glasgow in 1941. The spring was marginally wetter than normal with the following rainfall:

January – 0.76in
February – 3.17in
March – 3.46in
April – 1.98in
May – 3.28in[76]

An inch of rain represents 100 tons of water per acre. We tried desperately to imagine the scene depicted in the book *Double Standards*, with the Duke of Kent and various dignatories waiting at 'The Kennels'[77] for Hess to land. The airstrip was illuminated with landing lights and then they were suddenly switched off. We do not believe a word of it.

If one analyses the third party evidence that Stephen Prior produced, there is precious little save a photograph that he alleges proves Dungavel to be much more than the private airstrip it actually was. The said photograph shows one large hangar surrounded by a number of small sheds, no larger than chicken houses. They are certainly not hangars. They seem to us to illustrate a typical private airstrip of the 1930s.

The issue of lights is also interesting. Prior states that the lights were switched on and off from the house following various telephone calls. This is based on the evidence of two ladies who continue to remain anonymous. We have severe doubts that there were any lights at all (as indeed do Roy Conyers Nesbit and Dougal McIntyre). The statement that the lights were switched on and off from the house also seems questionable: Dungavel House must be at least 400 yards from 'The Kennels', on the other side of the road, and it seems unlikely that electricity would only come from the big house. If there were lights, a generator on site would have been the more likely power supply. Many private houses did not even have 'mains' electric lighting until long after the Second World War.

On 'front-line' stations the RAF adopted what was known as the 'Drem' lighting system in 1943, following development work by R.L.R. Atcherley (1904–1970). At the time he was a wing commander (subsequently an air marshal), but his relevance to this story is that he developed the standard runway lighting system whilst station commander at RAF Drem, East Lothian, in 1940.

While Dungavel was completely different to a mainstream RAF base, the point is that if the main RAF bases did not have effective lighting systems until 1943, we are quite sure that Dungavel, even if it were to have had lights, would have had only the most rudimentary, more likely to illuminate the hangar rather than the strip. The Scottish archives detail plans in 1940 for Dungavel House in respect of water supply, sewerage purification and electric lighting (RHP4167), so it appears that it may have been a recent innovation.

Therefore, already we have three main issues with Dungavel: location, condition of airstrip and lighting. That is before we even consider the aircraft. A Bf 110 could not have landed at Dungavel; the airfield simply was not long enough. Roy Conyers Nesbit states: 'It was certainly inadequate for a heavy aircraft such as the Bf 110.'

We have been trying for a number of years to find out the typical landing distance of the Bf 110. This has proved to be very difficult. Part of the difficulty is that there were many types of the Bf 110, from the 1935 prototype Bf 110 V-1, through to the Bf 110H-4/U8. Even between 1 January 1945 and the end of hostilities, forty-five aircraft were produced.[78] As with most aircraft with such longevity, as they became more powerful they also became heavier. For example, the prototype Bf 110 was originally built with two DB 600 engines developing 900hp. The Bf 110G-0 was fitted with two DB 605B engines, which increased output to 1,475hp. The normal loaded weights rose from 15,300lb (Bf 110C) to 20,700lb (Bf 110G).

The Hess type was fitted with the new DB 601N engine and so we would estimate the normal weight to be somewhere between the 15,300lb and 20,700lb previously quoted. Roy Conyers Nesbit specifies the weight as 14,850lb loaded.[79] This seems a little light to the authors by comparison to the other models.

However, as we had seen with our own eyes, a farmer's tractor (which would weigh less than half of the above) made a significant mess of the field in the spring. We therefore dread to think of the implication of a 7-ton aircraft landing at 90–100mph on a wet field in the dark. The landing speed is stated as being 87mph.

During the war, a Bf 110 was captured by the Allies and evaluated. John Vasco quotes the landing distance as being around 600 yards. Even if we include the field adjacent to the airstrip, and then look for the longest possible run, we struggle to reach 600 yards. We understand that the difference between a concrete and grass strip is approximately plus or minus 25 per cent in terms of distance; 25 per cent shorter when landing because of the lack of friction, 25 per cent longer on take-off, because of the additional friction. We know the Augsburg-Haunstetten airfield from where Hess took off was 1,202 yards long.

Captain E.M. 'Winkle' Brown, RN, who tested many German aircraft of the period, stated that, in the case of a Bf 110: 'The landing run was short as the brakes could be applied heavily without any tendency for the tail to rise.'[80] This test was, however, probably conducted on the hard runway of RAF Farnborough,[81] not a wet, undulating Scottish field. So we contend that, if Hess had attempted to land at Dungavel House on 10 May 1941, he would have crashed and probably been killed.

When arranging our flight, the proprietor of the company we used proved to be a follower of the Hess affair and he commented that the Duke of Hamilton had crashed at Dungavel in the 1930s while flying a Hawker Hart. At Lennoxlove, there are pictures of the four Hamilton brothers[82] in their RAF uniforms and of Hawker Harts from No. 602 (City of Glasgow) Squadron diving in formation. If an aircraft such as this was difficult to land at Dungavel, then the much heavier Bf 110 would have struggled far more. The Hawker Hart weighed approximately one third of the Bf 110. Hess would have been extremely lucky to land alive at Dungavel House. It may well be for the above reasons that the Marquis of Clydesdale applied in 1936 for the construction of a new airstrip at Kilnburnside, a small village between Strathaven and Glasgow. Was this because Dungavel was considered already inadequate at that time?[83]

PRO file AIR40/195 shows that, even if Hess had landed, he could not have taken off. The evaluation of the Bf 110 shows that there was a 'special loading chart' and weights of 18,739 to 20,944lb would only be permissible from a concrete strip.

The actual flight would also seem to back up our reservations. As we have said, we know pretty precisely where Hess actually went, but what we do not really have a clue about is where he was headed. We are convinced it was not Dungavel.

It is accepted, we think, that Hess flew past Dungavel on his east to west flight, before turning back inland when meeting the sea. Had there been lights on, as per *Double Standards*, then why fly on to the sea? If the strip was lit and Hess saw it, he could have easily turned his aircraft around (The Bf 110 handled well for its size) and attempted to land on the uphill slope (all other issues being disregarded for the moment).

The fact is that he had to go to the coast to try and get his bearings. Either he was lost, or there were no lights for him to see and he was collecting his thoughts; or he was actually heading elsewhere.

Parachute Escape

Rudolf Hess, in his 1941 letter to his wife describing the flight, says that when he parachuted from the Bf 110, it was his first ever parachute jump. Given the meticulous detail in which other aspects of the flight were planned, it seems most unlike Hess to not have at least considered his means of exit. As Hess later recounted: 'There was just one thing I had overlooked. I had never asked about how to jump; I thought it was too simple!'

What Hess does not go on to say is whether he actually intended to parachute, or whether his true intention was to land conventionally, somewhere, parachuting only being a last resort. Had he not asked about parachuting because it had never been his intention? Some authors have asserted that it was always his intention to parachute from the aircraft, citing the need to preserve the secrets of the Bf 110 from the enemy (interpreting an inference in the 1941 Hess letter). This we disagree with, but consider it necessary to study the evidence first.

The parachute is an ancient device in concept, but had only been developed militarily since the end of the First World War. At the beginning of the Second World War, both Germany and Russia had established large-scale airborne forces. Britain, too, had a fledgling parachute regiment. Germany had used their *Fallschirmjäger* (paratroops) to good effect in the Norway campaign, though the largest parachute deployment was yet to come, when just ten days after the Hess flight the airborne assault on Crete was successfully undertaken. The parachute had been developed to the point that it was not necessarily seen as a means of last resort. An Australian aviator had escaped from a crashing aircraft in 1916 by parachute and, since that time, the equipment had been developed and refined.

There were two main types of parachute used: the traditional 'backpack' and the seat type. The Luftwaffe seat-type parachute was combined with the dual role of a *Sitzfallschirm* (padded seat). An example of such a parachute is held at the RAF Museum, Hendon. The dual role also explains the spartan appearance of the Bf 110 seat — a basic metal bucket. The German and British designs were almost identical, on account of the German use of the ubiquitous Irving design.

Messerschmitt typically had also considered the issue, but perhaps, it is fair to say, not with the same degree of thoroughness as other parts of their design. Their instructions for emergency escape from the Bf 110 are as follows:

Fallschirmausstieg (parachute exit)
Führer (pilot)
Beobachter verständigen (inform observer)
Fahrt nach Möglichkeit verringern (fly to reduce necessity)
Nach Möglichkeit (if possible)

Netzausschalter drücken (press electrical system cut-out switch)
Zündungen ausschalten (switch off ignition system)
Brandhähne schliessen (close fuel cocks)
Losschnallen (un-buckle)
Führerraumüberdachung öffnen und Flugzeug verlassen: Vorsicht vor Luftschraube und Antennenmast (open cockpit roof and leave the aircraft. Beware of the propellers and aerial mast)

This is broadly the sequence that Hess followed, as detailed in his 1941 letter to his wife. He describes: 'Switching off the engines and turning the propeller indicator to null and … opening the cabin roof.'

It was at this point that the real problems began. The cockpit roof was in three parts: a top and the two sides. A single lever at the front of the cockpit released the roof, which hinged back to rest against the aerial. The two sides then folded down. Consequently, Hess was now sitting in an open cockpit, protected only by the armoured windscreen. The air pressure was far too great to allow Hess to exit safely.

Captain E.M. 'Winkle' Brown, the British test pilot of captured aircraft, anticipated the problem in a later report:

> The pilot's cockpit was entered from the port side by means of a ladder normally accommodated entirely within a slot in the fuselage aft of the port wing trailing edge, a button aft of the trailing edge being pressed and the ladder springing out to the extended position. The Perspex canopy over the forward seat was formed by three parts, the upper part hinging aft and the side panels folding down, and it could not be locked from the outside.
>
> I had always been intrigued to ascertain exactly how one vacated the Bf 110 in an emergency as it did not look in the least simple, yet Rudolf Hess, Hitler's deputy, had apparently achieved this operation with ease after making his notorious solo night flight from Munich to the outskirts of Glasgow. Studying the problem I had to admit that I was little the wiser and concluded that an element of luck entered into a successful bail-out from the aircraft. The cockpit upper panel could be jettisoned by unlocking it and allowing it to swing up into the airstream, but thereafter the pilot apparently had to roll on to the wing and risk getting blown back against the rather considerable empennage.

It is extremely unlikely that Hess planned to parachute from the Bf 110. There are many contemporary references to the problems of baling out from aircraft: reports often refer to 'after surviving baling out', and 'despite managing to bale out successfully'. This was an emergency procedure and one fraught with difficulty and danger.

Hess finally baled out by bringing the nose of the aircraft up to the near per-pendicular and falling out backwards, just before the machine stalled and fell to Earth. Hess later said that his friend, General Ritter von Greim, had told him to turn the aircraft over and fall out. We fail to see how this would present a solution to the problem of the air pressure.

So, if Hess is to be believed, he somewhat luckily managed to bale out. Given his description of the ordeal and the practical difficulties involved, we cannot believe that this was what he anticipated. The procedure was too hazardous and the risk of failure too high for it to have been part of any realistic plan. If Hess had intended to land and not draw attention to his visit, his Bf 110 crashing into a Scottish field was hardly a stealthy arrival.

More evidence to call the planned parachute arrival into question is to be found in the reports of 'papers' being found at the crash site;[84] Hess would not have left important items in his aircraft, he would have carried them with him.

The only point at which Hess chose to bale out of his aircraft was after he had missed his landing site and his mission was, to all intents and purposes, over. Again we have to discriminate between what happened and what was intended.

PART 3

THE HESS FLIGHT

After having detailed some of the parameters and constraints that Hess was subject to, we now present our detailed analysis of the flight using the evidence that we have gained to date and described in the earlier chapters.

15. GERMANY AND THE NORTH SEA

'I flew direct – save for some diversions made with the object of deceiving the English, in which aim I was successful.' Thus wrote Rudolf Hess to his wife whilst at Nuremberg, in response to an interview with Willi Messerschmitt first published in the newspaper *Frankfurter Neue Presse* in May 1947.[1]

The authors believe that the 'diversions' were certainly carried out during this part of the flight and that it is the 'diversions' that explain the near catastrophic delay in his arrival over Scotland. The following chapters will go on to explain the consequences of the delayed arrival.

Hess described the route he took as early as August 1941, when he drew his route map and gave timings. This was first published as early as 1947 as part of the J.R. Rees book.[2] The map shows that, on reaching the coast at Den Helder, northern Holland, he then flew over the Wadden See islands before turning out to sea when he reached the German island of Borkum, at the head of the Ems estuary. Thereafter, we are treated to the usual Hess descriptions: 'It was utterly lonely. But how magnificent!'

The map is of interest. Firstly, it is dated 8 August 1941 and was drawn while Hess was at Mytchett Place. It appears that, at the time, Hess was in the process of writing a report of his actions, as on 5 August 1941 one of his guards noted that he 'wrote page after page until dinner time'.[3] It seems that the map was part of a deposition that Hess had completed, in which he commented: 'I am partly betraying military secrets by making these statements.'

We believe we should also say a little more about deceit. Whenever Hess was later questioned about the flight, the standard reply was: 'I can't remember'. We have already analysed his mental condition (Chapter 1) and it appears to us that this is no more than a device to protect the operational and technical secrets of the Luftwaffe. Later, he may also have considered his own fate and that of the others involved on both sides of his quest.

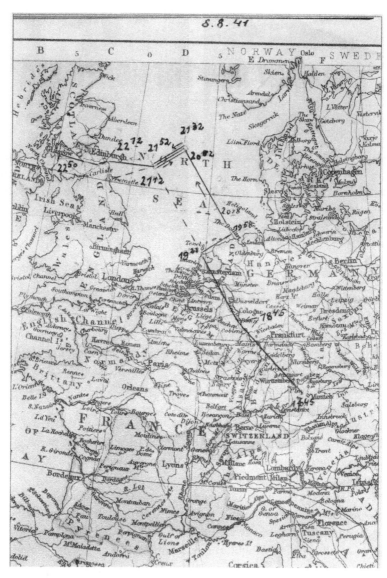

The Hess flight plan. Note its date: 8.8.41.

The cast-iron Den Helder lighthouse.

The Borkum Großer light.

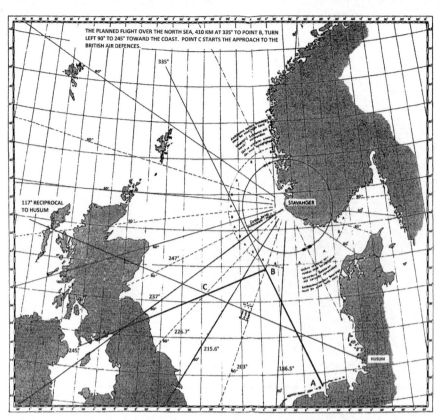

THE PLANNED FLIGHT OVER THE NORTH SEA, 410 KM AT 335° TO POINT B, TURN LEFT 90° TO 245° TOWARD THE COAST. POINT C STARTS THE APPROACH TO THE BRITISH AIR DEFENCES.

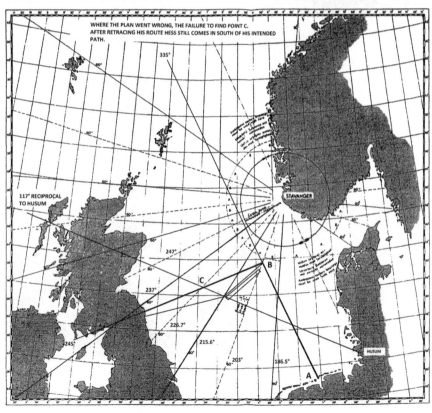

WHERE THE PLAN WENT WRONG, THE FAILURE TO FIND POINT C. AFTER RETRACING HIS ROUTE HESS STILL COMES IN SOUTH OF HIS INTENDED PATH.

In many parts of the Hess story, the truth has been obscured and muddled deliberately so as to preserve military secrecy as far as possible. If one studies the map carefully, there are further markings on the North Sea which have then been partially erased. It also appears to us that there are distinct similarities to the routes as described in the pilot's notes.

We should also record that there is a second, hand-drawn map of southern Scotland which Hess also marked up. This, too, first appeared in the J.R. Rees book of 1947. As with most things Hess, there are elements of the truth contained within the map, combined with elements of disguise or 'diversion' as Hess himself admitted.

Planning and Execution

In making the flight, Hess had to be mindful of three things:

— To be able to reach his target. A premature crash or interception would be a waste of much time and effort.
— To prevent Russian suspicion of an Anglo–German treaty (hence the covertness and the deniability of the 'solo mission').
— To preserve the secrecy of the Elektra system, which he considered to be a necessary part of his equipment. We suspect that this was the major military secret in his possession. That is why he was deceitful and why the flight has proved quite so difficult to subsequently understand and interpret for over seventy years.

Hess was clearly a 'planner' and his flight to Scotland, though it ultimately failed, is a testament to his thoroughness. As Hess later wrote: 'I had thought out half a dozen different courses, numbered them on the map and memorised them with care, but the one I eventually took was not among these!'[4]

This statement we believe to be true, as Hess had planned or considered at least four routes to get from Augsburg to the British coast, and further options as to how to cross Scotland. A combination of the various options gets very complex and, for simplification, we will concentrate on the planning for the route which we suggest was the most likely and the best fit for the evidence. Then we will venture our explanation of where and why he went wrong. Before analysing the parts of the flight, we will discuss the more routine planning concerns: the plane, fuel and oil.

The Aircraft

As we have seen, Hess had chosen a Bf 110 because Willi Messerschmitt thought the Bf 109 to be too difficult to handle and clearly did not wish to be any more responsible than he needed to be for the health and safety of the Deputy Führer. The Messerschmitt company was chosen simply because Hess knew the owner, it was close to his home and other manufacturers had apparently turned him down.

The Bf 110 was a sensible choice for the job as it combined the ability to be flown solo with sufficient range to get to Scotland, if fitted with the relevant sized auxiliary fuel tanks. If there was trouble en route, the machine had a good turn of speed and was faster than most aircraft flying at that time.

Fuel

The old problem of fuel capacity really is not an issue. With the usual 1,270l in the wing tanks, the aircraft had an endurance of two to two and a half hours, under normal conditions. Longer if at cruising speed.

However, again as we have seen, in order to fly for five hours twenty-four minutes (1745hrs to 2309hrs) the aircraft would correspondingly require approximately 3,000l of fuel. This capacity could be nearly achieved by fitting two 900l auxiliary tanks, providing a total capacity at take-off of 3,070l.

So, we do not believe there is any doubt, in fuel terms, that the flight was achievable with the fitment of the appropriate size of drop or auxiliary tank.

Oil and the Need to Land En Route

However, oil is far more difficult. Chapter 9 demonstrated to our satisfaction that the Bf 110, Werknummer 3869, did not ever have an auxiliary oil tank fitted. We can quite understand why. To fit the tank was not difficult as the aircraft had all the necessary fittings. However, with the auxiliary oil tank came the need to pump oil to each engine oil tank. The mechanics of this have been explained. A separate pumping system would have to have been installed in the front cockpit. We believe this did not happen.

The oil line on the Hess aircraft was blanked off and then wired. There never had been an auxiliary oil tank. Without such a fitment the aircraft would have to rely on the two 'rubberised' self-sealing oil tanks, which are stored in the RAF Museum reserve collection at MoD Stafford.

The *Flugstreken* for the DB 601N engine reveal an oil consumption of between 5 and 9 litres per hour, dependent upon engine power settings. Therefore, to use the oil in its entirety would take between three hours fifty-three minutes and seven hours.

The rate of manually pumping oil from the auxiliary tank to an engine tank is given as 7.5 litres per hour, which is nearly an average of the two extremes of oil consumption. At this rate of use, the engine tanks would give four hours forty minutes of flying time, before the engines seized.

It is for this reason that we are now convinced that Hess stopped en route somewhere in Northern Germany. Without replenishing his oil tanks, we do not believe that he had enough oil to sustain a flight from Augsburg to Scotland. This is no longer speculation, it is fact based on known engine oil consumption.

Consequently, Rudolf Hess chose to de-risk his flight in terms of oil consumption and the need to install a manual oil pump in the already crowded cockpit. He simply chose to land en route. As has already been explained, the pilot's notes we have been given lead us to believe that Giessen was the interim stopover. The part of the flight from Augsburg to Giessen is not recorded as part of the pilot's notes because it was not a variable, not a choice. A fully laden Bf 110 in terms of fuel and oil would be taking off from Giessen, whatever eventual route was chosen. That is when the notes assume their relevance.

It was Richard Wilbourn's revelatory discovery that had explained the pilot's notes and the problem of oil consumption simultaneously. It explained precisely why and what Hess had done. The map dated 8 August 1941 had never made sense to us as it appeared to indicate a speed of less than 300km per hour until he crossed the coast. This was much too slow and had actually been drawn to hide the fact of the landing.

In 1989, Helmut Kaden, the Messerschmitt test pilot, also appeared to doubt the map when he addressed the Rudolf Hess Society in Munich. He questioned as to why Hess would ever have chosen to fly over the heavily defended Ruhr/Cologne area and instead postulated a more northerly route, whilst not admitting to a landing.

The secret of the landing was, of course, vital in that it supported the 'solo flight theory', rather than the meticulously planned flight which it was. It also explains why Hess was dressed as a *Hauptmann* and not as the Deputy Führer. He was much less likely to attract attention from his own ground crew, who certainly would not be told that he was to land. Needless to say, the Giessen airfield records are no longer available for 10 May 1941.

So, we now believe that Hess took off from Giessen at around 5.45 p.m., flew to Giessen, arriving around 6.30 p.m. and then finally took off at around 7 p.m.

He then crossed the coast (as he stated) at 7.58 p.m., safe in the knowledge that he had ample fuel and oil to reach the west coast of Scotland.

Planning for Radio Direction-Finding

From a navigational point of view, Hess had one thing he had to get exactly right on this part of the journey: knowing when to 'turn left', his *Nordpunkt* (North Point), vital for him to avoid detection and interception, and approach the coast of Northumberland in approximately the correct position. Once there, the Farne Islands to Prestwick 'corridor', that part of the Lennoxlove Map that had been so carefully folded as evidenced by the 'grime marks', was virtually undefended.

However, if he were to come in too far to the south, Hess would put himself over RAF Acklington and RAF Ouston; too far north and he would arrive over RAF East Fortune, RAF Dyce and RAF Turnhouse. It was, therefore, vital that this turn was made at the correct time and position.

Hess could, especially if a navigator had been present, have used dead-reckoning navigation. As we learned when we recreated the Hess flight over Scotland, this entails adjusting a compass course for the effect of a crosswind. Distance travelled would be measured by a function of time and speed.

David Irving, in his book *Hess: The Missing Years*, makes particular mention of Hess asking to understand how the pitot tube is calibrated. The pitot tube is a device which measures air velocity, which is converted to airspeed and then is computed to an approximate ground speed.

The basic problem is that it is difficult to fly in a straight line over the sea, given the effect of a crosswind. Hess knew all of this and reacted appropriately. His Bf 110 was already equipped with a magnetic compass, as a standard fitting.[5] As mentioned by Len Deighton in his chapter for *Flight from Reality*, and as seen at Duxford, the aircraft also had a Siemens K4ü (*Kursstueurungen*), an advanced yaw axis control auto-pilot system, based on a gyroscopic compass. This rudder control system would greatly simplify his task of following a bearing. The compass, which was mounted in the rear of the machine, was 'salvaged' from the crash site. It is certainly not in the fuselage stored at Duxford. Hess also describes having a wrist compass,[6] which is currently on display at Lennoxlove House.

However, having three compasses, each independent of one another, was apparently still not enough. The critical part of the flight, as already stated, was to know exactly when to turn left. Consequently, Hess chose to utilise the state-of-the-art Luftwaffe technology – the Elektra navigation system.

As has been stated previously, it was the preservation of the secrecy of this system that led Hess to deceive the British in subsequent descriptions of the flight.

The Flight up the North Sea to *Der Nordpunkt* (Point B)

We have already seen that, as well as direction-finding, Hess would have to avoid the perils of the British Coastal Command patrols and 'Chain Home' radar. As such, irrespective of the merits of any radio-direction system, a flight plan that kept him over to the eastern side of the North Sea would be the more likely to help avoid detection. For direction Hess chose to use his auto-pilot, and for distance his radio navigation. The FuG 10EL was a standard fitment on a Bf 110. This was the receiver necessary to hear the long-wave (EL) transmissions; a beat frequency oscillator (BFO) in the device would convert the radio signal to the dots, dashes and tones in his headphones.

There are mentions of the radio equipment being modified to allow solo use. This is simply because the FuG 10 system was fixed to the bulkhead at the rear of the pilot's seat. A pilot could not normally reach the controls. There are references to the system being tested, so perhaps he was getting familiarised with its workings at his home in Harlaching. This is not surprising as the use of the system was not self-evident. Ilse Hess writes: 'A large brand new radio apparatus appeared in the workroom of our home.'

This is surely the genesis of the Kalundborg radio station theory that other authors have latched onto. Ilse Hess tells how she noticed that the apparatus was tuned into the Danish station. This we doubt very much. Kalundborg was (and is) a non-directional radio beacon based on the largest Danish island of Zealand and transmitting on 243kHz. We believe it much more likely that Hess was using the term 'Kalundborg' as a cover for the Husum Elektra (E2) station and 'Oslo' for Stavanger (E1). In any event, we do not believe that the Kalundborg transmitter was powerful enough to reach Munich from Denmark.

We have already seen how the pilot's notes gave a number of choices: the one that Hess detailed does not actually work in radio signal terms. We have presented our original graphical representation of the four route options. Two options entered the North Sea at Den Helder and two at or around Borkum on the Wadden See Islands. Both are viable entry points and both are marked by massive lighthouses. The lighthouse at Den Helder is named *Lang Jaap* and was the tallest cast iron lighthouse in the world when built in the late nineteenth century. However, we have learned that it had been sabotaged in 1940 and was still out of use on 10 May 1941.

The Borkum *Großer Leuchtturm*, built in 1879 and at a height of 60m (197ft) and the twenty-fourth tallest 'traditional lighthouse' in the world, served as the landfall light. The top was painted red, which provided a day mark for the Ems estuary and Emden. We interpret the first part of the pilot's notes as follows:

Leg	Kilometres
Augsburg to Giessen	300
Giessen to coast	370
Point A to Point B	410

Thirty minutes after Point A – switch on receiver, radio setting 0 (Δ) 3 for Stavanger (E1) station. (This is just before the first equi-signal line, but at that point it is navigationally unreliable, sounds could be heard from the transmitter).

First beam from Stavanger at 290km from Point A – bearing north east (Nord Ost) 186.5°, from Stavanger, 76 identifier (*zK, zur Kenntnis*).

At Point B – Stavanger 86.zk (information missing here), but this would be beam 203° from Stavanger at 410km (see Appendix I, Fig. 12, p. 291).

This gives a more detailed breakdown of one of the four options, column 1 - b and incorporates other instructions pertaining to the radio system. What it does not do is give a total flight time, combining time and distance. This we believe is simply to disguise landing in Northern Germany en route.

The notes appear to be calculated on a cruising speed of 410km/h. Point A to Point B is stated as being 410km and is also stated as taking sixty minutes. It would therefore appear to us that, with this option, the distance to Scotland was expected to be 660 + 410 + 170 + 40km = 1,280km. Referring back to tabulated notes, this compares with an anticipated total flight time of three hours seven minutes, giving a wholly acceptable 410km/h average speed.

This route, you will recall, was also contemplated by the pilot's notes, with the North Sea entry point being effected around Borkum; the radio bearings then work precisely.

By taking the Borkum entry point, Hess was farther to the east when travelling up the North Sea. A Den Helder entry would also have put him virtually in the range of the British 'Chain Home' radar. We are content that Hess first arrived at Point B at around 2052hrs, in the evening of 10 May. It was the next part of the flight that would lead to his eventual downfall. Even if he had no radio equipment at all, we suspect he could have had a reasonable guess when he was at Point B. If he was cruising at around 410km/h, then after sixty minutes over the sea, he should be somewhere close to the turning point that was designated as Point B.

Point B to Point C and the British Coast

The next instruction was, however, potentially far more difficult, critical for Hess and important in the explanation of the flight. To refer back to the pilot's notes: Point B to Point C = 170km. A 90° turn at Point B would bring Hess on to a heading towards the British mainland, at an approach angle to the Farne Islands of 245°, an angle that, perhaps coincidentally, would minimise his chances of meeting a Coastal Command patrol. Hess knew the importance of this vital turn as evidenced in the Messerschmitt works memorandum of 2 May 1941.[7] Here we bring the Lennoxlove Map into play: this angle is drawn accurately on the map at 245°, but annotated 255°; perhaps more deception?

Point C is on 'Oslo' bearing 226.7°, 170km from B and on a reciprocal bearing of 117° to Husum E2 or 'Kalundborg', as in the notes. Between the two he would have crossed the 216.5° beam, which appears at the top of the Pilot's notes as Koln No. 216.5; we believe this to mean Kolonne (line, band or column) Nord Ost (north-east) 216.5°.

This Point C is a waypoint, a marker along a course, but a very important one. Hess now had to deal with the two challenges of intercepting land at the correct point and minimising his chances of being intercepted by fighters. His main hazard here was the 'Chain Home' radar system. We described earlier how the procedure worked. Once detected, a 'raid' was given a designation and it was up to the filter officer to judge the level of threat and what was likely to happen next; a skill that was learned through experience of past raids. The aim was to get sufficient fighters into a 'box' in the air near the target to allow them to make a visual confirmation of the contact and act accordingly. The Hess 'raid' was initially set at three aircraft, which is normal, bearing in mind that the filter officer would normally expect bombers in formation rather than a lone aircraft.

Point C is important to Hess because he was preparing to act in a manner that the defences would not expect: instead of the steady progress of a bombing raid he was about to take actions which would confuse the defence and see him safely through the fighter shield. The pilot's notes again take us through the action. Our interpretation: 'After 10 minutes from C go to full throttle, 1.3 atm (atmospheres), manifold boost pressure and propeller pitch to automatic. Check cooling, jettison fuel tanks, lose height. After 12 minutes of this (fast dive) to Islands 40km'. He was now fast and low, beneath the range of the radar. The intercepting Spitfire from RAF Acklington would be climbing and expecting to meet a formation of enemy bombers.

His route would, if he had time to consider it, be bounded by the Elektra beam 237° (the line of blue triangles on the Lennoxlove Map) to the north and 226.7°

to the south; keeping to the centre of these beams would bring him in somewhere near the right place on the coast and within sight of his 'funnel features'. After that it is: 'Aim for (peilen) Cheviot, 255°' and Hess begins his journey over Northumberland and Scotland.

In this way Hess could beat the defences, although we do not think this is how it happened on 10 May 1941. This critical part of the flight was to prove his undoing.

The manoeuvres over the North Sea between Points B and C were on the original 1941 map and have been a widely accepted part of the flight, with various interpretations as to their meaning. A common suggestion is that Hess had made good time on the flight so far and was using the 'North Sea box' to use up time to wait for the light to fade. Hugh Thomas says this is the area where the first Hess was shot down, to be replaced with a Doppleganger.

We do not disagree that the flight was planned to minimise the amount of daylight left after the transition to British airspace and landing (this was an important part of the plan), but it will turn out that he miscalculated by a small but critical margin.

The more mundane answer – Hess was lost, as he had failed to find his waypoint at Point C. This is his reference: 'The compass point to give me the right bearings, which I needed so badly at the decisive moment – was just the one thing missing.' Without such a bearing, Hess would not know for sure where he was and how far he was from the Northumberland coast.

Consequently, as befitting an experienced pilot, he re-traced his course back to Point B. In attempting once again to find Point C, he would have travelled approximately the designated 170km, thus taking around twenty minutes there and twenty minutes back, returning to Point B at around 2132hrs for the second time and to the south of the original Point C much later, at 2152hrs.

Probably using his 'pilot's instinct' and trusting to a realistic bearing, Hess was now committed to his radar-beating dash; farther south of Point C by some 50km he turned due west, making landfall near Dunstanburgh Castle, some 20km south of his intended target.

The implications of this failure must surely have dawned on Hess. He had wasted time in the air: at 2132hrs it was now forty minutes later than he had anticipated leaving Point B. He had used up forty minutes more fuel than he had anticipated, probably 300l at least. He was now in deep trouble. The pilot's notes do not anticipate this manoeuvre at all – it certainly was not planned.

Some 106 miles behind him at Point B, sunset had taken place at 2144hrs. As he made his second approach to the coast, it was around 2152hrs. Hess was now in a desperate race to beat the light. By the time he crossed the coast it was 2223hrs. Sunset was at 22.00hrs.

Throughout this investigation we have been hampered by the lack of an Elektra system chart. This has not been through lack of effort and the British Library have lost the copy they held. Consequently, until quite recently, we had been unable to accurately test our theory. 'Google Earth' appeared to support our view, but we were held back by the 'True Cylinder'-type map projection used, which does not allow accurate bearings to be measured. Ideally we wanted to check the distances and bearings on a proper chart.

Luckily we do have the next best thing: Consol charts, detailing the Stavanger station. These came in the form of an RAF Conical Orthomorphic Projection Map, No. GSGS 4698, Sheet NW/48/12, 2nd Edition, 1951, from the British Library, also an instruction manual for a Sailor R110 marine radio of the 1960s and 70s. It will be remembered that the Elektra system developed into the Sonne system, which in turn was adopted by the Allies as the Consol system. The bearings were identical to the earlier systems. Sadly, the Husum station was not marked, but we attempted to mark up the map to scale. The results were revealing.

In 1941, Hess would have produced his chart from memory and with the desire to deceive. This chart is deceptive because:

It shows Hess flying over the Ruhr, so as to disguise the landing after fifty to sixty minutes.
It shows the dog-leg course over the Wadden See Islands to try and 'soak up' the time spent on the ground.
The use of Elektra is obviously not recorded.
It shows the 'box' as a strategy rather than a mistake.

Hess knew that his papers would be studied. There are certainly elements of truth contained in them, but equally on his own admission there are also many 'diversions'.

Hess wanted to disguise the fact that he landed in Germany, as that implied collusion, and he also needed to protect the integrity of the Elektra system. His pride may well have prevented his admission of failure in respect of finding the correct Elektra cross bearing.

The plan that Hess developed was very simple: it was mostly a straight flight along simple bearings and with few turns; its progress measured in time and by counting waypoints as he approached and passed them, and reference to the grid of radio signals. He had a tactical plan to defeat the British radar and the active coastal defences. 'But the one [course] I eventually took was not among these!' – despite his planning and different options, he ended up taking a course that he had not prepared. He did not choose his eventual route, it was forced on him by error.

Hess' deceptions and 'diversions' worked for more than seventy years. We will now move on to the climax of the flight and the implications of the fact that he was forty minutes later than planned and short of fuel.

16. THE FLIGHT ACROSS SCOTLAND

Unable to find Point C as described by his notes, Hess had retraced his steps, taking an extra forty minutes and approximately 400l extra of fuel in the process. We believe that these stark figures, allied to the fact that it was now technically civilian twilight meant that it was soon to be too dark to consider landing an aircraft anywhere other than a fully-lit airstrip. His planning, as shown on the Lennoxlove Map, was heavily reliant on the recognition of visual features along the way. Reportedly, a hand-written addition to the pilot's notes, which we have not seen, mentions the instruction to check the altitude of the cloudbase as he approached the coast; more visual clues at this now rapidly darkening and critical stage. These basic details go a long way to explaining his actions that night.

Returning to the pilot's notes, we find a line between SEE – DU 58/ and DU –Westk. Without access to the original it is difficult to be precise. Does the line represent a new page? Is it another option, perhaps? The last part of the notes, before this line, we are happy we understand. This essentially describes what Hess did:

CHEVIOT – on a bearing of 255° from the Islands (this is the same as detailed on the Lennoxlove Map).
ISLANDS to St Mary's Loch 100kms. Change bearing by 12° north (technically correct).
St Mary's Loch to DUNGAVEL 58kms (again correct).

Professor Simpson had referred to a railway map of the area which was 'very indistinctly marked with a number of courses across Northumberland and into southern Scotland'. The part below the line is, we believe, yet another option. This we interpret as another alternative route:

Fly to west coast, below Ayr and Prestwick – ISLANDS TO WEST COAST 220kms THIS IS POINT D.
POINT D to POINT E – heading northwards, is 28 kms.
POINT E to DUNGAVEL – 35 kilometers – boost pressure 1.3 atm at 1,000 metres.

Hess has considered two options as to how to approach Dungavel (if that really is the target). He either flies across the country westwards, making use of St Mary's Loch as a visible marker after 100km and then, by heading north a further 12°, Dungavel is discovered; or he flies across the lowlands, more southerly,

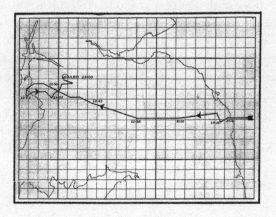

The 1953 ROC map.

Wenn im Fluge diese Kraftstoffmengen vorhanden sind, können im Horizontalflug folgende Flugzeiten und Flugstrecken erreicht werden.

Flughöhe m	Motorbelaſtung	Ladedruck ata	Drehzahl U/min	Kraftſtoffverbrauch l/h	Wahre Geſchwindigkeit ohne Wind km/h	1150 l h′	1150 l km	1000 l h′	1000 l km	800 l h′	800 l km	600 l h′	600 l km	400 l h′	400 l km	200 l h′	200 l km	Steigzeit bis 0 m Min.
300	Höchſtzuläſſige Dauerleiſtung	1,15	2200	590	405	1,34	635	1,25	575	1,13	495	0,52	355	0,32	220	0,12	80	05
	Größte Flugſtrecke	1,1	2000	525	390	1,44	680	1,35	620	1,22	535	1,0	390	0,36	235	0,13	85	
	Größte Flugſtrecke	1,0	1600	410	342	1,29	775	1,62	700	1,45	600	1,16	430	0,46	265	0,17	100	
1000	Höchſtzuläſſige Dauerleiſtung	1,15	2200	600	415	1,30	615	1,22	560	1,11	495	0,51	355	0,31	215	0,11	75	20
	Größte Flugſtrecke	1,1	1800	490	386	1,51	720	1,41	650	1,27	560	1,03	405	0,38	245	0,14	90	
	Größte Flugſtrecke	1,0	1600	420	352	2,10	765	1,58	695	1,42	600	1,13	430	0,45	260	0,16	95	
3000	Höchſtzuläſſige Dauerleiſtung	1,15	2200	630	445	1,24	620	1,17	570	1,07	500	0,48	360	0,29	215	0,10	75	60
	Größte Flugſtrecke	1,1	1800	530	415	1,41	715	1,32	645	1,20	555	0,57	400	0,35	240	0,12	85	
	Größte Flugſtrecke	0,9	1600	415	362	2,10	780	1,57	710	1,42	615	1,13	445	0,44	270	0,15	95	
5000	Höchſtzuläſſige Dauerleiſtung	1,15	2400	660	430	1,19	625	1,12	575	1,03	505	0,45	360	0,27	215	0,09	70	10
	Größte Flugſtrecke	0,9	2000	470	420	1,40	790	1,31	710	1,29	625	1,03	445	0,38	265	0,12	85	
	Größte Flugſtrecke	0,8	1600	360	367	2,22	885	2,10	810	1,57	710	1,23	510	0,50	305	0,16	100	
7000	Höchſtzuläſſige Dauerleiſtung	0,8	2200	600	435	1,24	610	1,18	565	1,09	500	0,49	355	0,29	210	0,09	65	13
	Größte Flugſtrecke	0,7	2000	510	393	1,38	640	1,31	590	1,21	525	0,57	375	0,34	220	0,10	65	

The Bf 110 *Flugstreken.*

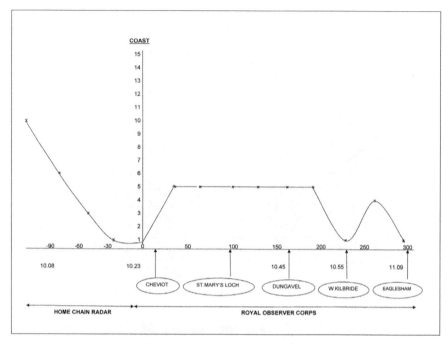

Height over Scotland from east to west.

meeting the coast at around Blantyre, heading northwards and then inland. The more northerly route allows for a landing approach into the wind, while the second option would mean landing with a following south-westerly wind.

However, we must return to the planning as we are about to discover how it is specifically referred to in the map that hangs in Lennoxlove House.

The pilot's notes had considered the flight across Scotland in two ways. Earlier, we described a line of blue triangles that are marked on the map from the Solway Firth to the Farne Islands. We then extended the line and found that it was a Stavanger Elektra line. Similarly, the pencil lines that pass through Ayr, if extended, also relate to Elektra Stavanger lines.

And finally, in a similar vein, we discovered that the markings '450' and '(450)' that were dotted about the map in apparently random fashion are also Stavanger and Husum Elektra lines. If the numbers are joined up, '450' become Stavanger lines and the '(450)' become Husum lines.

When planning his flight, Hess was at least contemplating the use of Elektra over Scotland. This discovery links the Lennoxlove Map to Elektra for certain – the lines are obvious, but perhaps, more importantly, it also links the map to the pilot's notes. We have been nervous of placing too much reliance on these notes, given what little we know about them, but we are convinced that they do indeed form a link with the Lennoxove Map, and so to Rudolf Hess directly. The figure 58, for instance, is drawn on the Lennoxlove Map between St Mary's Loch and Dungavel. On the pilot's notes SEE – DU 58 is the corresponding entry.

In order to complete our analysis, we still need to find an original Elektra chart. We believe this is the only missing part of the jigsaw.

Speed and Altitude over Scotland

In theory, the flight across Scotland should be relatively easy to analyse, given that it was accurately recorded by the ROC from the arrival of the aircraft over the Northumberland coast to the crash at Eaglesham exactly forty-six minutes later.

It is because of the British recording of the timings and altitudes that further analysis can be undertaken, which appears to contradict both the accepted version of events and even Hess' own later explanations. These details are taken from his letter to his son in 1941, just before his attempted suicide at Mychett Place, and secondly, his later correspondence with Ilse Hess in 1947.

Thanks to Peter Devitt of the RAF Museum, Hendon, we obtained a copy of the ROC map of the flight. The map has '24 Group – Edinburgh' printed on the back and so is a post-war recreation, as that designation only came into being in 1953.[8]

Subsequently, we discovered another ROC map of the flight, which we think is earlier than 1953. Contained within the file AIR 16/1266 is the record of the Hess flight, which appears to have sent to the headquarters of the ROC at Bentley Priory from 31 Group at Galashiels. Thomas M. Lees signed the accompanying letter as early as 13 May 1941, but the precise date of the map is unclear.

Nonetheless, in our opinion it is the most accurate representation of the flight, prepared from the individual ROC station reports. It forms the basis of the chart in the book *Attack Warning Red*, but there are some small differences upon close inspection, partly perhaps due to scale. Oddly, it uses a grid which appears to use 10km (or perhaps 6-mile) squares.

We have prepared this analysis of time, speed and distance directly from the ROC map. Some of the times may have a degree of overlap between the various

ROC stations, but we believe this to be a statistically fair representation.

Time (hrs)	ROC	Location		Time (mins)	km	Cum. km	Speed (km/h)	Height (ft)
1023	30/a2	Coast / Embleton	V	0	0	0	0	150
1025			V	2	11	11	336	

1030	31/f2	Jedburgh	V	5	50	61	595	5,000
1036	31/g1	Ashkirk	V	6	42	103	424	
1045	34/d3	Thankerton	S	9	49	152	325	5,000
1050	34/h3	Dunlop		5	49	201	586	
1055	34/g3	Off W.Kilbride	V	5	34	235	413	150
1100	34/f4	Kilmarnock	V	5	32	267	384	4,000
1109	34/h2	Crashes at Eaglesham		9	38	306	256	
				46			399	

(V –Visual: S – Sound only)

The above figures are taken from the ROC reports and demonstrate:

The total time taken is without doubt.

The kilometres flown are taken from modern mapping techniques (Google Earth) and are typically straight-line projections of the flight map. Further circling, for instance, would increase distance, thus lowering average speeds still further.

The heights given also come from the ROC reports.

Those sites marked (V) represent the locations where a visual (as opposed to a sound) bearing was taken.

PRO File AIR 16/1266 appears to add to the list of claimants as to who firstly identified the aircraft as a Bf 110. Apparently 'Charlie' Irvine and 'Dick' Oliver at Jedburgh reported the aircraft to their Galashiels centre as a Bf 110 as it had flown 'quite near the post'. They were told 'not to be so daft'. This claim is in addition to that of G.W. Green at Chatton, and Major Graham Donald, apparently on behalf of No. 34 Group.

Typical of any flight, there are marked differences in speed at certain times. A speed of 399km/h indicates that the aircraft was travelling slightly below its usual quoted cruising speed of 450km/h. However, on closer inspection, an average speed of 399km/h actually hides the reality of some very fast legs mixed with some quite slow legs. When getting ready to bale out, Hess is slowing to an average of 256km/h. (The landing speed of a Bf 110 is 140km/h.) As the table shows, the first part of the flight from the coast to Ashkirk is at an average speed of 522km/h. This is perhaps as expected, given Hess' later extravagant descriptions of diving down from 15,000ft to near sea level at the coast.

The engine performance charts reveal that, at 300m (*c.* 1,000ft), the *Dauerleistung* (maximum continuous power) at 2,200rpm produces a computed speed of 405km/h. In other words, the aircraft was flying very quickly for that altitude (and boost pressure of 1.15atm). The additional speed was presumably still being gained by reason of the diving manoeuvre coming in off the sea. (The maximum diving speed of the Bf 110 was quoted at 700km/h.)[9]

If Hess had really been travelling at 500km/h throughout the flight over Scotland, it would have lasted thirty-six minutes, not forty-six minutes. He would have covered 383km, not the measured 306km. We should also point out that the aircraft was quite capable of maintaining 480km/h, but only at a higher altitude. At 5,000m (c. 15,000ft) the *Dauerleistung* at 2,400rpm was 480km/h. However, at this speed the engines would consume an enormous 660l of fuel per hour. According to the ROC, at no time was Hess at this altitude over Scotland.

We now believe that Hess was virtually going as fast as he could, given the altitude at which he chose to fly. This certainly seems to be a sensible approach to take over enemy territory. Certainly the aircraft could fly faster, but only at a much higher altitude. We are now able to dissect each stage of the flight in terms of chosen altitude. Much then becomes clearer.

The *Flugstreken* chart shows engine rpm versus speed, height and fuel consumption. This was kindly provided to us by the Deutsches Museum, Munich, Germany. These charts were prepared by the Luftwaffe Research station at Rechlin and their purpose was to aid the planning process in terms of fuel consumption and time taken when flying at varying altitudes and with different loads.

The obvious point to note is the effect of altitude on speed. The maximum continuous power is produced at the highest sustainable revolutions of the engine that can be maintained. In combat conditions, for example, the Daimler-Benz engine could be 'revved' marginally higher, albeit only for short bursts. To analyse the effect on speed at the *Dauerleistung*:

Altitude (m)	Speed (km)
300	405
1,000	415
3,000	445
5,000	480
7,000	435 (the effect of thin air beginning to reduce engine efficiency)

Over the North Sea at 5,000m (c. 15,000ft), Hess would have been quite capable of covering 480km in one hour. However, when over Scotland at the reported altitudes of 50–1,600m (150–5,000ft) the performance of his machines was inevitably limited by the engine's capability.

Climbing from 50m (150ft) at the coast to the reported 1,600m (5,000ft) at Ashkirk took 12 minutes and covered 103km. Hess describes this part of the flight thus: 'So low did I roar past, barely higher than the houses at some 750km per hour.'[10] Clearly this is an exaggeration. Even if the dive speed really was 750km/h, the speed then quickly fell off when climbing back to 1,600m (5,000ft). To cover 103km in twelve minutes requires an average speed of 515km/h to be maintained. At low altitudes such as these, the speed would fall back to around 400–415km/h in level flight, let alone climbing back to 1,600m (5,000ft). We conclude that Hess was operating at *Dauerleistung* throughout this period, both while diving and subsequently regaining altitude. This equates to 103km in twelve minutes; 370km/h at 2,200rpm using 600 litres per hour equals 120l of fuel consumed.

Ashkirk to Thankerton

A flight of 49km, at 1,600m (5,000ft), at an average speed of 326km/h, took nine minutes. While still below the most efficient height of 5,000m (*c.* 15,000ft), this part of the flight appears to very slow indeed. We believe that this part of the flight required recognition of St Mary's Loch (The SEE as referred to on the pilot's notes). There are other stretches of water in the area, such as the Talla Reservoir (opened 1899) and the authors wonder if Hess struggled to identify St Mary's Loch. *In extremis*, did he double back to check his position or find the loch?

Hess merely states: 'The variometer told me I was ascending, until suddenly I was over my next point of orientation – a little dam in a narrow range of hills with Broad Dav the highest summit. Here my course bent to the left.'

The little dam we take to be the Talla Reservoir dam and Broad Dav to be Broadlaw hill, which are slightly to the left of St Mary's Loch. However, the actual course followed was soon to go to the right, certainly not the left. By reference to the *Dauerleistung* at 1,000m (1,000ft), the aircraft will fly at 415km/h, which is considerably faster than the achieved speed. At this rate the fuel is consumed at between 600 and 630 litres per hour. So this part of the flight is 49km in nine minutes; 326km/h at 2,200rpm using 615 litres per hour equals 92l of fuel consumed.

Thankerton to Dunlop

This appears to be easily (and surprisingly) the fastest part of the flight. From the ROC station at Thankerton, Hess flew north-westerly, directly towards the Firth of Clyde. He was travelling well above the *Dauerleistung* speed of 415km/h. He was also losing height quickly. At Thankerton he was at 1,600m (5,000ft); then approaching the Firth of Clyde he was at 50m (150ft). He had to be diving quickly so as to gain speed. At the same time he was passing over the Dungavel House area, albeit straying markedly to the north. Why might that be? Why fly over the supposed target at 588km/h?

We now believe that the Boulton Paul Defiant that had been scrambled from RAF Prestwick provides the explanation, in combination with the rapidly deteriorating light conditions.

At 2245hrs the Thankerton ROC station recorded: '1 @ 5000' (one aircraft at 5,000ft). It also stated: 'the sound plotting was confused by the Defiant in the same area.'[10]

Later, Hess reported to the Duke of Hamilton that he had seen the Defiant, but had thought it to be a Hurricane. While the Defiant had a top speed of 500km/h, the Hurricane was even faster, with a maximum of 566km/h (at a much higher altitude). Viewed from the front, the two fighters did indeed look similar and both were fitted with the Rolls-Royce Merlin engine.

We now contend that the reason that Hess was travelling at 588km/h was that he was fleeing for his life. The fact that the soundplot is confused was simply because the aircraft were in close proximity. The only means of escape for Hess was to dive as fast as he could – the guns on the Bf 110 were not loaded.

The RAF Ayr Operations Record Book – file AIR28/40 – tells of Cuddie and Hodge taking off at 2234hrs to intercept. The same file mentions that they failed to do so. We are surprised at the apparent short time between the order being given and take-off. We question the state of preparedness, or was there foreknowledge? What actually happened, we analyse later.

This is not a new assertion. On 11 May 1941, Major Graham Donald, the deputy commander of No. 34 Group ROC wrote to his commanding officer: 'There was a Defiant to the South of him, but it did not seem fast enough ...'[12] Roy Conyers Nesbit writes: 'All the time Cuddie was pursuing him [Hess].'

By contrast, Hess does not mention this part of the flight, but the statistical evidence is there for all to see. We believe that it was the Defiant that forced Hess to flee to the coast. He later tried to explain his action through the need to 'check his bearings' or 'to avoid all possibility of error' – this has to be bunkum. Why on earth fly another 100km or so, over some of the most heavily defended airspace in the UK, just to 'check bearings'? Similarly, why fly at 588km/h over the supposed target?

The Boulton Paul Defiant was peculiar in that it had no fixed, forward-firing guns. Instead, it was fitted with a rear-facing turret, mounting four .303in Browning machine guns. The turret could revolve to facilitate some forward firing, but upon its introduction the type had been successful against attacks from above and behind. As a night fighter, it therefore had to intercept by either being flown alongside or, more typically, below the target.

If we were being charitable, we could argue that Hess' reluctance to tell his wife of the dangerous situation was simply so she would not be alarmed at her husband's plight – albeit the letters detailing the flight were only censored and passed in May/July 1947. But, being realistic, we believe it was this part of the flight that, with the failing light, eventually culminated in the crash at 1109hrs. Hess was now straying into territory much farther to the north than originally planned.

We know this because the grime marks on the Lennoxlove Map reveal exactly how it was folded on his knee. The upper fold mark ends just above Ardrossan and Hess was now at least 10km above the fold mark. In contrast with the lower part of the map, none of the railway lines are marked, which indicates that Hess was not anticipating being in this area. He was 'off piste' and, furthermore, probably uncertain of his position.

This part of the flight is 49km in five minutes, quite possibly using a short burst of maximum power, consuming 700 litres per hour equals 58l of fuel consumed.

Dunlop to the Firth of Clyde (off Ardrossan)

A distance of 34km and losing altitude to 50m (150ft) at the coast, at an average speed of 408km/h, Hess is slowing down as he approaches the coast. He realises that to retrieve his position he must turn south when reaching the coast, and this he does when passing over West Kilbride and the ROC station on the hill adjacent to the cemetery. At this elevation we are quite prepared to believe the report that the observers could see the wing markings of the Bf 110 from above, as the site does have an uninterrupted view of the River Clyde and beyond.

Hess reports: 'The smooth sea lay beneath me, as calm as a mirror, lit by the rising moon. Just off the mainland, a towering rock, five hundred metres high, rose out of the water, magnificently illuminated, a pale reddish colour. All looked so peaceful and beautiful.' Again, oddly, instead of describing the peril that he was now in, Hess chooses to comment on the geography, which admittedly is stunning. Because he was now so far to the north, the towering rock would almost definitely be 'Goat Fell' (2,868ft) on the Isle of Arran.

He then flew south down the firth towards two of the most heavily defended areas of airspace in the UK: the Shell oil refinery at Ardrossan and, a short distance farther down the coast, the ICI works at Ardeer, the site of the largest explosives manufacturer for the British Empire. The heavy AA artillery was strategically positioned at the north and south of the site, and Hess was now flying straight towards Ardeer.

This part of the fight is 34km in five minutes at *Dauerleistung* flying at sea level, using 590 litres per hour equals 49l of fuel consumed.

From the firth to the crash at Eaglesham is 70km in fourteen minutes at an average speed 256km/h. Hess says: 'I flew a few kilometres along the coast until I reached a small place on a spit of land with what might have been a mole, as on my map. I turned east again and was able to pick out the railway and a small lake which was shown on the map with a road by it and south of the residence at Dungavel.' However, the statement just does not stand scrutiny.

It is fair to say he flew down the coast and we assume the small spit is Ardrossan. This is almost identical to the spit at Troon and it may well be that Hess had confused the two landmarks. Part of the problem was that he was still just above sea level, so his lines of sight were being impeded. The Bf 110 cockpit sat above the wings, so the view beneath was partially obscured. Whilst at sea level he could not bale out.

Of more immediate concern was the sight of the twenty-four barrage balloons marking the vast 100-acre industrial site at Ardeer. To fly over the site was surely suicide, particularly at low level, and so Hess chose to do the obvious and fly around, firstly to the north, while at the same time climbing. By the time he reached Kilmarnock he was at 4,000ft, according to the ROC station.

What also requires comment is the fact that, having avoided Ardeer to the north, Hess then headed south again. This, we believe, is significant and will be referred to again as it placed him in the Kilmaurs area. It is quite plausible that he did indeed see the Kilmarnock railway junctions (there were a number), but under no circumstances would he be able to see Dungavel House or Glengavel Reservoir, the 'small lake '(marked with a red arrow on the Lennoxlove Map) to which it has been assumed he refers. By this time, it was dark and Glengavel, 29km away and surrounded by hills, just would not be visible.

According to the ROC map (p. 204), Hess did not get remotely close to Dungavel, or Glengavel. By this time he was at an altitude which would allow him to use his parachute, but he was definitely heading north – not eastward.

The climb rate for the Bf 110 is given as 15m per second; therefore, to climb to 1,220m (4,000ft) would take approximately four and a half minutes, again at 2,200rpm. While climbing, the aircraft would be flying at 210km/h and would therefore travel 16km – approximately, the distance from the coast to Kilmarnock.

This appears to make sense. Hess turned south down the Firth of Clyde virtually at sea level (as noted by ROC West Kilbride) and then, on turning inland, eventually climbed back to 1,220m (4,000ft). It would appear that shortly afterwards the decision is taken to bale out and the engines were shut down.

This part of the flight breaks down as: at sea level 19km in two and a half minutes at 390km/h and 2,000rpm, using 525 litres per hour equals 22l consumed; climbing 16km in four and a half minutes at 210km/h and 2,200rpm using 600 litres per hour equals 45l consumed; at 1,220m (4,000ft) until the crash is 27km in seven minutes at 230km/h and 1,400rpm, using 350 litres per hour equals 40l consumed.

The total fuel consumed over Scotland is therefore 426l; this is an average of 555 litres per hour, owing to the relatively high engine revolutions being used throughout most of this part of the flight.

Altitude is revealing. From the diagram the reader can see that Hess flew over Dungavel at 1,600ft (5,000ft). This is indeed most odd if he were really intending to land. Particularly if there were lights being switched on, as is insisted in the book *Double Standards*.

We now know reasonably precisely where Hess went and what it meant in terms of time of speed and fuel consumption. The classic mistake is to believe that where Hess went is where he meant to go. If nothing else we hope the above chapter dissuades the reader of this. What is really interesting is why Hess then chose to describe his flight as going to plan, despite evidence to the contrary. We suggest that it was done simply to disguise his intended target.

However, our understanding of this part of the flight and, indeed, the whole Hess affair has been aided greatly through new information provided by Peter Padfield in his 2013 work *Hitler, Hess and Churchill*.[13] We are grateful to him for allowing us to discuss the same. In the chapter entitled 'Take off' he describes a letter that he received from Squadron Leader R.G. Woodman in 1991, whilst researching his earlier work, *Flight for the Führer*. Squadron Leader Woodman was a high profile officer and was involved in a later review of RAF Turnhouse and the Defiants of 410 Squadron RCAF.[14] It appears that Woodman had later also interviewed Wing Commander E.C. Wolfe about the Hess affair. Wolfe was the commanding officer of 141 Squadron on 10 May 1941, and in the week leading up to the Hess flight had been commended for shooting down an enemy plane over Clydebank.[15] In a surprising amount of detail, Woodman told Padfield that the Cuddie Defiant, T4040, had been given very precise instructions when taking off from Ayr. These were: 'Scramble Angels two five zero nine degrees. Dive and buster vector three five zero.'

Peter correctly interpreted these instructions as evidence of the intention to attack and destroy the Hess plane. We too believe this to be the case. However, we have gone further and have plotted the instructions on a map. Using a climb rate of 1,900ft per minute for a Defiant and an average speed of 200mph, the instructions actually can be interpreted as: climb to 2,500ft (by which time the plane would virtually be overhead Rosemount House – the Ayr 'operations room') and then, on a bearing of 350 degrees, dive flat out. Our reconstruction gives the following sensational result (see map opposite).

As can be seen from the diagram, the very specific instruction was given to seemingly attack an aircraft approaching RAF Dundonald, only some 8 miles away. Having constructed the diagram and knowing the approximate speed of a Defiant, we calculate that the plane would have been virtually at the end of the runway at around 1040hrs, no more than five minutes after take-off. At this time it will be remembered Hess was fast approaching Dungavel at 1,600m (5,000ft,) only some 32km (20 miles) away.

It is vitally important to consider that, at 1034hrs, when the command was given at Ayr to launch the Cuddie plane, all that Fighter Command had to go on was the ROC reports of a solitary Bf 110 that had 'been treated with derison'. These sightings were based on observations of a plane coming in off the coast and then coming across Lowland Scotland near Jedburgh and Selkirk. The plane, at that stage, could have been going virtually anywhere, with Clydebank being the most obvious destination. Yet the decision is given so precisely and seemingly in a rush – 'dive and buster' – to launch Cuddie towards RAF Dundonald. Quite extraordinary.

We also considered whether this was just wishful thinking on our part and that it was an instruction to perhaps protect the Ardeer explosives works. This we discount because why 'dive'? Ardeer was protected by heavy AA guns and the barrage balloons, and their placement were designed to force enemy planes to go higher, thus damaging their potential for accuracy. There was no need to dive if protecting Ardeer. A height of 2,500ft would have still enabled Cuddie and Hodge to have attacked a plane above them, assuming that it was heading their way of course. A more usual instruction would surely be to 'circle Ardeer and wait.' The other question that comes to mind is why were no other planes launched from any other west coast base. Why was Fighter Command seemingly so convinced

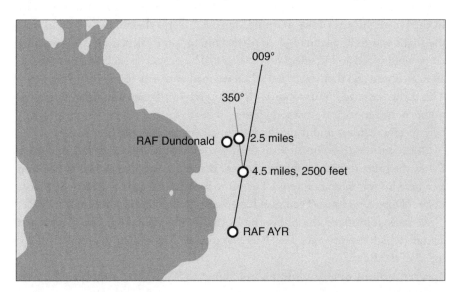

Cuddie map, 009°, followed by 350°.

the plane was heading towards RAF Dundonald/Ardeer? At 1034hrs there was virtually no evidence to base that decision on.

This new information, we believe, now proves for the first time that the British knew full well where Hess was heading and going to land. The Defiant, and indeed, RAF Ayr (which had just opened in May 1941) were there to protect the Clyde, Ardrossan and Ardeer. Of all the possible instructions and locations that Hector Maclean, the controller on duty on 10 May 1941, could have given, why did he choose to be quite so precise? This will be debated in the next chapters as it has significant implications when unravelling what actually went on and why.

Recreation of the Hess Flight, 2012

In the summer of 2012, we were engaged in trying to decipher the pilot's notes and were fascinated to discover how they were linked to the Lennoxlove Map. Therefore, we now think the two maps and flight notes (despite their near total lack of provenance) are completely genuine, or at least the information contained within them is genuine. We can now link the flight notes to the Lennoxlove Map and to the FuG 10 equipment and Elektra system.

For a while we had not been happy with the assumption that Hess was intending to land at Dungavel, for reasons that will become apparent. We came to the conclusion that another location had to be the intended target. In order to verify our suspicions we felt we needed to put ourselves in the same position as Hess.

Consequently, on 19 May we embarked on our flight from Carlisle airfield. In the pre-flight part of the morning, our pilot, Derek, helpfully showed us how the flight was to be planned by dead-reckoning, after calculating the prevailing cross-wind speed and its effect on the original bearing. The fuel requirement was also calculated and then exceeded when we made our way to the refuelling point. The flight was made in daytime, with good visibility. Derek also marked halfway points between various marked features so as to keep a check on our progress over terrain that was undulating and not at all aircraft friendly.

Our route was to go north from Carlisle to find St Mary's Loch and, thereafter, follow the route that Hess took. Please note that on no account should this be seen as where he was intending to go. The route we planned was: Carlisle – St Mary's Loch – Dungavel House/Glengavel Reservoir – West Kilbride – return to Carlisle.

We now reproduce the photographs that were taken from our Cessna 172 aircraft, which seventy-one years later was capable of travelling at around half the speed of the Bf 110.

After around ninety minutes and some 320km, we returned to Carlisle airfield. We believe the flight to have been extremely useful in that it demonstrated certain truths. Having found St Mary's Loch, the rest of the re-creation was reasonably easy and quite possible to perform visually. From the loch it is possible to see Arran in the distance, over the Firth of Clyde. Flying straight towards Arran we inadvertently came across Dungavel House and Glengavel Reservoir. Visually, Glengavel was much easier to find than Dungavel House.

Dungavel airstrip was very small and uninviting. To land there would require flying past the airstrip and then doubling back to land on the uphill slope. This would mean landing with a tailwind, not into the wind as pilots much prefer. En route to the coast the land is largely flat and undulating. Visibilty was good and it was possible to see a good distance, some 49km. Arran was a prominent landmark. In the light, there was no requirement whatsoever for radio navigation equipment – visual recognition was quite adequate and possible. We also made further important findings that will become apparent later.

St Mary's Loch.

View towards the Clyde from St Mary's Loch.

View towards the Clyde – Arran in the background.

Dungavel House.

Dungavel House – the old airfield.

Glengavel Reservoir.

17. SUMMARY OF THE FLIGHT

As we stated in the introduction, we do not wish to be seen as 'revisionists'. We have merely analysed the flight in far more detail than has been done to date. In so doing, we believe we have made a number of new discoveries. The Hess aircraft did not have an auxiliary oil tank fitted; consequently, Hess had planned to land in Northern Germany. Without the additional oil tank, his Bf 110 simply could not have completed the flight. The flight over Scotland was almost a fiasco. When Hess crashed, the sequence of events thereafter certainly became one. In truth, we are a little nervous in presenting such a different version of facts and details, particularly given their implications.

Using the clues provided to us by the pilot's notes and the ROC maps, we have discovered that, far from the controlled flight across Scotland that Hess chose to describe, the reality was that it was actually conducted in an ever darkening panic, until ended by a near-fatal parachute jump. We believe the aircraft had also either run out of fuel or was close to doing so.

We have also looked at the navigation systems available to Hess and feel sure that he attempted to use Elektra, then based in Stavanger and Husum. Eventually, it was this system that failed Hess and, in trying to recover his position, he wasted forty minutes of time and fuel. The events that ensued over Scotland were a direct result when Hess could not find the correct Stavanger beam, his Point C.

This was certainly not a triumph. It was actually a near fatal escapade. Heading for the coast and outrunning a Boulton Paul Defiant night fighter, Hess flew over Dungavel House at 1,600m (5,000ft) and at over 500km/h. He was never going to land there.

Having reached the Firth of Clyde, he quite correctly turned south as he realised he was too far north of his original plan. West Kilbride, where he crossed the coast, was not even on the 'folded' part of his flight map. Quite logically heading south, he soon came across heavily defended airspace.

In order to avoid Ardeer, Hess almost turned back on himself and headed back inland. A controlled landing was now out of the question, the main motivation was firstly to avoid the AA batteries and secondly to gain height. If a parachute exit was the main concern, his aircraft had to gain height as he was almost at sea level near West Kilbride.

By this time, it was almost pitch dark and we doubt if Hess was really sure of his position, or indeed what he was even capable of seeing. He may have still been able to discern the line between ground and sky, but by this time his main

The Actual Flight Plan

	Height	Engine revs	Litres	L/per hr	Speed	Time	Distance	Timing
Start Engines		2600	10	590		1		5.45
Climb to 300m	300	2200	10	590	210	1	4	
To Stopping Point	300	2000	500	525	410	58	406	6.45
			520			**60**	**410**	
RETANK AND REFUEL						30		7.15
Climb to 5,000m	5000	2200	190	600	205	19	65	
To North Sea	5000	2000	188	470	400	24	195	7.58
To Point B	5000	2000	423	470	410	54	410	8.52
North Sea Box	5000	2000	313	470	410	40	350	9.32
Final Approach	3000	2400	561	660	480	51	390	10.23
Over Scotland	1000	1800	336	530	415	37	256	11.09
Baling Out	2000	2200	90	600	210	9	32	
			2101			**234**	**1697**	
TOTAL			**2621**			**324**	**2107**	
Standard tanks			1270		Av. speed	435.1282		
Auxiliary			831		Av. fuel use	538.8034		

motivation was surely just to get out of the Bf 110 alive. Dealing with parachuting, Chapter 13 describes the difficulties he encountered in this regard, and the well-known sequence of events at Eaglesham indicates to us that Hess was certainly not expected in that area on that night.

We have not devoted much time to events at Eaglesham once the crash had occurred, simply because it seems to us typical of what would be expected to occur (various displays of 'rank pulling', errors in procedures and blatant propaganda; Hess captured by a pitchfork-wielding ploughman etc.). There is no doubt whatsoever that Hess was not intending to land anywhere near Eaglesham. The location was a random outcome occasioned by the previous errors of navigation. The only aspect of any relevance seems to be the arrival of Roman Battaglia on the scene at Busby, which certainly meant that the Polish government in exile knew of Hess' arrival, almost before the British government had confirmed it.

However, one further small fact deserves explanation. In *Double Standards*, the authors describe how Rudolf Hess gave Sergeant McBride his Iron Cross medal, the same Iron Cross that Stephen Prior eventually acquired. Prior quite properly wondered why this might be. According to the authors, McBride had a friend who was a newspaper editor and, quite extraordinarily, Hess persuaded McBride to telephone his friend from the cottage at Floors Farm. Having done so, Hess could be quite content that his presence would come to public attention; it did on 12 May. Hess knew by then that he had fallen into government hands (literally) and we suspect McBride might well have just saved his life, notwithstanding the extraordinary lapse of military security. Similarly, the fortuitous intervention of Battaglia at the Busby Scout Hall also provided unwelcome third-party evidence that Hess had arrived. The option of denial was becoming more difficult by the minute. Further interventions by the likes of Major Graham Donald would later not be treated as particularly helpful when he too claimed to have recognised the Deputy Führer.[17]

We also make the case that Hess landed somewhere in Northern Germany. This is done for two reasons. Firstly, it allows the flight to take place without recourse to the complications of the 75l auxiliary oil tank, and secondly, the landing justifies the opening lines of the infamous pilot's notes (fifty-five to sixty minutes). We were interested to learn that ZG142, an operational Bf 110 squadron, had moved to the airfield at Lippstadt in May 1941; though given the requirement for secrecy, we will also research Göttingen in further detail. We therefore, with some trepidation, present a completely different interpretation to the usual 'solo flight' theory. The main differences are:

A landing at an airfield in Northern Germany, around an hour's flying time from Augsburg.

The North Sea box was actually the result of a fundamental failure in Hess's navigation.

The entire flight was meticulously planned and we believe required significant assistance in its delivery – in terms of training, education and operation.

Given the light conditions, the flight across Scotland was a near fiasco and Hess was lucky to survive.

Hess was certainly not targeting Eaglesham or Dungavel. The British clearly assumed, or knew, RAF Dundonald when sending Cuddie to intercept.

The romantic post-flight descriptions can only be seen as a 'smokescreen', to hide the reality of the failure of the mission. In some ways, their divergence from the facts is among the most compelling pieces of evidence.

The Hess flight had failed and Hess was in the hands of Churchill's government; a feat that he could have far more easily accomplished by walking into an embassy or even flying to England, if that had really been his objective.

The flight had been well planned, but despite the planning and attention to detail it had still ended in near catastrophe.

As Josef Goebbels summarised the position: 'A fool, but a meticulous one ...'[18]

PART 4

AFTERMATH AND CONCLUSIONS

18. THE IMPLICATIONS

The previous chapters, we hope, make the convincing case that the flight was a complete failure in terms of what Hess was hoping to achieve. Despite much effort, Hess had merely ended up under the control of the Churchill government. After 2309hrs on 10 May 1941, the farcical, yet dangerous, situation was now virtually identical to that described in Peter Fleming's book *The Flying Visit*: a fictional, amusing account, describing the hypothetical aftermath of Adolf Hitler parachuting into England in 1940. 'It was above all a personal gesture, challenging, reckless, yet characteristically well judged ...'

The real analysis, however, is dependent upon an understanding of what Hess thought he might be achieving in choosing to fly to Scotland in 1941. Without doubt he did not achieve what he set out to achieve – but what could or might have happened?

Chapters 4 and 5 dealt with the variety of negotiations that were conducted prior to Hess deciding to fly. Albrecht Haushofer had spent much of the spring in 1941 travelling throughout Europe, from Stockholm to Madrid, via Geneva, in pursuit of his master's peace initiative. We may never know for sure what precisely was being negotiated, or even what information was being relayed, but clearly there was considerable activity. Hess, in turn, had spent the spring learning the finer points of the Bf 110 and Luftwaffe navigational systems. Politically, he had to wait until he felt he had the necessary logistics under his control.

What we now need to ascertain is precisely who Hess was dealing with, or who he thought he was dealing with. As a starting point, we believe it is important to ascertain where Hess was targeting, as this can clearly provide a significant clue as to who he believed he was negotiating with. On no account should this be confused with the actual result of the flight – Hess certainly did not plan to parachute from his aircraft over Eaglesham. Eaglesham is off the map, literally and figuratively.

In this connection we believe there are some clues as to the precise intended destination. They are marked on the Lennoxlove Map. There are also other marks on the map that we believe are disguised as to their true meaning. When these marks are analysed and understood, the true target location becomes more apparent.

There is, and has been, a lot of evidence to support the idea that Hess was targeting Dungavel House, the home of the 14th Duke of Hamilton. However,

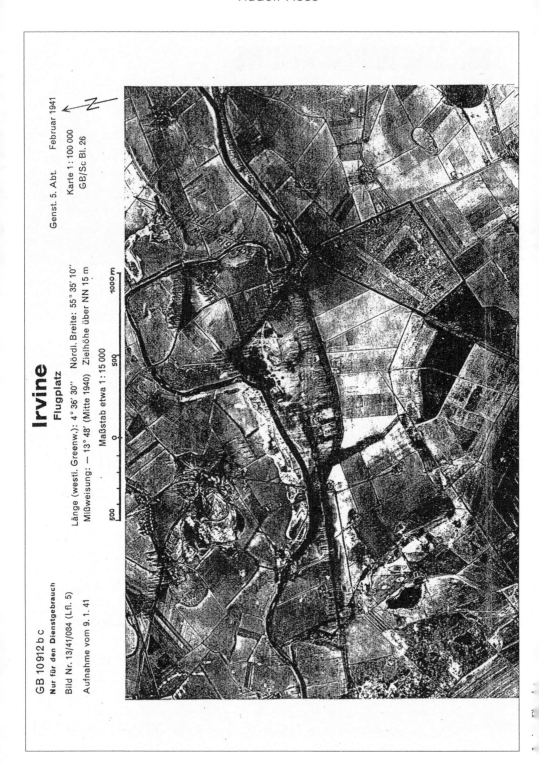

GB 10912 b c

Nur für den Dienstgebrauch

Bild Nr. 13/41/084 (Lfl. 5)

Aufnahme vom 9. 1. 41

Irvine
Flugplatz

Länge (westl. Greenw.): 4° 36' 30''   Nördl. Breite: 55° 35' 10''

Mißweisung: − 13° 48' (Mitte 1940)   Zielhöhe über NN 15 m

Maßstab etwa 1 : 15 000

Genst. 5. Abt.   Februar 1941

Karte 1 : 100 000

GB/Sc Bl. 26

RAF Dundonald, May 2012. Note the railway acting as a marker.

much of it makes no sense at all. Quantity of evidence should not necessarily assume quality of evidence. We hope we have made that point.

Most authors agree that a Bf 110 could not land at Dungavel House, the aircraft was simply too large for the airstrip. Those that even then still cling to the idea of a Dungavel House rendezvous claim that Hess was always going to parachute and, in so doing, destroy the Bf 110 and its secret equipment.

We simply do not believe that Hess, who was 47 at the time, would voluntarily choose to make his first parachute jump over enemy territory, without any basic training. Furthermore, if the mission was really to remain a secret, as we have already suggested, a German aircraft crashing in the South Lanarkshire countryside was not going to assist in the preservation of such secrecy. There had to be a viable alternative.

John Harris, in his book *Rudolf Hess: The British Illusion of Peace*, made the case that Hess was targeting Prestwick airfield. At the time it was extremely quiet in operational terms and the main runway was being extended in anticipation of the commencement of the Atlantic Air Bridge. As we have already seen, the adjacent RAF Ayr was also operational, having 'scrambled' Cuddie and Hodge in their Boulton Paul Defiant. Presumably, RAF Ayr must have had some form of runway lighting to allow night operations.

RAF Prestwick and Ayr both make sense in aeronautical terms: both are reasonably easy to locate geographically and, as Hess' adjutant Pintsch made clear, there are lighthouses in the Firth of Clyde that could be used as beacons to guide the approach. Both runways could easily accommodate a Bf 110, but the obvious inference would be collusion with the RAF. This option then completely alters the complexion of the flight. It is one thing for a mad German to target an airstrip that he could not land on, but it is quite another thing for a rational, sane German to target an operational RAF base. That choice has really quite profound implications and may well explain why the pilot has been thought to have been deranged ever since. We have, however, ruled out RAF Prestwick and Ayr simply because, if Hess was aiming to land at either base, we feel he would not have acted in the manner he did. When at West Kilbride he need only have flown down the Firth of Clyde to locate either RAF airfield. Presumably, Ayr also had some form of lighting in place so as to allow the Defiant to have safely landed.[1]

As already inferred from the very specific instructions given to Cuddie, we now believe that Rudolf Hess was actually intending to land at RAF Dundonald, which, from March 1940, had acted as a reserve landing ground for the Tiger Moths of 12 Elementary Flying Training School, based at Prestwick. We will attempt to make the case for the location shortly, but in truth, in the wider area under scrutiny there are very few airstrips at all.

The second controversial implication of this assertion is that whoever sanctioned the landing at Dundonald was perhaps, to some extent, in agreement with Hess and his objectives, or gave that impression. We doubt very much if Hess would have been allowed to land at Kenley or Biggin Hill. Otherwise he would have gone there – it was so much easier.

We are quite aware that this is the challenging part of this narrative, as it implies German collusion with the British. We have already demonstrated that the Hess flight was a meticulously planned German initiative that was dressed up as a solo flight in case it went wrong; we now wish to move on to assert that the actual target was an operational RAF airfield.

RAF Dundonald was not a major RAF airfield. In the later stages of the war it was a focal point of the Combined Operations and No. 516 Squadron in particular. However, in 1941 it was still a grass strip, albeit much longer and flatter than the Dungavel airfield, some 15 miles distant. In February 1941, the airfield had two runways: the SW/NE was 765 yards long and the NW/SE was 602 yards long.[2]

In 2009, we became interested in Dundonald for a number of reasons: firstly, and above all, we have never thought Dungavel made any sense. Secondly, Dundonald seemed almost perfect, with runway lengths adequate to safely land a Bf 110. It also shared the same first two letters, DU, and so we wondered if it was the DU specifically referred to in the pilot's notes. It was also quiet, so as to limit exposure, and was nominally controlled by Prestwick/Turnhouse.

However, the more we studied, the more we learned. We have described how the Lennoxlove Map had two types of marking: the conventional red and blue pencil marks that describe the visual features such as hills, mountains, lakes and corners of woods; and other markings that are specific to the Hess flight, in that they refer to the Elektra radio system.

Richard Wilbourn discovered three specific measurements that were not immediately obvious in their meaning: 108kms, 145 kms and 155 kms. Richard analysed the marks by reference to other places on the map. He performed this separation analysis and looked at the distances from a variety of possible locations.

Hess Map Markings   Separation Analysis

Map Mark		Map Mark/Place	Note	Distance km	Diff
250	km	Farne Insele		250	0
155	km	145km		40	115
155	km	145km	E–W	18	10
155	km	108km		118	37
155	km	Dungavel		127	28
155	km	Dundonald		156	–1
155	km	Prestwick		154	1
155	km	Troon		160	–5
155	km	Turnberry		170	–15
155	km	Dumfries		96	59
155	km	West Kilbride		175	–20
145	km	108 km		83	62
145	km	Dumfries		71	74
145	km	Dungavel		121	24
145	km	Dundonald		147	–2
145	km	Troon		150	–5
145	km	Prestwick		144	1
145	km	Turnberry		153	–8
145	km	West Kilbride		167	–22

108	km	Cheviot	122	-14
108	km	Farne Insele	160	-52
108	km	Dumfries	35	73
108	km	58 km	85	23
108	km	Dungavel	98	10
108	km	Dundonald	109	-1
108	km	Troon	108	0
108	km	Prestwick	101	7
108	km	Turnberry	97	11
108	km	West Kilbride	127	-19

The conclusion is simply that Dundonald is the point that most closely coincides with the four distances marked on the Lennoxlove Map.

Secondly, we were intrigued by the number of black pencil marks on the Lennoxlove Map, '450' and '(450)'. These appeared all over the map in an apparently random fashion, and, in particular there was a cluster of these marks just off the Northumberland coast in the North Sea.

After much headscratching we have deduced that the markings are actually radio beacon markings from Stavanger and Husum. The '450' markers align from Husum and the '(450)' markers from Stavanger. These markers are in addition to the lines already described – the blue triangles from Bamburgh to the Solway and the Stavanger line that passes through Ayr on the west coast. Whilst we understand Hess' wish for preserving the secrecy of the Elektra system, we wondered if the lines might give us a clue as to the actual target.

Drawing the lines accurately is quite difficult, given the fact that the Lennoxlove Map is not a gnomic chart. Hess would have also had this difficulty and so we anticipate him transcribing the lines from such a chart while at Harlaching, Munich. We obtained a Luftwaffe map of south-west Scotland and we assume that Hess marked up his 'road atlas' maps from the Luftwaffe map. The choice of map was simply to reinforce the idea of the 'solo' flight; a Luftwaffe map might, of course, have implied air force connivance and assistance.

In marking the Lennoxlove Map, Hess was demonstrating that he was at least considering the use of the radio beacons while over Scotland. The Elektra system certainly had the range. We therefore felt it important that we tried to interpret the '450' and '(450)' markers.

We remain mindful that the above map will have some variations due to the non-gnomic projection of the above diagram. However, the principle seems to hold true that there are two lines described from Stavanger '(450)' and one from Husum '450'. The intersection of one pair of these beams appears to be in the Ayr/Troon/Dundonald area. It is probably unwise to attempt to be any more precise than that, other than to say that, if Hess had not at least considered their use, then why would he go to the trouble of marking his map thus? There are also a number of marks *Ab hier zur küste* (from here to the coast). Again they also appear to follow the projection of the Husum bearing.

We were also particularly intrigued by a reference in the James Leasor book, *Hess: The Uninvited Envoy*. Leasor describes how 'RAF pilots under instruction would leave Irvine air base, near Prestwick, fly north to Renfrew, then south east to Dungavel and, using the hill as a landmark, turn south-west again for their base'.

We find this statement very interesting. Firstly, why should it be recorded at all? Secondly, and more importantly, it describes Dungavel Hill as being used as a marker for Irvine airfield. Irvine is of course RAF Dundonald. (Thirdly – who told Leasor?)

When we recreated the Hess flight, we too followed the flight route from Dungavel House to the Firth of Clyde. As we have already stated, even to our untrained eyes it really is very easy in terms of visual recognition. The Isle of Arran is clearly visible from Dungavel House. However, en route to the Firth of Clyde, we were naturally intrigued to examine the approach to RAF Dundonald. Again, even to our untrained eyes, we could pick out the landing strip without difficulty. The railway line from Troon to Kilmarnock, as Hess had also marked up on the Lennoxlove Map, almost provides an 'arrow' pointing the way, and in the mid-distance Troon harbour is easily visible. We are tempted to say, 'find Dungavel and you have found Dundonald'. The RAF appears to have thought the same.

RAF Dundonald is some 18 miles from Dungavel House.[3] Hess was at 5,000ft when passing over Dungavel, at over 311mph. Whether the speed was a reaction to the night fighter that was pursuing him, or the knowledge that he was desperately chasing the light, we do not know for sure. However, we do know that, by the time he reached the Firth of Clyde, he was flying at sea level in the anticipation of a landing.

There really is no other explanation: if, as others assert, Hess went to the coast to gain his bearings, then why would he lose altitude and, in so doing, lose a line of sight? Why would he overfly his target at high speed, to then fly close to heavy anti-aircraft defences and turn back into the darkness?

We also know from the ROC map that, in avoiding Ardrossan and Ardeer, Hess had doubled back inland and then turned briefly south. This manoeuvre would place him at the end of the approach to Dundonald airfield. It was only after Hess realised that it was far too dark to land that he acted quite logically and regained height, prior to baling out over Eaglesham.

We believe that Hess was actually targeting RAF Dundonald; we are also aware of the implications of this conclusion.

We are sure that Hess would be aware of the airfield. In February 1941, the Luftwaffe embarked on reconnaissance missions over south-west Scotland. We reproduce the picture of RAF Dundonald, which surprisingly was titled 'Irvine Air Base' – the same descriptor that James Leasor had used in 1962.

We noticed immediately that the German reconnaissance photograph of Irvine *Flugplatz* had been marked to show a NW/SE runway of 500m length and, importantly, a SW/NE one of 700m, confirming that there was plenty of room to land a Bf 110.

We had already come to and documented the above conclusions well before we obtained the Cuddie vector instructions from Peter Padfield in early October 2013.

Rudolf Hess had planned to land at RAF Dundonald.

19. THE 14TH DUKE OF HAMILTON

Given the conclusion reached in the previous chapter and our firm belief that Hess was targeting an operational 'RAF base, this fact, if true, widens the Hess affair to a true conspiracy.

While researching the Hess affair we have met many interesting people: Wolf Hess, Bill Kean, Andrea Schroder-Haushofer, some other descendants of the main players, and Stephen Prior.

Stephen Prior was one of the four authors of *Double Standards*. He and John Harris had met on two occasions. He was perfectly charming and, during the conversations, claimed to have worked for British intelligence. John remembers finding this particularly intimidating at the time, as Stephen had asked to meet him. He told John that he ran a hotel near to the Rosslyn Chapel, 7 miles south of Edinburgh.

Prior's interest in the Hess affair had apparently arisen by reason of his purchase of the Hess Iron Cross medal at an auction. Hess had previously given the medal to a soldier named McBride on the night of 10 May 1941. Prior appeared to agree with us in rejecting the 'lone-flyer' story.

His book, when published in September 2002, drew on an extensive amount of basic research, most of which we could only admire. In particular he had been granted access to the Hamilton Archives in Edinburgh, which, to our knowledge, was the first time this source had been used and quoted, outside of the Hamilton family. We were very saddened, therefore, to hear that Stephen had died in 2003.

However, when working on this book we have naturally gone over much of the same ground as Stephen and, whilst apologising in advance for any disparagement, we now think that some of his conclusions are badly flawed. In particular, the part of *Double Standards* pertaining to Dungavel House. We also do not agree with the conclusion that Hess died with the Duke of Kent in Scotland in 1943.

When John Harris met Stephen, he had invited him to visit him at 'his hotel' and, after beginning to have doubts, we did a little research of our own. It appears that Stephen was the manager of the Templar Lodge Hotel at Gullane, East Lothian. After his death in 2003, the hotel closed and is at the time of writing awaiting redevelopment. While under Stephen's control the hotel seemed to base its marketing strategy on attracting various groups of minority interests, the majority of which were linked to UFO research, the paranormal and the Knights Templar. One visitor commented: 'I had at that time contact with a music scene in Gullane at the Templar Lodge Hotel and the character who ran it claimed to be an ex head of MI5's department of parapsychology. There were reasons to doubt that, though, but he did seem, according to a guy who had been working for the UK's version of the NSA, to be operating a strange unit of people in some of the rooms that had computers and staff time dedicated to researching material.' The *Independent* newspaper reported that Stephen had arranged for a Japanese camera crew to film the nearby hills from the roof of his hotel for possible UFO sightings.

We suspect, but do not know for sure, that this is how Stephen met two of his co-authors, Picknett and Price, who appear to be well-known writers in the fields of the 'paranormal, esoteric and secret societies'. Robert Brydon, the third collaborator, is a more conventional military historian, even though his TV script credit is for 'The Occult Reich'.

Consequently, we fear that their heady mix of detailed fact and supposition has distilled into some wild theorising to produce a wholly flawed conclusion, albeit based on some really good basic research. Therefore, we would like to draw on this basic research, which we think was very well done.

Much of the life story of Douglas Douglas-Hamilton is well known and published, but as we have already seen there is much more still to be learned, as the section dealing with Prestwick airfield has hopefully already demonstrated. In particular, we believe that Hamilton was some kind of an agent of the Foreign Office, firstly pre-war as an overt intermediary and then, once the Foreign Office initiatives had run out of steam, he played the role of potential revolutionary, albeit with the script being ably written and supplied by British intelligence. He really was an ideal candidate for the part.

Douglas Douglas-Hamilton owned at least four aircraft registered in his own name in the 1930s:

G-ABPD: airframe No.AW133 – DeHavilland Gypsy Moth, August 1931
G-ACPK: airframe No.X9382 – DeHavilland Leopard Moth, April 1934
G-ADVC: airframe No.BB812 – DeHavilland Tiger Moth, October 1935
G-AELF: airframe No.VTA32 – Percival Vega Gull, July 1936

In addition, Scottish Aviation Limited registered seventeen Tiger Moths in December 1935, and there are also listings of similar aircraft registered in the names of his three brothers throughout the 1930s. All were types eminently suitable for the Dungavel airstrip, though it would be too short for the Percival, powered by a 200hp engine and capable of carrying four persons over 600 miles at 150mph. It appears to us that Douglas-Hamilton used his aircraft in much the same way as we would use cars today. Extensive European trips were undertaken as a matter of course.

Clearly, aviation played a large part in Douglas-Hamilton's life. He was made the youngest commanding officer of No. 602 (City of Glasgow) Squadron in 1927, was chief pilot to the Houston Mount Everest Expedition in 1933, and shortly after helped establish Scottish Aviation Limited with his close friend David McIntyre.

We think these details are reasonably well known and documented. We would now like to record his activities as effectively a foreign affairs agent; by doing so we hope to illustrate why he was targeted by Rudolf Hess. This role combined his aviation interests with that of a serving MP; Douglas-Hamilton had been MP for East Renfrewshire since 1930. Clearly he was a very busy man.

As has been discussed previously, the Everest flight ensured that both Douglas-Hamilton and David McIntyre became famous throughout the UK and Europe.

The *Tatler* magazine records Douglas-Hamilton as being in Klosters in early 1936, Davos and Kleine Scheidegg in 1939. Dougal McIntyre, in the book concerning his father, notes a skiing trip to Basle in 1934 by his father and Douglas-Hamilton, travelling in what appears to be a DeHavilland Puss Moth. However, James Douglas-Hamilton gives the most detailed listing of his late father's trips.

In 1936, he witnessed the Berlin Olympics and the Hess/Douglas-Hamilton 'did they/did not meet' banquet, hosted by Ribbentrop. Douglas-Hamilton was also present at a later banquet hosted by Adolf Hitler in honour of Sir Robert Vansittart. According to his brother, David, it was here that Douglas-Hamilton met Albrecht Haushofer for the first time. During August 1936, with Göring's express permission, Douglas-Hamilton was given a tour of the major Luftwaffe airfields, and again in October 1936. In January 1937, Douglas-Hamilton was again skiing in Austria, and met with Albrecht Haushofer on 23 January. Albrecht introduced Douglas-Hamilton to his mother and father.

In March 1937, Albrecht visited London and the two men met again. On 29 April 1937, Albrecht gave his address to Chatham House on the subject of 'Raw Materials and Colonies: A German View'. In June 1937, Albrecht returned to London yet again and the two met.

In November 1937, Douglas-Hamilton married Lady Elizabeth Percy, the daughter of the Duke of Northumberland. Albrecht Haushofer was invited, but declined. It is strange that Douglas-Hamilton invited a German diplomat, whom he could not have known for much more than a year prior to his wedding. David McIntyre was the best man at the wedding.

In April 1938, Haushofer returned yet again, this time spending time at Dungavel House, prior to moving to London in May 1938. We do not know precisely the relationship between the two men. What is absolutely clear, however, is that Douglas-Hamilton was certainly a very close acquaintance of the leading

German expert on British foreign policy. James Douglas-Hamilton comments on how his father was quick to report his findings; matters aviation to the RAF, matters diplomatic to the Foreign Office. Letters and correspondence continued to come from Haushofer; one in July 1939 was forwarded by Douglas-Hamilton to Halifax, Butler, Chamberlain and Churchill.

Douglas-Hamilton was essentially acting as a conduit to the British government from that part of the German government operating through and relying upon the Haushofer family. This role was confirmed by Douglas-Hamilton's attendance at a Foreign Office meeting in London on 9 June 1939. Among those present at the meeting were:

Lord Halifax – foreign secretary
General von Reichenau – a leading 'Hitlerite' general
Prince Adolf zu Mecklenberg – member of the International Olympic committee
Sir Robert Vansittart – anti-appeasement politician
Kenneth Lindsay – MP for Kilmarnock
Sir Louis Grieg – close friend of King George VI

The fact that Douglas-Hamilton was invited to attend what essentially was a European summit is actually quite extraordinary, were it not for the role that he was playing at that time; duke, governmental diplomat, a conduit for peace feelers and, not least, a front-line airman.

The truth is that, after 3 September 1939, nothing changed, except the means of communication. Direct communication, person-to-person, became more difficult for the reasons previously detailed and different alternatives had to be utilised. It only took a month. On 6 October 1939, the following letter appeared in *The Times*:

Sir,
Many, like yourself, have had the opportunity of hearing a great deal of what the men and women of my generation are thinking. There is no doubt, in any quarter, irrespective of any party, that this country had no choice but to accept the challenge of Hitler's aggression against one country in Europe after another. If Hitler is right when he claims that the whole of the German nation is with him in his cruelties and treacheries, both within Germany and without, then this war must be fought to the bitter end. It may well last for many years, but the people of the British Empire will not falter in their determination to see it through.

But I believe that the moment the menace of aggression and bad faith has been removed, war against Germany becomes wrong and meaningless. This generation is conscious that injustices were done to the German people in the era after the last war. There must be no repetition of that. To seek anything but a just and comprehensive peace to lay at rest the fears and discords in Europe would be a betrayal of our fallen.

I look forward to a day when a trusted Germany will again come into her own and believe that there is such a Germany, which would be loath to inflict wrongs on other nations such as she would not like to suffer herself. That day may be far off, but when it comes, then hostilities could and should cease, and all efforts be concentrated on righting the wrongs in Europe by free negotiations between the disputing parties, all parties binding themselves to submit their disputes to an impartial equity tribunal in case they cannot reach agreement.

We do not grudge Germany lebensraum, provided that lebensraum is not made the grave of other nations. We should be ready to search for and find a colonial settlement, just to all peoples concerned, as soon as there exist effective guarantees that no race will be exposed to being treated as Hitler treated the Jews on 9 November last year. We shall, I trust, live to see the day when such a healing peace is negotiated between honourable men and the bitter memories of twenty-five years of unhappy tension between Germany and the western democracies are wiped away in their responsible co-operation for building a better Europe.

Yours truly,

Clydesdale

This letter was originally going to be a group letter from all MPs serving in the armed forces. However, Chamberlain decreed that it should come solely from Hamilton, lest it be construed as showing a lack of support for the military. It was co-written by Kurt Hahn, the post-war founder of Gordonstoun School and subsequent guardian of Karl Haushofer's grandson. Alasdair Douglas-Hamilton details how members of the Hamilton family were close friends of both Hahn and the Duke of Brunswick.

With respect to the eventual outcome of the Hess affair, this letter effectively marks the end of Douglas Douglas-Hamilton's active involvement with governmental peace initiatives. Thereafter, he was still fully involved, but we believe in a non-governmental role, or to be even more precise, a quasi non-governmental role.

It appears to us that this letter, which purports to come from Hamilton but is written for him, is effectively a letter to Albrecht Haushofer, not the editor of *The Times* newspaper. We know that the letter received publicity in Germany at the time and seems to us to be an attempt to blame Hitler for the war that was about to be unleashed.

Be under no illusion, the 14th Duke of Hamilton and his brothers were seriously involved in pre-war attempts to foster relations and communicate with Germany. Stephen Prior believes that the duke was a member of the Anglo-German Fellowship, having discovered a receipt for his subscription. This would come as no great surprise. That said, we are totally convinced of his patriotism. Prior to the war he was led by his conscience. We suspect he was then being used, knowingly or not, by the same persons who had gained control of the Haushofer letter to Mrs Violet Roberts, dated 23 September 1940. This theory that Hess was responding to British Secret Service contacts first appeared in the magazine *Liberty* as early as 12 July 1941: 'Rudolf Hess ... fell into a British secret service trap.'[4]

The government of course knew all about Hamilton's pre-war activities – he openly told them himself. These are hardly the actions of a fifth columnist. As we have already seen, the government also knew that he had been contacted through Mrs Roberts in September 1940. The censor had done his job well.

Once the war had started Hamilton's priorities changed. He was an active member of His Majesty's armed forces and was appointed commanding officer of RAF Turnhouse, a position to which he had been appointed at the onset of the Battle of Britain in summer 1940.

Earlier in May 1940, the then Duke of Hamilton was also appointed as Lord Steward after Churchill had taken the honour away from the 8th Duke of Buccleuch on account of his overt 'peace mongering'. Whilst the position is largely ceremonial, with the actual role being performed by the Master of the Household, the Lord Steward also has certain rights and duties in connection with the Royal Sign Manual, the autographed signature of the monarch. Given that Hamilton was already in the RAF (serving in France at the time), we are a little surprised that he was given this honour. There were plenty of alternative dukes and earls in Scotland at the time. A perusal of the list of holders shows no discernible family preferences; all the major names have been present over the years. Interestingly, Wulf Schwarzwaller records Hess specifically debating with Karl Haushofer precisely what this honour actually meant in practice.[5]

The summer of 1940 was spent fighting the Germans and then, as we have seen, in September 1940, nearly a year after his letter to *The Times*, Albrecht Haushofer tries to make contact with Hamilton. The attempt fails, with the letter being intercepted by the censor, realistically in mid/late October 1940 (it had to come from Lisbon, Portugal and pass through the British censor).

The letter from Albrecht Haushofer to Mrs Roberts was dated 23 September 1940. The censor, we know, had the letter no later than 6 November 1940. By 22 November 1940, MI5 had written to the Foreign Office asking if they could send the duke a copy. On 7 December, the reply comes back: 'Yes, the letter can be forwarded.'

On 12 November 1940, Hamilton had taken ten days' leave from RAF Turnhouse. Apparently the Hamilton diary for 1940 is missing, so we cannot be sure as to his destination. On 20 January 1941, Hamilton met the Duke of Kent for lunch and, again on 23 January, the two men met at Prestwick. It is around this time that Tancred Borenius was travelling to Geneva.

On 26 January 1941, a further ten days leave were taken. Stephen Prior discovered that, according to the Hamilton archives, the leave was taken at Lesbury, Northumberland, the ancestral home of the Percys, the Duchess of Hamilton's family.

In March 1941, a further period of leave from RAF Turnhouse was taken, but this was apparently to do with an approach by RAF intelligence to Hamilton, requesting that he attend a meeting in Lisbon with, presumably, Haushofer. The last recorded 'sighting' of Hamilton was on 28 April 1941 when *The Times* recorded Hamilton greeting a contingent of Empire airmen at a 'British port'. The port is not recorded, but the airmen were subsequently taken to a depot near London.

At this time, James Douglas-Hamilton also reveals that his father was taking advice from Lord Eustace Percy as to how to avoid being used, and presumably abused, by RAF intelligence. The choice of confidant is intriguing. Lord Eustace Percy was a cerebral member of the Northumbrian family and a recently retired MP. In 1935–36, he had been a member of the Baldwin cabinet as minister without portfolio. From 1911 to 1919, he served in the Diplomatic Service. As such, he would be well experienced in governmental wartime machinations and competent to advise his Scottish relative in his hour of need.

However, we suspect that there was already another intelligence operation underway; one that did not really require any active involvement from Hamilton, but did ultimately rely upon his passive acquiescence. He and the Duke of Kent were probably the only two men in Britain who could combine RAF authority with a right of access to the monarch. That is why Hess flew to Scotland.

The interesting question is when was the duke 'let in' on the game, if at all?

20. THE NATURE AND EXTENT OF THE CONSPIRACY

This book started with the basic premise that to instigate a parliamentary revolution in Great Britain, without an outright military victory, one needs the acquiescence of the King. Whether to prorogue Parliament, or to directly appoint another prime minister, requires the active consent of the monarch.

Had Germany successfully invaded Britain in 1940, the conqueror could, of course, impose whatever system was deemed appropriate. Therefore, what follows presupposes that a peace settlement was to be negotiated and not imposed after military humiliation. So far, we hope to have demonstrated:

– To effect a change of government, Hess would have to be in a position to either meet with, or influence, the King.
– Hess was targeting Dundonald airfield, making use of state-of-the-art German navigational equipment. The flight was meticulously planned and required assistance from within Germany that was elaborately hidden so as to be able to give the realistic impression of a solo flight, if necessary.
– Germany was under growing pressure to neutralise Britain prior to unleashing Operation Barbarossa; 15 May 1941 was the appointed date. The British, through their use of 'Ultra', were quite aware of this fact.
– There were a whole host of individuals within the UK who would be willing to negotiate with Germany for a whole host of reasons.

There had been many approaches from the Germans, ever since September 1939. The major stumbling block had been Hitler as German leader. The British could see through his 'game plan' and did not like it at all. Once Russia was conquered, Britain would again be vulnerable, and this time German supplies and raw materials would be secure.

Rudolf Hess and Adolf Hitler desperately wanted the West to be neutralised before heading east. The Luftwaffe had failed twice: firstly by losing the Battle of Britain in 1940, and secondly by failing to bomb Britain to the negotiating table in the spring of 1941. The German Foreign Office had also failed to the extent that they had even made matters worse. The German nation, so far, was still reasonably firm behind its victorious leader, but now the stakes were about to get higher. Much, much higher and, as far as we can see, without a fallback position should Russia prove harder to defeat than envisaged. The brutal orders that were being distributed to the army made the nature of the conflict clear. There would be little chance of any compromise – it really was to defeat or be defeated.

Rudolf Hess had initiated the Haushofer/Hamilton letters in September 1940 and, as described, we suspect that this had led, in turn, to Tancred Borenius somewhat bizarrely travelling to Geneva in January 1941 on the say-so of Claude Dansey and MI6. The book that he was carrying was, we suspect, an intelligence plant, following their discovery in November 1940 that Haushofer was trying to contact Hamilton. There may well have also been forged letters, but we are struggling to see how they would have plausibly passed the censor and yet continue to be seen as a non-governmental reply. They would also have to be transmitted through a non-governmental channel.

We are fascinated by Borenius and the fact that he was close to the Lascelles family, Queen Elizabeth and the Duke of Kent. Is this the reason that he went to Geneva? We have also yet to discover if he brought anything back with him. We suspect we never will.

If Borenius was really appearing to represent the Queen/Kent/Lascelles then much actually does makes sense. These people, along with Hamilton, certainly had direct influence and access to the King and Hamilton even had some archaic form of power over the King's signature, should the need arise. The Von Hassell Diaries even reveal that Carl Burkhardt had met Tancred Borenius in London.[6] The diary entry does not make clear when this meeting took place – we can only assume that it was pre-war while Burckhardt was in pursuit of the beautiful Lady Diana Cooper. Philip Ziegler, in his biography of Diana Cooper, states that Burckhardt's last visit to London had been in October 1939.

Borenius was obviously well connected. We have discovered that he also acted as art adviser to George Holford (1860–1926). Holford was extremely wealthy, having inherited a fortune based on the water supply to London. He was the stepfather of Stewart Menzies, the wartime head of MI6. While Menzies was not Churchill's preferred appointment as head of MI6, would he really be prepared to unseat a government?

It also explains Haushofer's interest in Samuel Hoare. If the King were to dissolve Parliament, then an amenable replacement would have to be installed. According to Hoare: 'My staff and I made it clear beyond a doubt that the British Government would have nothing to do with any peace negotiations ...'[7]

What is not perhaps so clear is whether Hoare gave the impression that *he* would have nothing to do with peace negotiations. Surely, if Hess was acting on the supposition that he was about to ignite a coup, he would have to have some idea as to who might be installed in Churchill's place. That, we believe, is the role that Hoare was assigned and played with skill. In 1919, Hoare had been an intelligence agent in Russia, so was already well used to the 'game'.

There is a line of thought that Hoare was working alongside Montagu Norman, the Governor of the Bank of England, in an attempt to impose a 'Pan European' super state, ruled over and governed by bankers and industry, not governments. Subscribers to this view point to the Hoare-Laval Pact as an example of Italian appeasement, the installation of Hitler as Chancellor of Germany, the formation of the Bank of International Settlement in 1930 and the loss of the Czechoslovak gold reserves to Nazi Germany in 1939.

Max Aitken (Lord Beaverbrook) is also cited as being part of this 'coup attempt' and it has been suggested that his resignation as Minister of Aircraft Production on 1 May 1941 was as a marker or prelude to some form of action. In the book *Hess: The British Conspiracy*, John Harris also made note of the fact that Burckhardt had been visited by a representative of the City in March 1941 (yet another meeting for Burckhardt) and certainly the diary of Montagu Norman during the spring of 1941 makes very interesting reading, with meetings with the Red Cross and Campbell Stuart, former head of the Political Warfare Executive (PWE).

However, whatever they were doing, clearly Hoare, Haushofer, Hess, Hamilton and Burckhardt were very busy doing something in the spring of 1941. If nothing else, their diaries and itineraries demonstrate too much activity for the Hess flight to be adjudged the solo initiative of a deranged man. We now think that these meetings, on both sides of the English Channel, were held to finalise the various details of what could be a coup attempt appearing to emanate from the very highest levels.

The British were in the convenient position that they could play Hess in a number of ways. We know that Borenius was acting as an MI6 agent; his son had no reason to lie to John Harris when he reported his father being briefed by Claude Dansey. What we do not know is the full intent behind the action. Was the intention merely to buy time? Dansey and MI6 knew that a German invasion of Russia was imminent and would be a good result for Britain, and so did they merely play for time by initiating false prospects of peace and governmental change? Did the nature of the 'sting' perhaps change when the knowledge of Operation Barbarossa became clearer?

Or, more controversially still, was the intent really to unseat Churchill, using Hess' peace proposals as a catalyst for change? Was MI6 working with the royal family to overthrow the Churchill government, or was it merely giving that impression? No option need be exclusive of another. The extent of the actual royal involvement is the challenging part of this book, and in order to make a considered opinion, we need to look for more details.

21. ROYAL INVOLVEMENT IN THE HESS AFFAIR

Without wishing to be sensationalist, there is no doubt that the British royal family (or the illusion of its participation) was involved in the Hess affair; quite simply, it had to be – in order to give sufficient encouragement to Hess, or to provide the constitutional authority for a change of government. That is precisely why he flew to Scotland and not England.

By the spring of 1941, it had been clear for some time that a Churchill-led government would not make peace with Nazi Germany, despite the almost impossible position, so any compromise peace would have to be without Churchill. If Churchill would not stand aside, constitutionally the King alone could remove him.

However, it is quite possible that MI6, or another intelligence service, was simply orchestrating the illusion of royal support for such a course of action, perhaps even without the family's knowledge. Actual royal participation was not therefore vital, but the illusion of their involvement, at the very least, certainly was. Firstly, we should analyse the actions of the various intelligence agencies.

We know MI6 were involved in the Hess affair, through their tutoring of Tancred Borenius. The story of the oversized cyanide pill is too outlandish to be made up. However, we were disappointed, but not wholly surprised, when the name Rudolf Hess did not even feature in the index of the official *MI6: The History of the Secret Intelligence Service 1909–1949* by Keith Jeffery.[8] He wrote to the authors, stating: 'I have found no evidence (so far as SIS is concerned) to support your contention that Hess was lured to Britain as part of a British Intelligence ruse.'[9]

When challenged, as we had evidence to the contrary, Professor Jeffery did later admit to there being 'some details about Hess' and included some brief references in the paperback version of the book. John Scarlet[10] commented at the book launch that 'secrets that prejudice relations with other nations would have to remain secret'.[11] So, to date, MI6 have never admitted involvement.

It is also clear, by their subsequent behaviour, that MI5 were not involved in the Hess affair, even though they knew of the Haushofer letter to Hamilton in September 1940. They were given a copy of the subsequent censor intercept. In our estimation, they reacted as someone in a state of ignorance might do, by rushing around and arresting possible suspects such as the Marquis of Tavistock and placing the Duke of Buccleuch under house arrest. They also paid Mary Violet Roberts a visit.

Lochgreen House.

The Crown Jewels of Scotland were re-hidden in Edinburgh Castle on 12 May 1941.[12] These seem to us to be the actions of a body unsure of what was really going on.

Conversely, SO1, the recently created black propaganda department could certainly write letters on behalf of others – they were past masters and their pre-war skill sets made them experts in the field. There is also the coincidence that Dalton and Eden were at their HQ at Woburn Abbey when Hess flew in. Previously, John Harris had thought it most likely that the ruse had emanated from the minds of Sefton Delmer or Leonard Ingrams, and this may indeed be the case, especially given the fact that Walter Stewart-Roberts was closely associated with Mary Violet Roberts. However, because we know of the involvement of Claude Dansey and MI6 (through Lars Borenius), we now doubt this. We also doubt that SO1 had the means to run such an operation. Being relatively new, they were not particularly liked, or trusted, by the established agencies.

Lastly, whilst looking at the potential 'organisers' we have to look at the RAF intelligence service. Very, very little is known of this section of the force, save that there are some well-known 'Hess affair' names closely associated with it. Fred Winterbotham, Baron de Ropp, the Dukes of Kent and Hamilton have all been linked to it, and the duke's brother 'Geordie' Douglas-Hamilton was head of Fighter Intelligence and lived at Prestwick. In the absence of any disclosure, we cannot be any more specific, but equally we should not be labelled as conspiracists merely for detailing the links. In the absence of official admission of involvement we have chosen to look at the movements of the potential participants to try and elicit clues.

Firstly, the odd behaviour of the Duke of Kent's archivist and the royal archivists at Windsor raises far more questions than they provide answers. The fact is that we do not know where the duke was on the evening of 10 May 1941. Given his mode of daily transport, he could conceivably have been anywhere in the UK. When the present Duke of Kent's secretary was asked whether his father's diaries were available, we were told they were at Windsor in the Royal Archives. The Royal Archives told us: 'We do not hold a diary or a Season Kalendar …' We can only believe what we are being told, the implication being that we may never know where the Duke of Kent spent the night of 10 May 1941.

In just the same way as the 14th Duke of Hamilton, the Duke of Kent's pre-war sympathies were well known, but the fact of the matter is that neither duke could bring about a peace. They could perhaps facilitate the start of the process, but they did not alone have the ability to negotiate and seal a peace, even if they had wished.

It is interesting to consider what the Duke of Kent might have been hoping to achieve. Some have made the point that the duke was acting as emissary for his brother, the King, throughout much of the late 1930s, but on 5 August 1937 the *Canberra Times* newspaper in Australia had reported that the executive of the Polish Monarchist Party had offered the Polish throne to George, Duke of Kent, in an attempt to develop the ties between the British Empire and the oppressed Polish nation. The Polish throne had been vacant since 1795 when Poland had politically ceased to exist, only having been recently recreated as a consequence of the 1919 Treaty of Versailles.

In 1939, following the Nazi invasion of Poland, the government in exile moved firstly to Angers, in France, and then after the May 1940 invasion, the government moved to London, based at the Rubens Hotel in Buckingham Palace Road. Thereafter, the Polish Army moved northwards and became responsible for the home defence of Lowland Scotland.

The Duke of Kent, in his role as airfield inspector for the RAF, quite naturally came across Wladyslaw Sikorski, the prime minister of the Polish government in exile, and there are numerous pictures showing the two men reviewing troops and other units. There are unevidenced rumours that Sikorski had also offered the Polish throne to Kent.[13] It would certainly have been politically expedient. The Second World War technically began because of the Nazi invasion of Poland. In so doing the Anglo-French guarantee of Polish independence dated 31 March 1939 was activated and Britain and France declared war. Any peace settlement between Britain and Germany must at the very least have been mindful of the initial cause of the conflict. Sikorski had flown back from the US on the morning of 11 May 1941, landing at Prestwick, no more than 7 or 8 miles from RAF Dundonald. John Harris, in *Hess: The British Illusion of Peace*, made the point that Sikorski, in flying back in a Consolodated B-24 Liberator bomber, was making a groundbreaking VIP flight. He had travelled out to the US on a much slower, but safer British destroyer. Did he choose to return by the untried and untested Atlantic Air Bridge because the stakes warranted such a mission? Was the Duke of Kent part of that mission, or the process? We had to learn more.

The location of the Duke of Kent on 10 May 1941 has been the subject of speculation for some time. This will continue for as long as the truth is withheld, or just lost. According to *Double Standards* and Stephen Prior, he was at Dungavel airstrip. We find this very hard to believe because Hess was not going to Dungavel; we do not think that Prior actually had any evidence to support his theory. The Countess of Sutherland has written to us stating that he was at Dunrobin Castle.

However, we should record that we are not particularly convinced by any of the above claims. Adding to the confusion is the fact that Martin Allen then apparently 'invented' the fact that the duke was involved in a road accident with a coal lorry the following morning, just outside Dungavel. This was part of the National Archives 'document insertion scandal', but nevertheless placed another hurdle between the researcher and the truth.

In September 2008, we placed an advertisement in the *Daily Telegraph* newspaper, enquiring if any reader knew the whereabouts of the Duke of Kent on 10 May 1941. We had nothing from the Royal Archives or the Duke of Kent archivists and so tried to get independent evidence.

Helen, our long suffering secretary, was somewhat taken aback when she answered a very prompt call from Elizabeth, Countess of Sutherland, informing her that the Duke of Kent spent the weekend of 9–11 May 1941 at her home, Dunrobin Castle, some 40 miles north of Inverness. Apparently, during the war, she had been working at Raigmore Hospital in Inverness, but came home occasionally. We asked the countess to put in writing what she had told us and this she was kind enough to do. Her letter was postmarked 3 September 2008:

> Thank you for your letter [John Harris had written previously, to thank her for her trouble]. Dunrobin was a hospital in both World Wars. A very small part of it was kept for the family – only my Uncle and Aunt who had no children & me (their niece). I was working in Raigmore Hospital, Inverness but came home occasionally for a few days. I happened to be there when the Duke arrived for the night.
> The visitor's book has a hand written notice saying,
> 'War period 1939–1944 Book not kept.'
> [King George VI and the Duke of Kent stayed at Dunrobin during this period.] After he was killed he was brought back to Dunrobin and his coffin was kept in the front hall until the King arrived to accompany him back south. I remember how amusing he was – very easy to talk to – nice to everyone.

We were delighted to receive this letter and it confirmed some things that we already knew: the fact that the Duke of Kent's body was taken to the castle after the aircraft crash in 1943 and that the castle had been used as a hospital. However, we looked at Raigmore Hospital in Inverness and found it did not open until September 1941.[14] Moreover, the countess said that she was there 'when the Duke arrived for the night', rather than 'the weekend'.

The real problem here is that the official records are yet again lacking. The Duke of Kent had been engaged on important work, visiting wartime airfields throughout the length and breadth of the UK. With this duty in mind, he had been created an air commodore in April 1940, with the role of a staff officer in RAF Training Command. National Archive File Air33/7 gives voluminous detail of the many visits carried out by the duke in the above capacity, but does not cover the period we are interested in. There are forty-two files covering the Duke of Kent during 1941–42, but not one covers the weekend of 9/11 May 1941.

We think we know where the duke was on the Friday 9 May, and we think we know where he was on Monday 12 May. It seems to have passed into legend that the duke was at RAF Sumburgh on the Friday and at RAF Wick on the Monday. Sumburgh is on the Shetland Islands and a notoriously difficult airfield on which to land. For this we have to rely on Norman Glass in his book *Caithness and the War 1939–1945*.[15]

We felt we needed to check further and so duly despatched a researcher to Kew to look at the Operational Record Books (ORBs) of the two stations. Surely they would record the fact that the brother of the King had visited? There was no record of any visit.[16]

So, we have a real problem. The ORBs make no mention of any visit, the Countess of Sutherland, with the greatest respect, may have made a mistake and we do not really understand why he would choose to stay at Dunrobin. He obviously flew into the airfields so as to carry out his visits and surely, if he was going anywhere, he would then have flown back to Pitliver House, Fife, where he, his wife, Marina, and children had moved at the outbreak of the war. There were plenty of airfields, both RAF and Royal Naval Air Stations (RNAS), close to home, which would allow the duke an easy 'weekend with the family'.

The duke used a DeHavilland DH-85 Flamingo twin-engined transport aircraft, which had a range of 1,345 miles at a speed of around 200mph, to perform his duties. In other words, he could quite easily have flown to anywhere in Scotland or England. There is no airfield near Dunrobin that would take a relatively large aircraft such as the Flamingo, so presumably the duke would have flown on the Friday to RAF Wick and then driven down the coast for 50 miles to the castle. It just all seems a bit unlikely, but may of course be quite correct.

So, we tried another approach. When the duke died in 1943, unfortunately all of his immediate staff also died. They were John Arthur Lowther, private secretary, Michael Strutt, equerry, and John Hales, valet. We tried to ascertain where each of the three men was on 10 May 1941. We failed. John Lowther's papers are in Suffolk Record Office.[17] The family of Michael Strutt did not reply to our request, and the family of John Hale in Norfolk were kindness personified, but again were unable to help. So, we do not know where the duke was on Saturday 10 May 1941. We do doubt Dunrobin, but feel that location to be more likely than Dungavel, for that makes no sense at all.

What we were able to discover, however, was that the Duke of Kent did have friends in and around Prestwick (15 miles from Dungavel). When planning the Duke of Kent's 1941 trip to Canada,[18] the question arose as to where he might stay the night before flying from Prestwick. A note states that there would be no problem in that regard as the duke has 'a friend with a house no further than 1 mile from the end of the runway'. Intrigued, we contacted the Carnegie Library in Ayr, whose staff was very helpful.

We enquired of Sheena Taylor, the librarian, which houses in the area might be possible venues for the Duke of Kent. She gave us the following names: first, Orangefield House, Prestwick. Orangefield House has already been mentioned as the Georgian house converted in the 1930s to the control tower for the aerodrome. It was requisitioned in June 1941; second, Eldo House, which was adjacent to Orangefield House and was occupied by 'Geordie' Douglas-Hamilton; third, Adamton House, occupied by W.L. Carlow, prior to its being used by the USAAF as an officers' mess; and finally, Lochgreen House, an attractive mansion, now a five star hotel, on the Monktonhill Road, between Prestwick and Troon, just about a mile from the airfield.

We had already ascertained from Sheena Taylor that the owner of the house in 1941 was Sir Fergus Morton, a High Court judge. She also mentioned in passing that the tenant was Loel Guinness. Loel Guinness was a famously wealthy member of the banking side of the Irish brewers and bankers, and, we knew from previous research, a close friend of the duke and duchess of Kent. When Loel Guinness was married for the second time in November 1936, the Duke and Duchess gave him a pair of china birds and Tancred Borenius gave his usual present of a book.[19]

Loel Guinness was also an aviator, entering the 1930 'King's Cup Air Race' flying a Blackburn Bluebird IV. A fellow competitor was Lord Malcolm Douglas-Hamilton, brother of the 14th Duke, also in a Blackburn Bluebird IV. He was a regular at Cowes, owning a large ocean-going yacht, *Atlantis*.[20]

The reason he was in Prestwick, however, was that he was a serving officer in the RAF and, in May 1941, was in charge of the newly commissioned fighter station at RAF Ayr. Hector Maclean, his station controller:

In early 1941, Hector was posted as a Controller to RAF Station Ayr, a new fighter base in the course of being constructed at Heathfield near Ayr. The Station Commander, who was also the Sector Commander, was Wing Commander Loel Guinness, an Auxiliary Officer who had commanded No. 601 (County of London) Squadron. It was said that when he came to Heathfield – shortly before Hector arrived – that things had ground to a halt. When Loel contacted the contractors he was told the Air Ministry were dragging their feet and the contractors had not been paid. Loel Guinness asked how much was owed, wrote a cheque and buildings began appearing almost like magic![21]

So on 10 May 1941, we have the Duke of Hamilton in charge of a large Scottish Air Sector including RAF Ayr, RAF Prestwick, RAF Turnhouse and RAF Dundonald, which in turn is under the immediate control of Loel Guinness. Loel Guinness is a close friend of the Duke of Kent whose precise location on 10 May 1941 is uncertain. Tancred Borenius is a close friend of Loel Guinness, the Queen and the Duke of Kent. Tancred Borenius travelled to Geneva in January 1941 to see Carl Burckhardt.

The only part of Scotland not under the Duke of Hamilton's direct control (the east coast) was under the control of J. O. Andrews, a recently appointed (February 1941) German specialist. Include the duke's brothers, both are RAF intelligence officers, David McIntyre and the fact that all of the above are congregated in Lowland Scotland on or around an airfield actually owned by the Duke of Hamilton and his family – we think we are entitled to wonder what was going on. We know far better than to claim that the above proves a conspiracy, but we do feel entitled to question the extent of the association and ask the reader to decide.

It appears to us that the Duke of Hamilton and Duke of Kent, having spent much of 1939 and 1940 trying to avert war, then allowed their names to be used in an MI6-inspired operation which, if nothing further, bought the British war effort more time. Prince Ludwig von Hessen-Darmstadt[22] wrote the following description of the Duke of Kent in 1938: 'Duke of Kent, very German friendly. Clearly against France. Not especially clever, but well-informed. Entirely for strengthening German-English ties. His wife is equally anti-French.'

MI6 learn that Hamilton is being targeted through the mail censor and launch an operation allowing the Germans to believe that Hamilton (and the Duke of Kent) will facilitate a meeting between Hess and the King, with a view to a change of government. Hess is told he is to be given the status of Parlementar, thus guaranteeing safe access and return. We wonder if documentary confirmation was given to Hess to support this statement. It may well explain the rush to retrieve papers from a ditch at Floors Farm on 11 May 1941. They had crashed with the aircraft. We know from the testimony of Mrs Baird (the farmer's wife) that there was a panic to find them. We also wonder about the rush to send

Anthony Blunt to Germany in 1945 to retrieve sensitive letters to and from the royal family's German relations. In order to discover the modern-day whereabouts of these papers, John Harris made a Freedom of Information request. Needless to say, all that came back was a list of current PRO files where Hess documents reside. These are all well known. In other words, the papers 'from the ditch' have either been destroyed or filed somewhere beyond the reaches of the Freedom of Information Act.

As far as the Germans are concerned, this course of action would get over the stumbling block of the Churchill government not negotiating with Hitler; firstly the Churchill government would be replaced, and secondly the replacement would be negotiating with Rudolf Hess – not Hitler.

Consequently, Tancred Borenius, being one of the few necessarily qualified messengers (not British, based in Britain, knows the participators) is sent to Geneva to relay to Burckhardt the plan/ruse. Burckhardt tells Haushofer/Hess. Haushofer checks out Hoare to make sure it is viable and that there is a potential British Quisling/Petain type of person in place.

It may well be that there are other minor messengers who gave the necessary appearance of a non-governmental operation: Count Machamilton and Baron Knut Bonde in Stockholm come to mind in this respect,[23] but really, once Hess knows where to go, relatively little information needs to be relayed to the British – realistically just a date and time of arrival. We also wonder who actually marked up the Lennoxlove Map; local knowledge in matters aeronautical would surely have gone a long way.

Ernest Bevin was supposed to know that Hess was coming via the Messerschmitt factory in Augsburg, but given that the 'Enigma' code machine had been compromised in 1940, Bevin's story could be just a cover to protect the 'golden goose'. It may or may not be true.

It appears to us that the arrival of Hess was really no more than an unwanted by-product of the British attempt to buy as much time as possible until her enemies started to fight each other. That was the important result, certainly not Hess' captivity. His capture was a potential embarrassment that could cause huge damage if handled badly.

Having discovered that we would probably never be in a position to disclose where the Duke of Kent was on 10 May 1941, we transferred our attention to King George VI. As we have stated previously, any peace negotiation would have to be sanctioned by the King, if against the wishes of the prime minister.

King George VI and Queen Elizabeth's early dislike of Churchill is well known. Both the King and Queen were known to be admirers of Chamberlain and both wished for Halifax to succeed him in 1940. It is quite easy to understand why. While

Churchill was speaking defiantly of 'fighting on the beaches', the royal family would have been a prime target for any German invasion, and the King probably would not survive as head of state if the invasion was bloody but successful. Also, Churchill had made himself unpopular with the King and Queen on account of his support for Edward VIII in 1936.

We have therefore attempted to ascertain the location of the King and Queen and their advisors over the days following Hess' arrival into the country. If they really were to be involved in a coup d'etat, surely there would be some visible sign, or indication of planning? The King and Queen's movements according to the Court Circular were as follows:

9 May (Friday) – Privy Council – attendees: Anderson, Reith, Sinclair and Wood.
10 May (Saturday) – Windsor Castle.
11 May (Sunday) – Divine Service.
12 May (Monday) – No details given.

On 9 May, Churchill had written to the Queen concerning 'Operation Tiger', the movement of 306 tanks across the Mediterraean to North Africa. The Queen's reply appears to have come from Windsor Castle, dated 12 May 1941. Queen Elizabeth makes the point that the day is 'that of the coronation', which of course it was, some four years earlier. We also wrote to Windsor Castle, seeking confirmation, which we received on 22 May 2012: 'King George VI was at Windsor during this weekend in May, but went up to Buckingham Palace for a Privy Council meeting and other meetings on 9th May.'

The King recorded in his diary that 250 out of the 306 tanks had arrived safely, the SS *Empire Song* having struck a mine in the Gibraltar narrows. Eighteen men were killed. William Shawcross, in his 2009 official biography, quotes the King's diary as reference RA GVI/ PRIV/ DIARY. Consequently, we know the King kept a diary. If that is the case, the following issues arise: why does the archivist state that 'King George VI was at Windsor during the weekend'? Why does William Shawcross state that on 9 May 'she [the Queen] had probably left for Windsor'?

We wish to categorically state that both the King and Queen might have spent the entire weekend of 10 May and 11 May 1941 at Windsor Castle, but if they did, why does the evidence not simply and clearly state that fact? At present it does not.

The archivist, with the benefit of the King's diary, states that the King was there during the weekend, and the official biographer says that the Queen was probably there. This does not appear to be very satisfactory to us, but we wish to emphasise again that the King and Queen may well have spent the weekend at Windsor, replying to their letters on 12 May (Monday).

Given the unsatisfactory nature of the above responses, we started to look at those close to the monarch. Sir Alan 'Tommy' Lascelles, the assistant private secretary to His Majesty maintained a diary which is now held at Churchill College, Cambridge. In it he records that, on Friday 9 May, the King lunched with Mrs James, 10 May was recorded as 'Blitz', on 11 May he dined with G. Thomas and on Monday 12 May he lunched with 'Bessborough', who we take to be the former Governor General of Canada. On Tuesday 13 May he was at Windsor. G. Thomas we take to be Godfrey Thomas, (1889–1968), the former private secretary to the Prince of Wales, who had resigned when George V died in 1936.

From this sequence of entries we conclude that Lascelles was not with the King over the weekend. The King's private secretary was Sir Alexander Hardinge and we have been unable to gain access to his papers, which are held in the Kent History and Library collection.

Perhaps thinking too laterally, we then researched the means by which the King would make a broadcast to the nation – for surely if peace were to be openly declared this would be a prerequisite. We looked firstly at the whereabouts of Lionel Logue, who earned posthumous celebrity following the release of the film *The King's Speech*. He accompanied the King when making broadcasts. In this connection we were disappointed as the preson who holds the appointment diaries did not respond to our letters.

In addition to Lionel Logue, we also learned about R.H. Wood, a BBC outside broadcast sound engineer, through whom the radio broadcasts were arranged and supervised. While Sir John Reith had supervised the abdication speech in 1936, it was Wood who would provide the technical 'know how' for what was still a relatively recent innovation. Robert Wood's autobiography is interesting on two counts: firstly on page 137 it states, 'I happened to be visiting the Central War Room in the early days of the war on the occasion that Rudolf Hess, Hitler's right hand man, dropped by parachute …'

Wood places Churchill in London on 10 May, not Ditchley. Secondly, the book lists the various outside broadcasts that Wood made during the war. On 12 May 1941, between 0039.30hrs and 0041.50hrs, he was responsible for broadcasting the words of Queen Marie of Yugoslavia, who was exiled in England, having acquired the Mill House at Great Gransden, Cambridgeshire. This was clearly pre-recorded as the recording exists to this day on the Pathé Newsreels website. In it, the Queen speaks from the porch of her new home, in both English and French. So we know very little as to the precise location of the following: King George VI; Queen Elizabeth; the Duke of Kent.

We have been told where they probably were, by those that should know, but we doubt very much the evidence so far presented would stand scrutiny in, say, a court of law. That is not to say that the persons concerned were anywhere other than where it is assumed they were, but we feel it only fair to point out that we have no definitive evidence either way. This uncertainty is not helpful in making further analysis.

We know we have an MI6-led operation which has contacted Hess, through Burckhardt in Geneva. We believe that, in doing so, Borenius is seen to be representing the 'clique' to which Churchill later referred to in 1942.

Trying to gauge the extent of royal involvement is therefore very difficult indeed, but, real or illusory, we do believe it a prerequisite to convince Hess to fly.

22. QUESTIONS AND ANSWERS

On 2 November 1942, Richard Stafford-Cripps wrote a memorandum to the War Cabinet entitled: 'Facts as regards Herr Hess's arrival in Great Britain so far as known to His Majesty's Government.'

However, in his note to the cabinet members, Stafford-Cripps prefaces his memorandum by stating: 'I was asked to get out a note on the Hess incident of the kind that might possibly be shown to the Russians, or, if necessary, even published here.' We reproduce the note below.

This small memorandum highlights precisely the problems in ascertaining the truth as regards the Hess affair. Stafford-Cripps was Lord Privy Seal at the time, but spent most of his time liaising with the Russians, essentially as a minister without portfolio.

Clearly, Stafford-Cripps was very mindful as to what was being said to the Russians and this is the problem; Churchill, of course, always had to be careful which version of events he told to his various allies. In 1942, when the memorandum was being written, Russia was in the process of defeating Germany and the knowledge that the British had been negotiating with the Germans as to a peace settlement in 1941 would be potentially explosive. Clearly, Stafford-Cripps was not sure the 'Russian version' would be suitable for the 'War cabinet minutes version'.

Similarly, in 1941, Churchill and Eden were rightly fearful that, if handled badly, the Hess affair had the potential to fuel the isolationists in the US. Why should the US get involved with Britain if she was about to 'throw the towel in', or even worse, side with the Germans? Most Americans in the spring of 1941 were content that their logistical support and the supply of armaments, at that time, was an appropriate level of support – rather than actual participation. So Churchill said nothing, the necessary image at that time being that of Britain standing alone.

The comparison to Peter Fleming's *Flying Visit* is almost uncanny. In the 1940-based novel, the British government did not know what to do with the unwanted guest and the reality a year later was much the same. Fleming's book concluded with Hitler being dropped back into Germany, but that was really never an option in the case of Hess. Once back in Germany, Britain had no control over what Hess might say. Churchill had written various drafts of what he might say, but eventually thought silence the best riposte.

Instead, the British naturally attempted to extract any information they could from Hess. For nearly a year after May 1941, there was relatively little in the

SECRET.

Copy No. 23

W.P. (42) 502.

November 2, 1942.

WAR CABINET.

THE FACTS ABOUT RUDOLF HESS.

MEMORANDUM BY THE LORD PRIVY SEAL.

I was asked(¹) to get out a note on the Hess incident of the kind that might possibly be shown to the Russians, or, if necessary, even published here.

I attach the note, which I have purposely kept as short as possible.

R. S. C.

November 2, 1942.

(¹) W.M. (42) 145th Conclusions, Minute 2.

ANNEX.

Facts as regards Herr Hess's Arrival in Great Britain so far as known to His Majesty's Government.

Herr Hess flew to Great Britain in a Me. 110, from which he landed by parachute in the evening of the 10th May, 1941, at Eaglesham in Scotland. He was wearing the uniform of a captain in the German Air Force. He gave his name as Alfred Horn and stated to the Home Guard and the Police that he was on a "special mission" to see the Duke of Hamilton, and that he had intended to land at Dungavel, 12 miles distant from the spot where he landed.

The prisoner was taken to Maryhill Barracks and amongst his possessions were found photographs of himself and of a small boy, also the visiting cards of Dr. Karl Haushofer and Dr. Albrecht Haushofer, his son. No other documents or identifications were found on the prisoner.

On Sunday, the 11th May, at 10 A.M., Wing-Commander the Duke of Hamilton arrived at Maryhill Barracks and visited the prisoner with the interrogating officer and the Military Officer on guard.

At the prisoner's request the latter two officers withdrew. He then stated to the Wing-Commander that the latter had lunched in his house in Berlin at the time of the Olympic games in 1936 and added: "I am Rudolf Hess." The Wing-Commander had no recollection of the prisoner and was not aware that he had ever seen or met Rudolf Hess.

The prisoner then proceeded: "I am on a mission of humanity. The Führer does not want to defeat England and wants to stop fighting." His friend Haushofer, he stated, had told him that the Wing-Commander was an Englishman who would understand his point of view. He had tried to arrange a meeting in Lisbon.* He had three times before tried to fly to Dungavel, the first time being in December 1940, but had been turned back by weather or various other reasons.

* NOTE.—The Duke of Hamilton had in fact received a letter dated 23rd September from Haushofer suggesting a meeting in Lisbon but without any reference to the presence of Hess. This letter was brought to the attention of His Majesty's Government at the time of its arrival. As Sir Archibald Sinclair stated in the House of Commons, the Duke's conduct in relation to Rudolf Hess had been in every respect honourable and proper.

11886 [24568]

The Stafford-Cripps memorandum.

way of British/German fighting; some authors have speculated that Churchill was pretending to hold 'mock discussions' with Hess, so as to buy more time.

It seems to us that this is unlikely, for while Churchill sent Lords Simon and Beaverbrook to interview Hess, and Hess spent the summer of 1941 preparing a written manifesto, the more likely truth was that Germany was fully committed to the invasion of Russia and had simply prioritised the Eastern Front. Germany knew that Britain was certainly not in a position to launch an invasion, or even threaten the Reich, as Dieppe would so disastrously prove in the summer of 1942.

We are also interested in the Frank Foley discussions with Hess, as they were an attempt to understand the state of the German atomic weapon programme. Foley, as senior MI6 agent and head of the German section, was billeted with Hess while incarcerated at Mytchett Place. We suspect Hess had anticipated this approach and used the subject as a way of gaining attention quickly. The rooms were 'wired', but on 23 May 1941 Hess had opened up to Foley, telling him: 'In addition there are also new bombs with stronger explosives.'

This, Foley knew, was a reference to the German atomic program. Hess continued: '… if we really believe that the war will carry on, we can be relaxed in the face of this coming war.' On 19 November, Foley tried again and Hess replied: 'He knew there was one, but had no idea what it was, but Hitler would not use it unless as a last resort.'

This we believe to be true. In May 1941, the Germans, while being ahead of the Allies in their research, were in truth slowly becoming confused and divided. No doubt the Nazi leaders would have been told of the potential, but not the detail. The atomic threat was still the great unknown, the potential 'trump card'. As the war reached its climax, Hess's confidence was shown to be unfounded. The Germans did not have a viable device.

The next challenge for the British government was the Nuremberg trials. Some analysis of the charges is worthwhile. There were four counts:

1: Common plan or conspiracy.
2: Crimes against peace.
3: War crimes.
4: Crimes against humanity.

Hess was found guilty on counts (1) and (2) and sentenced to life imprisonment. Typically, but not exclusively, if he had been found guilty on counts (3) and (4), the sentence was death. Speer, Funk and von Neurath provided the exceptions.

While comparison of relative wickedness can be trite, Funk and Raeder were given life sentences, but neither served the term due to supposed health issues. Doenitz was guilty of three counts yet served 10 years and Speer avoided the gallows, despite being found guilty on counts (3) and (4). Looking at the relative sentences and the period that was subsequently served, it does appear that Hess was treated harshly. No other prisoner condemned to a life sentence served the complete term of such a sentence. James Owen, in his book *Nuremberg: Evil on Trial*, states: 'Many of the sentences were, to say the least, perplexing. No reasons were given …'

We suspect that Hess' apparently bizarre behaviour did not help his sentencing. Completely unrepentant ('I do not regret anything') and contemptuous of the proceedings, he admitted that:'The reasons for simulating loss of memory were of a tactical nature.' Feigned amnesia and illness had been used as a defence whenever necessary since his captivity in 1941. In his rambling final speech, he talks of 'glassy eyes' and we wonder if this is a coded message for the use of drugs. Given the presence of Ewan Cameron – a Scot who practised in Canada in the fledgling field of brain washing – at Nuremberg, almost anything was possible.

Once Hess was incarcerated in Spandau Prison, there was no chance of further public utterances. When the author Desmond Zwar worked with Eugene Bird to publish *The Loneliest Man in the World*, the intelligence services even travelled to northern Australia to ensure that publication was controlled. Bird's career was over.

From 10 May 1941 to his death in 1987, Hess was completely controlled. When he finally agreed to meet his immediate family, physical contact was controlled, conversation was also controlled. To what end? What threat did Hess pose? After 1966, Hess, prisoner Number 7, was the sole inmate in Spandau, which gave Russia an excuse to retain a presence in that Berlin sector on a rotational basis. Was that really sufficient justification to continue the imprisonment?

The usual reason given for the prolonged incarceration is that the Russians were vetoing any pleas for clemency or release. On one level this is quite understandable, given that the Hess flight was aimed at making the annihilation of Russia easier and quicker. We wondered if this was actually the case, given what we had learned of MI6 involvement.

Alfred Smith, in his book *Rudolf Hess and Germany's Reluctant War 1939–41*, deals with this part of the story very well. Smith knew Wolf Hess well and acted as his British representative. His view is quite clear. Mikail Gorbachev had softened the Russian view, purely on humanitarian grounds. *Glasnost* was the new international buzz word, which in fact disguised the fact that Russia was bankrupt. However, Alfred Smith obtained the following information from Rhodri Morgan MP:'The British then vetoed it [the release] while always hiding behind the Russian refusal to release Hess.'

Again we are not surprised. The British had controlled Hess since 1941, if not before, and they were not going to lose control now. Hess died on 17 August 1987, while still in Spandau. We make no comment on the cause of death.

The Basic Conundrums

(a) What made Hess fly?
One thing is for sure: Hess decided to fly of his own volition. It was his initiative and had been from August 1940. No one was forcing him to fly. He had assimilated the various pieces of evidence that had been presented to him.

He then decided the probability was that, by flying, he would achieve a peace settlement between the German and British nations. In coming to this conclusion, we believe he drew on the following pointers.

The impact of 'Flying Missions and Achievements' on history was great: the Everest expedition, the flights over the Atlantic, and even Chamberlain's 'peace in our time' flights all had immense impact on the population. Aviation was very much part of the spirit of the time. Hess was present in Berlin in 1939 when Hitler, in a panic, had ordered Göring to fly to London to make peace.

The Churchill-led government was in trouble. On 7 May 1941 there had been a vote of confidence which, although it had been won, shocked Churchill and Eden. The fact that a vote was even taken was a reflection of the mood of Parliament. Beaverbrook had resigned the week before the flight. Churchill really had few friends apart from the British population.

The British were slowly being battered into submission, despite the German failure in the Battle of Britain; London was looking like 'A battered old war horse'.[24] In the Atlantic, German U-boats were still in the ascendancy and the winter 'Blitz' had wrought terrible damage throughout Britain.

MI6, through Borenius and others, were telling Haushofer/Hess that a coup attempt was in the offing, emanating from the highest levels and detailing how Churchill could be circumvented. Supporting the plot, Hess had pre-war evidence of German sympathies from much of aristocratic Britain. The fact that the apparent approach was 'non-governmental' made it more likely to succeed as there was no precondition of the removal of Hitler. In Spain, Hoare was saying the same thing, but possibly for different reasons. Again, Burckhardt would no doubt relay back the 'City' intelligence of March 1941 to Haushofer.

The psychological impact of his arrival exactly one year after the invasion of the Low Countries and France, together with one of the worst nights of bombing during the Blitz and also the targetting of the Houses of Parliament by German bombers, would be increased.

The German intelligence service in Britain was pretty hopeless and did not provide any useful intelligence of its own. Hess was blind in intelligence terms. Haushofer was his best bet, but could he even be sure of Haushofer?

There were doubts about Germany's war machine, their industrial ability to maintain supply and doubts about Hitler's ever more radical policies.

Hess' own position was in doubt. Here was an opportunity to shine once again and put Göring, Bormann, Himmler and Von Ribbentrop back into the shadows.

And lastly, there was a fundamental doubt about Germany's ability to defeat Russia. In reaching his decision to fly, Hess was swayed too much by the following:

Information coming from Geneva, Madrid and Stockholm (and via Burckhardt/Haushofer).

The desperate need for a settlement before 15 May 1941.

The potential for enhanced status should he succeed.

The knowledge that his family would be 'looked after' should he fail.

b) Why a solo mission?

The impression of a solo mission made the whole thing deniable if it failed. It did not appear to be a government initiative. The Russians would not automatically calculate that an invasion was imminent. This is why our analysis of the flight is significant. We believe it completely dispels the notion of a solo mission.

If Luftwaffe involvement could be demonstrated, such as Hess flying in a formation or part of a raid, then immediately the mission becomes government-led. If the mission were overtly governmental then Stalin would straight away be suspicious. Why would Hitler wish to make a peace with Britain? This is why the Cuddie flight vectors are so important: the British knew too.

(c) Did Hitler know?

Yes, Hitler knew. Perhaps not from the earliest stage of the preparations, but certainly he went with Hitler's blessing. Hitler 'looked after' the Hess family throughout the war and we suspect Hess told his Führer of the finer details whilst in Berlin at the start of May 1941. There are various stories of Hitler's acting abilities and we suspect that he gave a masterclass on receipt of the news that Hess had flown. The anger displayed was because Hess had failed, not because he had flown. As far as Hitler was concerned, it was an acceptable risk to take, given the prize. As the US magazine *Liberty* stated: 'Hitler, aware of his Deputy Führer's intentions, prepared to hail him as an angel of peace if he succeeded – and to denounce him if he failed.'

Leading on from the above, it also appears that Hitler knew about the flight much earlier than the accepted date of the late morning of 11 May 1941, when Pintsch delivered his master's letter of explanation. Fresh evidence has recently emerged.

Firstly, *Udet, Des Teufels General* reveals that Ernst Udet, the English-speaking Luftwaffe development chief and ace, was telephoned by Hitler personally on the evening of 10 May, while the flight was under way. This is earlier than previously reported and, although it has been taken as an indication to support the view that Hitler did not want Hess to get to Britain, it could have another, more hopeful meaning.

Secondly, Wolf Hess records that Lippert, Hess's driver, was arrested at 05:30hrs on 11 May, hours before Hitler was supposed to have learned of the flight.

Josef Goebbels' diary seems to confirm the German statement that Hess was insane, but later seeks to blame others, Karl Haushofer and, interestingly, Ilse Hess in particular. It does appear contrived and contradictory:

13 May 1941 (Tuesday): Appalling news comes in the evening: Hess, against the Führer's orders, has taken off in a plane and has been missing since Saturday. We must presume him dead. His adjutants, who were the only ones aware of his intentions, have been arrested on the Führer's orders. The Führer's statement gives delusions as the reason for his action, some madness to do with illusionary peace-feelers ... We are forced to issue the statement immediately. A hard, almost unbearable blow ... I receive a telephone call from the Berghof. The Führer is quite shattered. What a sight for the world's eyes: the Führer's deputy a mentally disturbed man. Dreadful and unthinkable. Now we shall have to grit our teeth.

14 May 1941 (Wednesday): The Führer is waiting for me. I read the letters that Hess left behind for the Führer: totally confused, schoolboy amateurism, saying that he is intending to go to England, make the hopelessness of their position clear to them, bring down Churchill's government with the aid of Lord Hamilton in Scotland, and then make a peace which would save London's face ... A fool like this was a Führer's deputy. It is scarcely conceivable. His letters are littered with the ill-digested occult theory. Professor Haushofer and Hess's wife were the evil geniuses in this affair. They pushed their 'great man' into this role. He is supposed to have had visions, had horoscopes drawn up, and so on. Rubbish. And this is one of Germany's rulers. The whole thing can be traced to his mystic obsession with healthy living and all that nonsense about eating grass. Totally lunatic. I would like to give a good thrashing to that wife of his, his adjutants and his doctors. ... The business is so squalid and ridiculous that one can hardly credit it. And it had to happen now, when the Führer has received Admiral Darlan and is about to carry out his coup in the East.

... Then I have to get back. Affectionate farewell. I regret very much that I must leave the Führer.

The timings here do not hold true. Gerhard Engel, Hitler's Army Adjutant, gives a detailed account of the receipt of the news at the Berghof on 11 May at around 11.00 a.m.[25] According to Engel, Hitler's first call was to Göring at Nuremberg, demanding that he come to the Berghof. (The reader will remember that Göring had given orders to Adolf Galland to shoot Hess down the night before.)

Again, this charade does not stand too much scrutiny. Galland was at Guipavas, in Brittany, France, when the call came 'in the early evening' to go and try to shoot down Hess. Galland was obviously nervous, 'for reasons practical and personal' but the biography then tellingly states that 'it would be dark in 10 minutes'. We would place the call at around 8.45 p.m. to 9.00 p.m., by which time Hess was in the process of getting lost, trying to find his Point C. Even aircraft at Westerland on the

Island of Sylt (the then nearest base to Hess) were an hour away. It was a hopeless task. Göring had telephoned Galland in the far west of Brittany with ten minutes of light left, instructing him to go and shoot down a Bf 110 somewhere over the North Sea. This seems to us to be nonsense, purely to enable him to back up the solo flight myth that was shortly to be officially communicated to the world.

Then, as can be seen above, Hitler apparently waits until the Tuesday 13 May to inform his propaganda minister. Even Ciano, Mussolini's foreign minister heard 'the announcement of Hess's death in a plane accident' on 12 May (taken from a German communiqué).

The fact that Hess had crashed in Scotland was going to put the Nazi Party under terrific pressure, in just the same way as it had Churchill. As Ciano states: 'Mussolini considers the Hess affair a tremendous blow to the Nazi Regime.' Von Ribbentrop was sent to Rome to allay any Italian fears of a separate Anglo-German treaty. Goebbels:

> 15 May 1941 (Thursday): I am suffering acutely from the Hess Affair. One feels as if one has been dealt a personal blow, and one would prefer not to show one's face on the street … But we shall get through it. I instruct the press and the radio to devote vigorous attention to other things and act as if nothing had happened. This is the best remedy.

The affair had massive 'news management' issues. Hitler was desperately nervous about the Russian campaign and, above all, the fate of his deputy could not be allowed to jeopardise Operation Barbarossa.

The mission was effectively a German sanctioned peace attempt which failed. The complexity of the flight in terms of equipment and a landing in northern Germany implies official connivance. It was an officially sanctioned mission, covertly planned.

(d) Did the British know?

Yes, Britain knew that Hess was coming as he was effectively invited. If there really was a coup attempt underway – we doubt Churchill would have gone to the cinema on hearing the news of Hess' arrival. We suspect, however, that probably no more than ten Britons knew that Hess was coming that night: amongst them, members of MI6, Churchill, those at RAF Prestwick/Dundonald, the Duke of Hamilton and J.O. Andrews. We are intrigued as to whether there may be Ultra transcripts that detail radio traffic concerning the flight. Needless to say, none have yet surfaced, but the British were reading Luftwaffe traffic by May 1941. This may possibly explain the odd story of Ernest Bevin receiving word of Hess' flight from trade union colleagues at the Messerschmitt works in Augsburg.

As Peter Fleming later wrote: 'Strategic deception is to make your enemy take – or refrain from taking – a particular course of action; and thereby to improve your chances of defeating him. Merely to gull him – to implant in his mind a false picture of the true situation – is only half the battle; it is not enough, even that "he should do something about it". He must do what you want him to do.'

(e) Were the major British protagonists loyal?

Yes, we think so. This was definitely an intelligence-led operation. We are however interested in the Duke of Hamilton's actions following Hess' arrival.

The new Cuddie evidence can only demonstrate the fact that the British knew where Hess was heading. Ultimately, however, the RAF failed to shoot him down and he became 'public property' – the worst of all outcomes. Sgt McBride would soon inform the press and the 'genie was out of the bottle', a secret military operation had just become public property.

Consequently, we find Hamilton's subsequent rush to explain to Churchill odd. Hamilton flew by Spitfire to Churchill as soon as he feasibly could on 11 May and stayed overnight at Ditchley with the prime minister. Later in the week he met with the King.

This is odd on a number of counts. Firstly, whilst the duke was the sector commander, ultimate responsibility rested with J.O. Andrews, head of RAF 13 Group. Hamilton was Andrews' junior in RAF terms. On one level we are tempted to ask why Hamilton saw the need to report anything. It was not really his job. Furthermore, he chose to do so before the news got out; the public were to learn of the flight on 13 May, albeit a significant number of persons already knew in Scotland (the Poles and those involved at Eaglesham). It appears to us that there are really only three explanations.

Firstly, that Hamilton was explaining what had gone wrong and how to manage the outcome; why Hess had not been shot down or captured and controlled as planned. This explanation, which we now think most likely, implies Hamilton knew Hess was coming, as did Churchill.

The second explanation is that there had been a coup attempt that had just failed and Hamilton was flying for his reputation at the very least. This we do not believe.

Thirdly, Hamilton genuinely knew nothing of the operation which had just failed so publicly, albeit making use of his personage.

In extremis, in 1941, we do not think the King would have signed anything against Churchill's wishes. Churchill was too popular with the country. If the King had really wished to depose Churchill, then constitutionally he could have done so at any time, and he had the opportunity of not approving his appointment in May 1940. We know that, at the time, the King and Queen would have much preferred Halifax. Whether he wished to or not, would the King have had the popular support of the country to support such an action? In contrast to Churchill, the King and Queen had been booed on some early visits to bomb-damaged areas. We suspect they were also feeling vulnerable.

Looking at the Hess debate some seventy years on, it also appears to us that the affair essentially marked a watershed in the war. Subsequent to May 1941, there were no further Anglo-German peace feelers until much later, when Nazi-Germany was essentially beaten. In repudiating Hess, Churchill had made the Anglo-American alliance his only option. There was to be no going back and the Second World War would then be a fight to the end. It is quite understandable that many were not happy in this choice of a 'New World' and old alliance and we suspect that many in Britain would have preferred an Anglo-German treaty. This debate still rages today.

Franz Halder's diary is illuminating and fundamental. He states that once Russia was defeated, Germany could deal with Britain on her own terms. That is why Churchill actually had no choice but to fight. Those in Britain who thought they could side with Germany and trust Hitler were fools.

(f) Why did the British do it?

We believe to buy time. A 1941 German/Russian war was definitely a 'good outcome' for Britain, with two of its ideological enemies engaged in brutal combat. Better than an invasion of Great Britain. Waiting for the German/Russian war to begin was a sensible military and political decision by the British, who knew it was going to happen through Ultra intercepts. When the Haushofer letter was intercepted in October 1940, it could well be that the motives were different, but they certainly developed into a strategic wait for the Russian invasion.

The war was fast becoming a race for the atomic bomb or, failing that, overwhelming arms production. The danger of the 'wait for the Russian invasion' strategy was obvious should Germany defeat Russia, but even then the intervening time would allow for increased arms production.

(g) Why did the British not exploit the issue?

Simply because Churchill was petrified of losing US support. If the American population at large thought the British were suing for peace, Churchill's only hope would be extinguished. Britain really would be on her own. Imagine, too, the reaction if Germany started to release evidence of British peace feelers. Even Goebbels questioned the British tactics, on 16 May 1941 (Friday): 'It seems that London has not hit upon the idea of simply issuing statements in Hess's name without his knowledge. This is the big, most alarming danger so far as we are concerned. The thought of it makes me shiver. But it seems as if we have a guardian angel watching over us. We are dealing with dumb amateurs over there. What we would do if the situation was reversed!'

(h) Why did the Germans not say that Hess had been tricked?

Hitler and Hess had just been outwitted. They had made a terrible mistake in believing that King George VI would depose his sitting prime minister. This is quite understandable, particularly if Hess had written evidence to support such a supposition, but still a mistake. Moreover, in the 1920s there had been a strong sense in Germany that the First World War had been lost partly on account of the almost 'supernatural' influence of British intelligence services. To resurrect such feelings would be dangerous. At Nuremberg, self-preservation would preclude such allegations, although Göring did taunt Hess to 'tell of his secret'. A second reason is that the Hess affair became irrelevant on 22 June 1941, with the invasion of Russia. Peace negotiations had failed and the Second World War was to be a fight to the death. The failure of this mission was a true turning point of the war.

(i) Was it Hess that crashed at Eaglesham?

Of course it was. If not, there certainly would not have been the subsequent furore. We have also looked at the photographs of Hess, pre- and post-war, and can see no difference. Hess did not appear to have ear lobes in either set of pictures. As to Spandau, we have no idea and no way of telling, but logically, yes, it was Rudolf Hess. Apart from Hugh Thomas, there have been no other suggestions of doubles; from colleagues, family or subsequent correspondence.

(j) Was Poland involved?

Yes. Poland would have to be involved in any settlement, or illusion of the same, as Poland was the reason Britain declared war. The Sikorski flight into Prestwick is just too much of a coincidence. This would be part of the operation, especially given that Prestwick had barely commenced cross-ocean operations.

We are also unsure as to the role, if any, that Polish intelligence may have played. The Poles saw intelligence almost as a national sport, given their proximity to both Russia and Germany, and while there was an agreement that Poland would share its intelligence with Britain, its wartime host, the suspicion remained that Britain was only told what Poland thought it should be told. That having been said, Poland did of course share 'Enigma' machine intelligence with Britain.

(k) Was Hess a 'Martyr for Peace'?

We do not believe Hess was a martyr for peace, or anything else for that matter. Nuremberg made it clear that he was wholly unapologetic and he made the flight in the hope that he could neutralise Britain, so that the subsequent Russian anni-hilation (about which Hess knew) would become that much easier. That motive alone surely precludes the description of a martyr.

However, to answer the question posed in the preface to this book, there is no doubt that 'he dared'. Despite becoming something of a fiasco, what he tried to do was without doubt daring, meticulously planned and brave.

The final analysis remains that Hess had spectacularly failed to complete his mission; a mission that was a purely self-interested Nazi act of war.

APPENDIX 1. THE DEVELOPMENT OF GERMAN RADIO-NAVIGATION SYSTEMS

The authors are certainly not experts in radio direction-finding systems from the 1940s. What became clear to us through our research was just how early the systems had been developed and how sophisticated they had become. Consequently, rather than be accused of poor paraphrasing we have obtained kind permission from Mr A. Bauer of Diemen, Netherlands, to reproduce his treatise on the development of the various systems that were available to Rudolf Hess when planning his flight.

Abstract

Some historical and technical aspects of radio navigation in Germany during the period 1907 to 1945. Radio navigation, in the broad sense, has become of the utmost importance since the end of the 1930s. Warfare, without navigation by radio signals is, today, nearly unthinkable. It is therefore useful to look back in history to get some understanding as to how, why and when some aspects of this technology came into being.

Navigation by radio as an aid has been practised in Germany since 1907. Scheller invented the complimentary dot-dash guiding path, which can be seen as a 'landmark' for several decades of navigational aids. Some aspects of the Lorenz civilian 'Blind Approach' apparatus and several technical details of the relentless Beams over Britain will also be discussed as will the principles behind Sonne (or Consol) used for long distance navigation and some other related subjects.

Arthur O. Bauer
Diemen, 26 December 2004
The Netherlands

Introduction

Already in the early days of the German wireless industry, it was Telefunken (fifty-fifty shared [owned] by AEG and Siemens & Halske) and C. Lorenz (the latter hereafter to be called Lorenz), who dominated Germany's market. The latter company was owned, since May 1930, by the American ITT company and, after WWII this company was also known as Standard Elektrik Lorenz (SEL). Around 1990 it was finally sold to the French Alcatel company.

From the beginning of the wireless industry, the German government was keen to keep both major companies in business, to avoid the possibility of the internal market becoming one company's monopoly.

In 1907, both companies were testing their first *Funkbaken* or radio beacons. It is not known to me who really was the first to construct such radio beacon(s) but, from the beginning, the developments engendered by the Lorenz Company showed signs that indicated the likely development of their product over several decades to come.

Scheller's patented No. 201.496 [1, p. 490] of 1907 was based on the idea of creating a particular radiation pattern caused by two identical crossed antenna loops. It is quite interesting that, according to Kramar [2, p. 155], the original patent application did not yet employ crossed loops but four vertical radiators, connected in a way similar to that suggested by Adcock 10 years after!

This figure shows in the centre the crossed loops and its well known radiation pattern. But his real invention was to feed both antenna loops from the same signal source, whereby each loop was switched (connected) on and off in such a manner that each loop was fed with complimentary currents. One loop was transmitting in the rhythm of: dot-dash (. -) which stands for the Morse character A, and the other loop was transmitting in the inverse sequence dash–dot (- .) which in Morse code stands for the character N. This keying application became well known later as the 'A/N system' and formed the cornerstone of many other Lorenz applications.

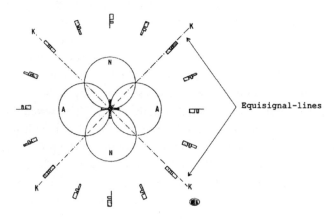

Fig. 1 Scheller's virtual 'A/N' path (1907) (Esau, [1, p. 348–349]).

It is evident that the field strength at the equipotential-lines KK are both influenced by the crossed antenna loops, so their electromagnetic field components are identical at this virtual line. It is obvious that there will be, subsequently, only a continuous signal remaining at both crossed KK lines as long as we ignore the obligational keying clicks.

The next important step, patented by Scheller, was to virtually rotate the radiation pattern, by the integration of a goniometer into the system. For this he had designed a special goniometer device, to avoid the distortion of the radiation pattern. According to Trenkle [3, p. 85], two special goniometers were utilised and the complimentary keying was executed in such a manner that only one single keying circuit was employed. A pair of toroid transformers (although these were called chokes then) were wired in such a manner that the two toroid cores were alternately brought in or out of saturation, by a keyed DC current. Whilst one antenna loop was radiating RF energy, the second loop was kept without current.

Subsequently this beacon, when not virtually being rotated, created, on a map, fixed A & N sectors. According to Esau, the aperture of equisignal sectors, when these were monitored acoustically, was approx. between 1° and 5°.

In 1908, Telefunken erected a different type of navigational beacon, which became known as the 'Telefunken-Kompass-Sender'. [Trenkle, 4, p. 80–81]

It shows the circular construction of the antenna system. Thirty-two wires were fed from the centre and were wired as for sixteen dipoles, installed as a sort of 'inverted V' or umbrella. Each antenna dipole was sequentially connected to a spark transmitter. The radiation pattern, for each dipole, was in the form of two lobes, perpendicular to the antenna wires. The shape of the lobes was influenced by the ratio between the length (l) of the dipole and the wavelength (λ) of operation (l : λ).

The north marker signal was generated by connecting all sixteen dipoles onto the exciter at the same time. Then, after a certain interval, during which the call sign was being transmitted in Morse as well, the virtual rotation of the radiation pattern was started. The virtual rotation of the antenna diagram was carefully synchronised, so that it became possible to utilise a specially designed watch in which only one indicator needle of double length was used. This watch had to be triggered just after the north marker had been switched off and the virtual beam rotation had been started. The watch had to be stopped at the point when the signal reached its maximum value. Though an ordinary watch (when all system parameters were taken into consideration) could manage this job too, it became evident that only one double length 'watch' needle could be utilised because the dipoles had symmetrical radiation patterns.

The first and necessary improvement was that, due to the relatively broad aperture of the antenna radiation pattern, the antennas had to be connected to the beacon transmitter such that the minimum radiation indicated the correct bearing. Hence, the antenna (or dipole) wires were pointing straight at the direction of the receiving apparatus.

A whole range of improvements came into operation, but the basic principle was in use for about a decade. The beacon had still one major disadvantage due to the symmetrical antenna pattern, it was not always possible to determine whether a bearing was at + 180° or – 180°!!

During the First World War, due to this disadvantage, the Zeppelins had to counter check their bearings by comparing two beacon stations. In Western Europe, the stations Cleve and Tondern were widely used for this purpose. It was also possible, for such a moving platform, to compare and/or by control the trend of the change of the true bearing, and thus to determine its correct quadrant.

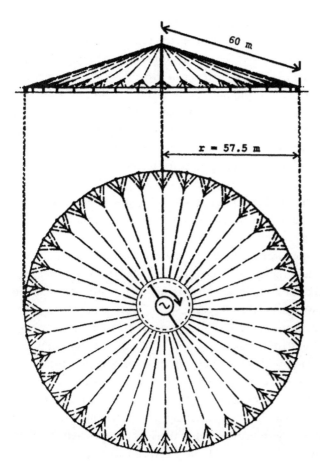

Fig. 2 The antenna array of the 'Telefunken–Kompass-Sender'.

Some developments during the 'interbellum'

The American Bureau of Standards experimented in 1921 with Scheller's type of beacon. Two years later the US Army set up technical trials with similar beacon devices. In 1926 a technical commission ordered the introduction of beacons that could be used for navigation and utilised a simple wireless receiver only [1, p.349–350].

As we already have noticed, the early Lorenz A/N system was widely tested in the US. But, due to the devastating economical situation during the first years after Germany surrendered at the Western Front in 1918, it took nearly a decade before Lorenz was really commercially back on stage.

In 1928/29, an improved beacon type was erected in Eberswalde, near Berlin. The utilised frequency was 385kHz and the beacon had a radiated power of approx. 800W. [1, p. 350–351], [4, p. 81] The first practical trials took place in co-operation with the Luft Hansa (today known as Lufthansa).

According to Esau's paper [1], the great advantage of this Lorenz equipment was the keying method, which absolutely guaranteed that both A and N signals were, under all circumstances, completely complementary. This was in contrast to the system utilised in the US, whereby two separate transmitters were employed.

Towed antenna wires, widely used by aircraft in those days, were a great disadvantage due to the fact that the antenna was forced (by drag) into a position somewhere between vertical and horizontal polarisation. Hence, both the vertical as well as the horizontal field components were picked-up by this antenna, thus creating an unacceptable distortion of the bearing. The solution, to prevent this unwanted effect, was found by placing a fixed vertical antenna rod of 1.5 metre length onto the fuselage of the aircraft.

Secondly, it became obvious that, although acoustical observation of beacon signals was theoretically quite effective, there was a great need for a left/right bearing indicator. (This will be discussed later.)

From aviation authorities around the world there was an increasing interest in 'Blind Approach' facilities (hereafter to be called BA), but, for over a decade a combination of national pride combined with commercial interests prevented the development of a worldwide standardised system.

The first attempt came from the American Bureau of Air Commerce around 1930 and resulted in an instrumental BA system by Diamond and Dunmore. The American aviation industrial complex was in those days already the largest in the world; nonetheless, even at the end of the 1930s they still were not certain enough to standardise BA for commercial use. [Esau, 5, p. 4] Handel suggested (in the same paper) that one of the resulting advantages for Germany was that the German Aviation Authorities were (at the end of the 1930s) not therefore strictly constrained by an already developed and definitive standard system.

In my opinion one aspect too often neglected by historians has been that the early introduction of new system standards, which although very sophisticated at the time, can soon become very outdated and are often kept operational for a decade or even sometimes much longer. We can call this phenomena the disadvantage of being advanced, and nearly all nations were, and sometimes still are, suffering from this limiting effect. For example, in the US their 115 power voltage and NTSC CTV standard, and in Britain their 405 line TV norm, up until the 1960s ...! Even today, all PCs (DOS computers) are victims of the 640kB memory phenomena!

Subsequently, the aviation standards in Germany could continually improve, as previously noted, without being limited by the existence of absolute standards. But, during the Second World War, it became more and more evident that German industry could no longer develop new technology and were not able to cope with the demands of their authorities. Thus they were forced into a position of standstill in respect of the introduction of really new and advanced apparatus and systems design [Bauer, 6 p. 76–82].

The Lorenz *Ultrakurzwellen-Landefunkfeuer* (LFF) or VHF, BA beacon

Technically there are two elements to be taken into consideration for a BA system: these are the horizontal and the vertical system components. Both of these are of great importance.

Let us consider the Figure 3 drawing (*Zeichnung*) 1. The horizontal system component for navigation (*Leitstrahl*) has to indicate the true course towards the landing strip (today called runway). It is evident that, whatever the glide-path conditions may be, an approaching aircraft needs to keep pointing straight onto the centre of the landing strip axis.

The Lorenz BA system proved to be most useful for this purpose. It was Kramar who brought this system to maturity. Let us take a brief look at what the basic elements of this system were.

Basically, the complementary dot-dash antenna lobe switching created an equisignal-line that was on the axis of the landing strip. Figure 4 shows the principle of such an antenna switching circuit.

First of all, let us take a look at the keying circuit: it is obvious that both reflectors are switched on and off in a complementary fashion. Its time pattern is shown left and right from the virtual guiding path.

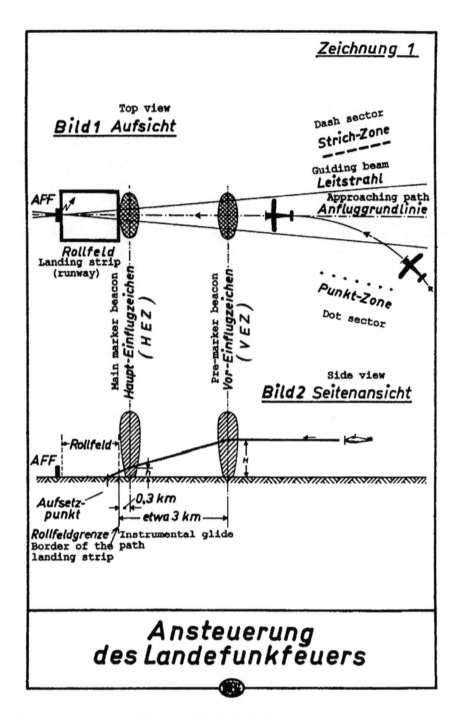

Fig. 3 Lorenz instrumental BA system (*Blindlandeanlage*).

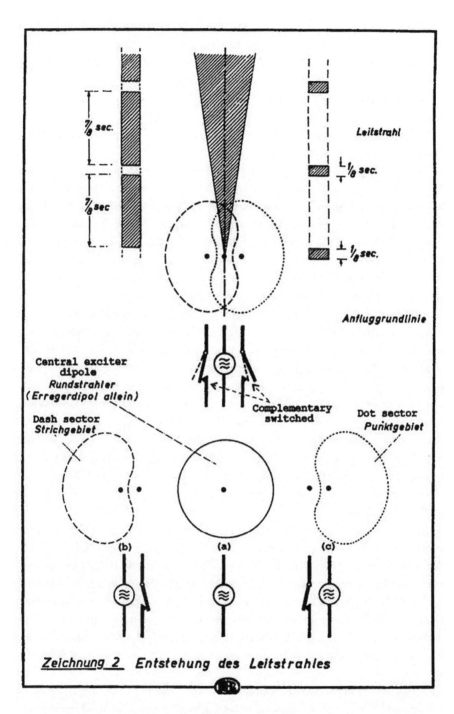

Fig. 4 (a, b & c) Beam forming of the virtual approaching path.

Figure 4a shows the omni-directional radiation pattern, when none of the reflectors are (electrically) actuated to half wave reflectors (these were then equal to ordinary dipoles of $\lambda/2$). It is known that, generally, quarter wave conductors are not good reflectors for electro-magnetic waves.

Figure 4b and c show the radiation patterns when each particular reflector is activated.

It is evident that the antenna lobes will virtually move in a particular sequence from left to right and vice versa.

As we have noticed before, this lobe switching had to occur in a complementary manner. To simplify operation a dot-dash sequence was chosen to distinguish between left and right of the centre of the virtual guiding beam path. Which side will be demodulated (either the dot or dash sector side) will depend upon the direction a plane is approaching – the Germans called this the 'green and red direction'. Until now, we have assumed that an acoustical observation would be used to determine left or right, but this would have posed difficulties, because the lobes were never operating at the same moment, due to the complementary keying. The difference of the received left–right amplitudes had to be distinguished in some alternative way. To overcome this disadvantage a left–right indicator was introduced. Its instrumental circuit reacted to different impulses from the demodulated left–right signals. As long as these were of equal value, so the antenna was pointing to the centre of the virtual guiding path and a moving coil instrument was indicating the centre, or zero, position. When the impulses were uneven in value, the meter circuit was wired in such a manner that the pilot would easily recognise what action he had to take. The left–right meter reading was most sensitive near its centre or zero position. The same instrument was combined with a second cross meter section that indicate the amplitude of the received signal.

Further information was, however, necessary before an aircraft could initiate its glide-path procedure.

It was Kramar who introduced a marker beacon that allowed the initiation of a controlled glide-path, as is shown in drawing (Bild) 3. (See [7], [8], [9]) The two specific beacons, for the so called pre-(VEZ) and main (HEZ) marker signals, were operated all at the same frequency of 38MHz, with a special shaped, upwardly (vertical) directed, antenna diagram. The radiated power was limited, to avoid interference with, or between, the other adjacent beacon signals. Both marker signals (VEZ and HEZ) were picked-up by a dipole antenna that was installed parallel to the axis of the fuselage of the aircraft. Only one spot frequency was utilised so that only one receiver frequency setting had to be employed for this purpose. Each marker beacon, both the pre- and the main signal, could be recognised by its particular manner of keying and its particular modulation tone. The sensitivity of the utilised marker receiver could be kept quite limited.

It is evident that two signals had to be monitored, by the pilot, at the same time. The main approaching course could be tracked, if necessary, for several kilometres (often up to 30km) before the glide-path procedure had to be initiated, at a point 3km before the landing strip. The pre-marker (VEZ) signal and the main marker (HEZ) signal, were than heard in the headphones and indicated visually by a flashing light (often a neon bulb) incorporated in the left-right meter indicator. The specific modulation (2A2), as well as the individual keying of the marker beacons was designed to alert the operators and so avoid misinterpretations. The pre-marker was modulated for 700Hz and the main marker was modulated for a tone of 1,700Hz.

Finally, let us take a brief look at Fig. 3 again. All system parameters such as the dot-dash sectors and the position of the pre- and main glide-path marker beacons are clearly shown. The aperture of the antenna lobes facing towards the landing strip are smaller than those perpendicular to the axis of the system, so as to ensure that if the aircraft was a bit off course it did not fail to pick up a marker beacon signal.

I am not suggesting that this technology was utilised in Germany only, far from it; this system was also adopted for use in Britain as well. Kramar also presented several papers in the US at meetings of the IRE., and other places, in the 1930s. Some aspects of this technology were utilised during the famous X- and Y-beam guidance for bombers during the 'Blitz'. However, knowledge of the system made British response, to counter these threats, a much easier job!

Navigation by 'Doppler-effect'

In 1935/36, the DVL (German Aviation Research Establishment) tested the world's first fully operational Doppler aircraft apparatus. To simplify matters we will follow the block diagram shown in Fig. 5.

To utilise the Doppler effect we require two different signals that have to be compared in phase and/or frequency. The reference signal here was generated in a quartz controlled time base and was send by two different routes towards the deployed Doppler indicator. The reference signal was linked (after being multiplied with the factor 16) to the front-end of the receiver in the aircraft. The second route was via the transmitter (by wireless) to a ground transponder. This transponder multiplied the RF frequency (without demodulation) sixteen times and, the signal was retransmitted after amplification, towards the aircraft. The reference, and the Doppler modulated signals, interfered somewhere at, or near, the front-end stage of the receiver and then passed through in the usual way. After demodulation the resulting signal was fed to the indicator apparatus. This indicator

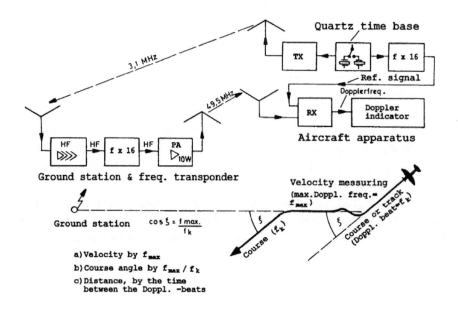

Fig. 5 World's first operational aircraft Doppler-Navigation apparatus, 1935–36 (DVL).

used a paper strip to indicate and store the received Doppler information. It was then possible to obtain several system parameters from this information.

The Doppler frequency reached its max. value when the aircraft was flying exactly towards the ground transponder (f_{max}). It should be noted that, if the aircraft happens to be following a circular track around the location of the ground transponder then it is not possible to demodulate the Doppler signals.

The third option would be the true state of affairs for normal navigation when the aircraft is following a certain track or course. The demodulated Doppler frequency (beat notes) will in this case always be of a lower value than the case of direct approach to the transponder. The ratio between both values for f_{max} / f_k indicates or creates cos ξ (see fig. 5).

It was, in my opinion, only possible theoretically to evaluate situation c) (in fig. 5), to distinguish the distance between the aircraft and the ground transponder. This would have had to be managed by fast switching between the two (build in) quartz references (although, a triggered oscilloscope could have determined the time delay, without a second reference frequency).

The first trials were very successful from the start and indicated the significance of both the theory and technology. However, it also showed that it was not very easy to handle this apparatus as a navigational aid. For instance the interpretation of the Doppler beat notes, when airborne, proved to be quite difficult. Due to this disadvantage, the project was put 'into cold storage'.

Although many more projects were being initiated in Germany during the 'Interbellum', we will turn to perhaps more familiar aspects of navigational technology!

The X Programme

This section of my discussion will sound more familiar, especially to those who experienced the relentless Blitz over Britain. This was an historical phase of development including the widespread adoption of civil technology for military purposes. An avalanche of publications has appeared since (see reference: [3], [4], [10] and [11]).

Plendl of the DVL in Berlin-Adlershof had suggested to the Luftwaffe, already in 1933, that it would be possible to adopt radio navigation as a 'blind bombing aid'. The first attempts were undertaken using two commercial Lorenz BA apparatus. Basically, the crossing point of two antenna beams marked the pre- and/or main points, at which the bombing procedure had to be initiated.

It soon proved that the antenna aperture was approx. 5° and, hence, for long distance guidance, useless. At a distance of 100km the beam aperture was already enlarged up to 8km! Subsequently, attempts were initiated to reduce the beam aperture to approx. 0.1°.

The new X-antenna arrays consist of two 3.5 wavelength spaced vertical dipoles ($D = 3.51\lambda$) (sometimes other versions were utilised as well) and these were fed in counter phase and created a total of fourteen (guiding) beams. Each virtual beam had an approximate separation of between 2° and 4°. As we have already noted, such a beam lies, in fact, inbetween two maximum antenna lobes. The minimal aperture of such equisignal-line is perpendicular to the array axis and at approx. 0.05°. We have also to consider that the beam aperture is dependent, as for all phased antenna arrays, on the ratio of the length of the antenna radiator(s) and wavelength of the signal ($1:\lambda$), as well as on the spacing of the antenna elements.

The dot-dash sectors were sequentially switched by a motor driven phase shifter. According to Trenkle [3, p. 60–62], the carrier was modulated by a sinusoidal 2,000Hz for this purpose.

Later, the deployment of antenna reflectors increased the radiated power in the forward direction and enhanced its effective range of operation. During the war, sometimes, very comprehensive antenna arrays were deployed.

To decrease the dimensions of the antenna array, the frequency band employed was increased up to 66–77MHz. Precise navigation along a virtual path became possible in 1935/36; extensive trials were set up to estimate the effective range of such guidance beams. It was found that ranges up to 500km could be achieved

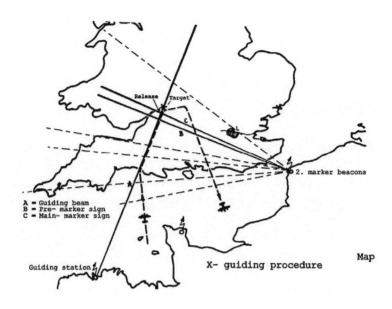

Map 1.

at flying altitudes of 6,000m. The standard altitude for German bomber aircraft during the Battle of Britain was at about 4,000m.

First practical trials in December 1936 proved that it was possible to get most of the dropped bombs within a square of 300m by 300m over a guidance range of 350km.

Map 1 illustrates an example of a typical 'X- Beam' over Britain. The dot-dash *'Leitstrahl'* path was transmitted from France, somewhere from the Breton coast. The pre- and main marker signals were transmitted from or near Calais. Although everything seems to be quite easy, as we know there was not only one main virtual beam path being radiated, but, due to the inevitable antenna lobes several equisignal-lines which had to be crossed (the dashed line on the map), before the first pre-marker ray was reached!

To start with, the pilot had to distinguish the correct beam A and had to keep on this virtual path until the marker signals B and after C were crossed, and until they passed the target. Crossing a certain equisignal-line was not the point that determined the moment of the bomb release, but the point at which a special computing 'X-Uhr' or 'X- Clock' had to be triggered to initiate computing of the exact release moment.

As we have noticed (and will be discussed later), several inevitable side lobes and their generated equisignal-lines had to be crossed before the chief B and C marker rays could be reached. This was done by counting the dot-dash zones being crossed.

Telefunken developed, during 1939/40, a system that became known as 'Knickebein' (Crooked leg). It consist of an antenna array of, sometimes, huge dimensions. One of the first antenna apparatus was constructed on a large rotatable undercarriage and was mounted on a circular rail track, having a diameter of approximately 90m! The vertical height was nearly 31m. The antenna array was crooked in the centre about an angle of 165°, which explains the German word: -Knick(e), and: bein, the latter stands for leg. The maximum range, at an altitude of 6,500m, was up to 500km.

Already, in autumn 1939, there were three operational stations under construction. Again, the commercial VHF (UKW) frequency band (30 to 33.3MHz), of the well known 'BA system', was being used, although certain special military equipment was being used with it. However, system components of the Lorenz system could be adopted for 'Knickebein' as well. The first attempts still had one major disadvantage, because the system still adhered to the techniques of the X-beam apparatus! [3, p.66–68]

In the archives of the Foundation for German Communication and Related Technology 1920–1945, a manual exists of a German mobile 80kW UKW (VHF) Sender, type S 561a, equivalent to Philips type DR 85. When AM modulation was used, the carrier output was reduced to 20kW. The frequency range was between 30MHz and 34MHz. For what purpose was this transmitter being ordered? One thing is certain: Philips managed to delay this project until 23-3-1944, as indicated by the signed date (and modifications) on several diagrams. I believe this transmitter had been ordered in 1940 or early 1941 for deployment with offensive X- and/or Y-beams. [12]

The X-procedure never became quite successful, but its basic idea created, after the implementation of more sophisticated technology, a variety of further systems.

We will not discuss here the knocking-out of the X- and Y-beams because this story has been told many times already.

The Y Programme

The basic principle of nearly all German 'Y-' related subjects is that distance measuring, by a controlling ground station, became possible. But it was based on Koulikoff's basic idea, patented in 1929, that it was possible to determine the distance between two wireless stations, by measuring the time delay between a periodically transmitted signal, and its instant retransmissions towards the station of origin. Today such retransmitting apparatus is called a 'transponder'. The content of the British translation was, originally, worded in the following manner:

The distance between two wireless stations may be ascertained by causing an outgoing train of waves from the first station to be automatically retransmitted from the second station back to the first, and so on, the periodic note set up at the first station being a function of the distance separating the two.

According to the present invention, an oscillating valve is interposed between the transmitting and the receiving circuits at the first or active station, and serves to interrupt or modulate the outgoing wavelength at a definite frequency, the receiving circuit being rendered sensitive only during those intervals when the transmitter is quiescent.

The distance between the local or active station and a distant or passive station is then determined by adjusting the oscillating valve or modulator until maximum reception of the retransmitted wave is obtained. This period corresponds to the time taken for a wave train to reach the distant station and return. A. Koulikoff, France, convention date was: 15th December 1929, No. 302602. [13, p. 528]

It is evident that what Koulikoff was suggesting was that, by the means of the summation of two signals, the maximum output will be reached, and so measured, when there is no phase difference between these two signals. This may be achieved by the careful control of the phase of the signal source (reference). We will discuss this subject later.

The introduction of new devices by the Luftwaffe was already underway in 1939. It was evident that more advanced systems had to be developed. Ideally only one guiding beam should be deployed, thus no extra confusing beams or signals were radiated towards the target. The aircraft merely had to keep onto this virtual track (path) and had to follow the instructions from the controlling stations.

To gain some understanding of this subject, we firstly take a brief look at the theory.

This drawing shows the content of a Y-system unit (although, the state of the art system used since 1943 is shown). From the transmitter (TX) the modulated carrier (wave) A, is sent towards an aircraft, where this signal is then retransmitted, with an offset of 1.9MHz, by the wireless set FuG 16ZY (transponder). Though, a FuG 17E was deployed over Britain during 1940/41. The re-transmitted carrier B is received by a shore station and was, after demodulation, sent on to the e-measure console. The character e stands for the German expression *Entfernung*, meaning distance. Let us return to the signal A, a fraction of the generated energy was picked-up from the antenna circuit. The envelope of this demodulated signal was being sent to the e-measure console to act as the system reference. With the DF receiver, bearings could also be taken on the retransmitted signal (B) as well.

We have now learned about the two major system components of a 'Y' station: firstly, the measuring of e (distance); and secondly, the bearing information of

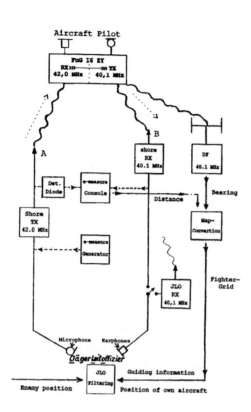

Fig. 6 Operational e-measure guidance.

the aircraft. Within a certain accuracy this expressed the position of the aircraft. In the bottom of this drawing we note the filter room of the fighter control (JLO = *Jägerleitoffizier*). The transmission of the wave A could also be used for regular radio communication (control) as well. The measuring tone and the voice modulated signal could be received simultaneously, in the aircraft radio apparatus, without disturbing the spoken content.

To understand what type of 'e-signals' were being deployed, we take a look at fig. 7. A 300Hz sinusoidal tone was used as a coarse measuring signal. The wavelength (λ) of a 300Hz signal is determined by the very simple equation: $\lambda = c/f$ (c = the velocity in a medium, f = frequency). Hence, this gives a 1,000km wavelength, which has to be divided by two, because the distance between both stations has to be passed twice (vice versa). The transfer delay in the transponder (e.g. FuG 16ZY, FuG 16ZE, FuG 17E ...) and the ground receiver were a, more or less, constant factor and were being taken into consideration.

It is evident that, for a distance of 250km between the two stations, the 300Hz signal phase has rotated over 180°. If, for instance, a precise location was needed,

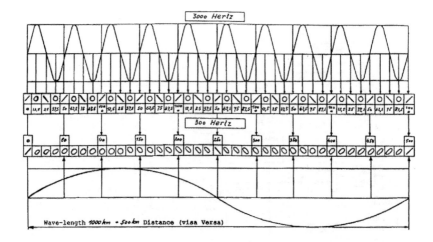

Fig. 7 Signal phase - distance correlation as was used for Y-distance measuring.

based upon the coarse measuring information, it was likely that the system accuracy was only of the order of several km. This would have been completely unacceptable, even in those days. So, a second measuring frequency of 3,000Hz could be selected, which allowed a measuring range of 50km. (For the Y-beams deployed over Britain, the more precise value was obtained using 7,500Hz.)

The demodulated reference signal, originating from the transmitter, was fed, via a cable, into the e-measuring console and passed through a calibrated tuneable time-delay circuit. This device delayed the reference signal and was fed after to the deflection plates of a CRT (cathode ray tube). The other deflection plate circuit was supplied with the received signal. On the CRT a 'Lissajous' figure was painted (there were different types of comparison displays being deployed). This procedure permitted the comparison of both signal phases. (Some examples are roughly illustrated in the middle sections of fig. 7.) There were two different e-measuring console types deployed, one was produced by Siemens and the other by the Greatz Company.

This explanation does not pretend to be comprehensive, as a great number and variety came into service during the war period.

The Y-facility allowed the (night) fighters, as well as other aircraft, to be guided (by wireless communication) onto the Allied bomber stream. But the Y-procedure also made it possible for a pilot, having left his operational area, to obtain his position on the map from ground control. For example, a night fighter might take-off during the late evening from, for instance, Munich airport. It could have been quite likely that he would have to refuel near Berlin or Hamburg then his Y-apparatus would enable him to do so by giving him his position on the map grid.

Following this brief example, let us to return to the Y-beams, as these were being used over Britain. Already in September 1940 (raid on Portland), the first Y-beams were operational.

As we have noticed in a previous discussion, the deployed guiding X-beams and the Lorenz approach beacons were both keyed in a dot-dash sequence, which sometime lead to interpretation errors. These originated due to the various virtual beams and the inevitable antenna lobes (over the British Isles).

To counter this phenomena, a newly developed, sequentially switched antenna pattern was put into service (although the first version still utilised a dot-dash sequence), as is shown in fig. 8 (see next page). The procedure was as follows: each antenna pattern radiates without interruption during a certain, equal time period. After both antenna lobes were sequentially being switched on and off, a short non-radiating interval was introduced, in a ratio of 8:8:1. This newly designed antenna array avoided the foregoing phenomena, due to a complicated switching and placement of several dipoles and its reflectors, in such a manner that: one main lobe, or a cardioid pattern was being radiated, with only a few rudimentary side lobes left. The two main radiation patterns are clearly visible in fig. 8. The virtual path is not in the centre of the forward antenna lobe, but, at the equisignal-line, just where the electromagnetic forces both have equal field strength. Consequently, the usual acoustical left-right discrimination could not be employed any longer. A special designed receiver device (FuG 28a), based on the FuG 17 aircraft wireless set, was introduced and this device could distinguish the dash sequence, and convert its data into left-right commands for the auto pilot. The silent interval (gap) was incorporated in such a manner that it could be used to synchronise the system control. The regular left-right indicator in the cockpit could still also used for this purpose as well.

The main guiding beam was transmitted by the station Anton in France. The beam was pointed at (over) the future target, before the operation was commenced. If we assume that an aircraft found the beam path as shown on the map, he had to steer himself in such a manner that he could keep on this virtual track (path). From this moment onwards several e-measure or Y-stations were being alerted to help control the flight. They could track the position of an aircraft by taking bearings and measuring the distance between the ground station and the plane. One of the requirements for the pilots was keep flying at a constant altitude, as well as at a constant ground speed. His course or track was monitored by one or more ground control stations. Let us assume the aircraft is arriving near to the point where the pre-phase of the dropping procedure had to be initiated. When this point was reached, the X-Uhr (or X-Clock) was triggered by the operators at the ground control station (the X-Uhr was mounted at the e-measure console). From now on, over a distance of approximately 18km, sequentially measuring impulse

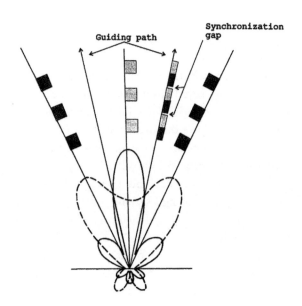

Guiding path

Synchronization gap

Fig. 8 Dash–dash keying of the Y-beam.

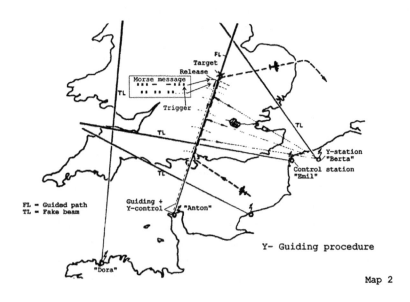

FL = Guided path
TL = Fake beam

FL
Target
Release
Morse message
Trigger

Y-station "Berta"
Control station "Emil"

Guiding + Y-control
"Anton"

"Dora"

Y- Guiding procedure

Map 2

Map 2.

trains were sent, to control the exact position on the map. From a certain point on that map, approx. 6km before the bombing target was reached, the X-Uhr switched a contact that initiated the transmission (2A2) of several pairs of dots as: ....Another section of the X-Uhr calculated the real bomb release moment and started the transmission beginning: ... - - ... (V B). The last received dot had to trigger the bomb release by the responsible crew member(s). The Morse message is shown inside the cadre on the map. [4, p.145–156]

Nearly all 'Beams' we have discussed before had as their main purpose the guidance of an aircraft on a certain virtual path but, for general navigation, the real azimuth bearing is a requirement. Many shore station beacons, worldwide, were in use for several decades, but for long-distance purposes these beacons were (due to skywave errors) often quite useless.

The determination of the azimuth by wireless

From the mid-1930s onwards, several quite sophisticated beacon apparatus were designed by, or with, the co-operation of the Lorenz Company. Two names were associated with various developments, namely Kramar and Goldmann. The latter joined the company in 1936 after leaving Siemens and Halske Central Lab. [14, p.6] In 1940 he joined the development team that worked on a project called 'Elektra', which was initiated by von Handel, who worked for the DVL as well (see previous information).

Elektra

Elektra was a long wave navigational beacon that generated guiding beams similar to those being used for the VHF Lorenz BA systems. As we have seen before, the spacing of the antenna radiators over several wavelengths creates, inevitably, a radiation pattern consisting of a number of antenna lobes. To understand the nature of these radiation patterns, we briefly take a look at the associated antenna theory.

When one vertical radiator is fed with energy, and no other electrical elements are in the vicinity, an omni-directional pattern will be generated, similar to that shown in figure 4(a).

When two vertical radiators are spaced for $D > \lambda$ and fed in phase from the same power source, the radiation pattern will create a main forward lobe perpendicular to the centre of the array base line. If we neglect the created lobes, and the two antenna radiators are now fed in counter phase, the maximum and the minimum patterns will have changed places. This is just what is happening for most of the antenna arrays, when these are being switched between main or split-beam operation (see later). The direction of rotation depends on the mutual phasing of the (two) radiators.

Until now, we have only discussed the condition of being in phase or in counter phase but, inbetween both limits there can be a changing phase shift (rotation) and hence the virtual rotation of the concerned radiation pattern. This is just what Goldmann did: he converted the Elektra apparatus into the Sonne, or Consol beacon apparatus, well know to the Allies as well.

Figure 9 shows the circular (polar) radiation pattern for a 6 λ spaced pair of vertical radiators, according to Sonnenberg [15, p.4–10] the station 'Stavanger' utilised a spacing of 5.75 λ (base length of 5.4km!), which slightly distorted the above illustrated pattern. The radiation pattern for two radiators spaced for D = 6 λ is arrived at without entering into the proof, by the wave path difference between two arriving electromagnetic waves in free space and distribute, at a certain point in the plot e.g. for d = 6 λ sin α the phase difference between the two arriving waves is n = 12 π sin α.

Figure 10 on the next page shows the principle diagram of the station 'Stavanger'. Until the 1980s, it operated with the Norwegian call sign LEC. The Germans named this station S1 when it was deployed as a Sonne beacon, and E1 when it was used as an Elektra beacon. Although I am not certain that there have not been other official German military call signs as well. [3, p. 154]

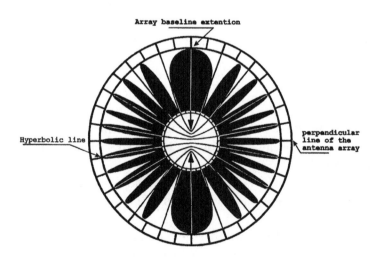

Fig. 9 Radiation pattern of an antenna array of two vertical radiators, fed in phase, with a spacing of 6 wavelength, for the horizontal plain.

The antenna radiators 2 and 3 are similar to those we have previously noticed in figure 9. Hence, their radiation pattern will be more or less similar. The motor driven phase shifter rotates for one minute from 0 to 180°. After the phase shifter has reached the connections with the feeders of antenna 2, the transmission (radiation) of antenna 2 and 3 will be stopped automatically, but the motor driven phase shifter will continue its rotation (for 60 seconds) until the new measuring sequence has been initiated (started).

Antenna 1 plays a crucial role, because its radiation pattern will now interfere with that of the two outside antennas 2 and 3. As we know, when two electromagnetic field components are equal and having the same phase, this results in the addition of both field components. When the phase difference between both field components is 180°, then both field components have to be subtracted (mathematically expressed by vector summation). Hence, theoretically, when at a certain point in free space two equal electromagnetic field components (waves) result in a particular field strength then, when one of the field components changed its phase by 180° vector subtraction of both field components will result in a cancellation (vanishing) of the resulting field. Thus, no signal will be observed. According to Stanner [16, p. 72] was the power ratio for the antennas was 1 : 1.7 : 1 (antenna 2 -1- 3), although, Goldmann stated, during his interrogation in May 1945, that the power ratio was: 250 : 1,000 : 250w. [14, p.8]

If we return to the purpose of Sonne or Consol apparatus, this is just what the aim of the centre antenna is. If we look at figure 9, it is feasible that the outside antennas, whatever their mutual phase difference is, will sequentially interfere in a positive or negative sense. This phenomena is due to the interference hyperboles which result in the so called 'Consol lines'. When the switched phase inverter, is

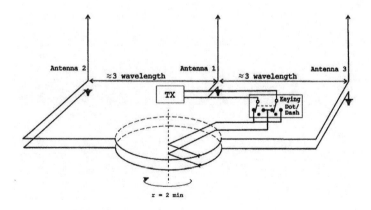

Fig. 10 Simplified diagram of the Sonne or Consol apparatus.

'keyed' in a dot or in a complementary dash sequence, the result is an on and off reception with the same content. If the shifter is changing its phase, this will obviously result in a transposition of the interference pattern in free space.

This type of beacon apparatus was only reliable at distance excess of approx. 40 km from the antenna base line, due to the influence of both ground and sky wave interference.

This figure explains, using abridged impulse diagrams, the interaction between the variable system parameters that were deployed for both Sonne and Consol. The upper row (a) shows the sequence of the dot and dash switching or keying.

Row (b) expresses the continuous rotation of the goniometer. Row (c) starts at an important point just where both field strengths are (becoming) equal and, as we have seen before, this would be the equisignal–line or point. Between Z 6 and Z 7 the resulting dot sequence had nearly disappeared.

The final row (d) shows, at the right edge of Z 5, the point were the rotating equipotential line marks the virtual bearing (equisignal or Consol line).

The bearing procedure was kept quite simple. A regular long wave receiver, equipped with a bfo (beat frequency oscillator), was the only instrument necessary on board an aeroplane or ship. The discrimination of the virtual bearing was fully acoustically executed. A special map was employed, which indicated at what equisignal or Consol line the particular bearing was taken.

An operator had to wait until the dot–dash signal sequence had vanished and no signal was being transmitted for a few seconds, followed by period with a constant (continuous) carrier. For this purpose both outside antennas 2 and 3 were

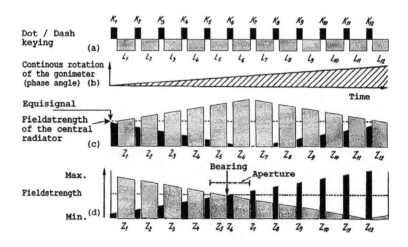

Fig. 11 Simplified dot-dash sequence of a Sonne or Consol system.

switched off from the system (electrically disconnected). A few seconds before the constant signal stopped, the station call sign was transmitted. Figure 11, row (d) shows the sequence of events if we were not at an equisignal line. A train of impulses in dot or dash sequence was received first and, after a certain period, these impulses would get weaker and weaker until no keying could be distinguished. Shortly after this, a second impulse train would begin to get louder and louder. Due to the nature of the system, the dot or dash impulses were, after passing through the equisignal-line, interchanged (see later). For the station Stavanger a total of 60 pulses of all types were transmitted. By simply counting the total dots or dashes before and after passing through the Equisignal line (Consol line), a simple calculation could be carried out with the aid of a Consol map.

The symbols for: A 1 – A 3, are similar to those used in figure 10. Each dot and dash zone (sector) is separated by an equipotential- or signal-line, just before the virtual beam rotation was being initiated. This line will start its virtual rotation in the displayed direction until it reaches the next sector or zone. Some publications, dealing with this subject, suggest that the entire radiation pattern would rotate over 180°. That certainly is not true!

According to von Handel, the average accuracy of 'Elektra' was during daylight up to 0.14° and this decreased, during night time, to approximately 2.5°. [17, p. 368]. The code name 'Sonne', what stands for: – the Sun, had to express that the system only worked reliable (optimal) during daytime.

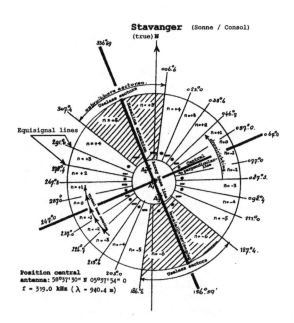

Fig. 12 Dot-dash sector patterns at the start of each virtual rotation.

Author's note: This key diagram ties in the pilot's notes and the Lennoxlove Map to the ELEKTRA system.

This map shows finally the effective range of several Sonne or Consol beacons, which were in service at the beginning of the 1950s. But, on the continent these stations had already been erected during the Second World War (The stations in Spain as well). According to Trenkle [3, p.154] there were, during the war, up to 7 Elektra – and 12 Sonne stations operational.

The British copied and built, already during the War, their own Consol apparatus although they were not able to solve all the technical problems as became obvious during the interrogations held shortly after the German had surrendered. Thus, they were very keen to interview Dr Goldamm about this and, of course, many other subjects as well. [14, p. 6–9]

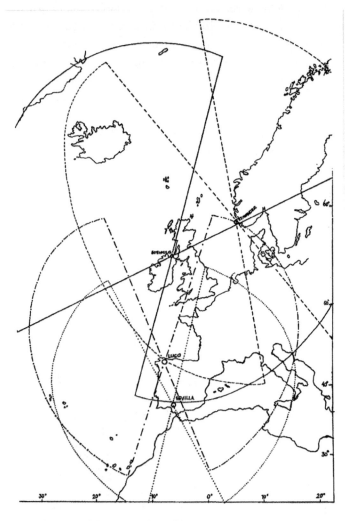

Map 3. 1,000-mile range of the Sonne/Consol beacons.

'Hermes' (although it also was called 'Hermine') could be deployed as a VHF air-navigation '*Sprechdrehbake*' or talking beacon, for instant navigational azimuth bearings, to be utilised by aircraft pilots. It consisted of two transmitters, one was deployed with a constantly spoken text, as follows: one — two — three — and so on, up to — three-five. The north marker was identified by the call sign of the particular station, as for instance, Berolina. (Berlin). [3, p. 100–102] The virtual rotation was completed in exactly 60 seconds. The general picture is outlined in figure 13.

It is evident that each number group had to be multiplied by the factor ten for angle as bearing. The bearing information was radiated from a vertically polarised dipole, placed in the centre of a rectangular group of four vertically polarised dipoles. These latter dipoles were fed via a goniometer which was connected in such a manner that the radiation pattern was cardioid shaped and was modulated so as to jam the content of the spoken information. Only that sector which was in the virtual null of the cardioid was free from jamming. The rotation of the entire antenna system was coupled with an endless film sound strip, in such a manner that the cardioid null was virtually facing toward the particular direction that corresponds with the content of the spoken message. The bearing accuracy was

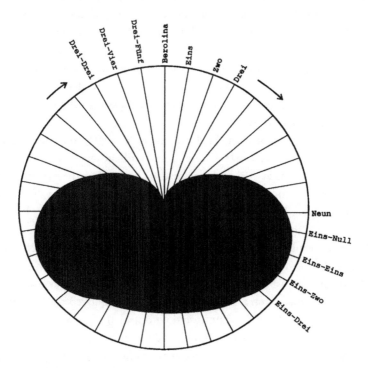

Fig. 13 'Hermes or Hermion', the 'Talking Beacon'.

limited to approximately 3° to 5° and its effective distance range was, depending on the flying altitude, up to approximately 250km. This beacon could be monitored by the remote controlled BA receiver EBL 3F in the aircraft. According to [14, p.21–22] this receiver ('Hermine' = FuG 125) had to be slightly modified (to increase the audio bandwidth) by an additional remotely controlled switch. The beacons were stationed near, or at, airports, so as to make it possible to home in on a site without the need for additional DF equipment. In my opinion this was very much an auxiliary device.

Bernhard' and 'Bernhardine

In the summer of 1935, Telefunken initiated a project to develop a navigational aid called 'Bernhard'. Its purpose was to increase the achievable azimuth bearing accuracy of radio beacons, as measured from aircraft or by other platforms. This concept proved to be able to take bearings of the order of 0.1° accuracy. The frequency utilized was 300MHz which, in those days, was a quite short wavelength (λ = 1 m). The maximum achievable transmitting power was approximately 200w being limited by the lack of adequate high power valves although, the power gain from an effective antenna array increased the power being radiated.

In 1937, a wax printer device was introduced, to store the bearing data. Ranges between 260km up to 340km could be covered (depending on flying altitude) with a bearing accuracy of approximately 0.25°. It proved that the system was not influenced by any ionospheric phenomena at all, as for instance that which occurred during twilight or sunrise.

Shortly after this, special Siemens 'Hell' printers were employed to store the bearing data on a paper tape, and bearings were logged with an accuracy of up to 0.3°.

A disadvantage was that two receivers had to be used in the system, one to receive the correct azimuth bearing and the second to demodulate the contents of the 'Hell' message. The actual bearing data was constantly reported in 'Hell' characters, in much the same way as was in use on a compass rose.

Rudolf Hell invented, at the end of the 1920s, a printer device which enabled facsimile as well as ordinary characters to be sent and then after being received, printed by means of an inked helical spindle. Every character was scanned in a particular matrix; quite often a 7 x 7 dot-matrix was employed for this purpose. Nearly every character could be transmitted within such a matrix, even Chinese! This system became very popular in Russia and in China, up until the 1970s!!

Due to the disadvantage of the need for two additional receivers on an aircraft, the Bernhard system was, more or less, put into cold storage but with the proviso that if needed such apparatus could soon brought back in to service again.

In 1941 the system was adopted by the *Luftwaffe*, but, employing the regular BA frequencies between 30 – 33.3MHz so that the ordinary EBL 3 receivers could be utilised and the system was renamed 'Berhardine'.

As we have noticed, two different signals had to be deployed and these were transmitted within the same audio frequency channel. A special auxiliary filter box separated the two demodulated audio signals.

If we look at this figure the particular system parameters are clearly visible. The two rotating beacon arrays were each fed by a separate transmitter but, mounted on the same chassis or frame. One was radiating its maximum energy in the forward direction, whereas the second antenna radiated, due to its split beam operation, its bearing null.

The receiver on board an aircraft reacted first to the modulation from the split beam radiated signal which triggered the paper transport and this was kept-on by a delaying circuit (to overcome the instant stop when the bearing null was reached). At the same time, the main forward looking antenna lobe was constantly radiating (reporting) actual 'Hell' data. This message was originated from a device that was linked to the azimuth scale of the rotating antenna array. Using an optical device coupled to a photo electric cell 'Hell' impulses were sent to the modulator of the particular transmitter.

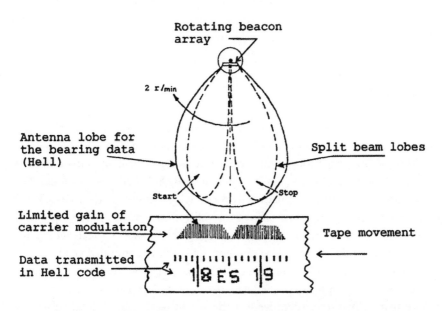

Fig. 14 'Bernhardine' FuG 120a bearing, displayed on a paper tape, by a 'Hell' printer device.

We have noticed that, there were two different audio frequencies being employed by the aircraft apparatus. In one case, for the split beam, a continuous sinusoidal tone modulated carrier was used. After reception its demodulated envelop was fed onto the upper 'Hell' printer section, which operated the transport mechanism and employed a small inked, milled edged wheel, similar to those used for regular Morse printers. Beneath a certain signal level, its printing ability vanished and at this point the bearing null was indicated (as originated by the split beam operation). At the same time (secondly) the main forward antenna lobe was constantly reporting (transmitting) the corresponding 'Hell' data. This data was sent to the lower printer section. The time interval left for an entire azimuth bearing to be taken, was between 3 and 5 seconds only.

From 1943 onwards, until the end of hostilities 2,500 printer units FuG 120, including variations were manufactured. Its average bearing accuracy was of the order of "0.5°.

The antenna arrays, together with all auxiliary apparatus, were mounted on a very heavy undercarriage that moved (rotated) on a circular rail track. Its total weight was approx. up to 100 tons! This huge device rotated twice p/m. The rail track had a diameter of 19m. To rotate a device of 100 tons, mounted on such a rail track, within 30 seconds, is quite amazing. Additional information can be found in [3, p. 94–96] and [4, p. 83–87].

Finally, these 'Hell' signals could, apparently, be activated by special command instructions, as well. This became of increasing importance after the Allies systematically jammed German ground to air communications. The very powerful 'Bernhardine' transmitters often helped to reduce the hampering effects of jamming.

Summary

Due to the number of subjects to be corralled, I have to make a very brief selection from amongst the many interesting topics. We have seen briefly some aspects of radio aids to navigation as these were initiated in Germany during the first half of this century. The initial steps were taken by Scheller's invention employing interference between radiation patterns, which could create a virtual path (bordered by two complementary sectors of dots and dashes), allowing one to distinguish between left and right. In my opinion, this was of great significance because it paved the way for developments which have continued right up until today. The Instrument Landing System (ILS) was certainly based on some aspects of these early developments, initiated by the Lorenz Company in 1907.

The main BA systems deployed in the world were nearly all based on this Lorenz principle. It is apparent that the fundamental idea of virtual path guiding, by keyed antenna diagrams, was due to be adopted for several other sorts of navigation applications.

In the 1930s, there was a growing support by the aviation authorities all over the world to engender scientific research on BA. The latter system consists of two main system components: firstly, the guidance onto the axis of the landing strip, and secondly, the creation of a virtual glide-path. Some comments on the latter subject we have not discussed, but, according to Handel's paper [5, p. 4–21], several early BA glide-path facilities were based upon the determination of a constant field strength, that had to be tracked during the approach procedure e.g. as initiated by the US Bureau of Air Commerce. This proved to be very difficult, due to a number of uncertainties, such as the conductivity of the soil, the condition of the local environment, as well as the square function of the vertical radiation pattern. Subsequently, this idea was dropped. In France, they followed a competitive route, which proved to be equally unsatisfactory.

It was Kramar who solved the glide-path problems in the early 1930s by the integration of two marker beacons into the system, at 3,000m and 300m ahead of the landing strip. These marked the two stages of the glide-path procedure. Britain and the US, both adopted the Lorenz BA system in the second half of the 1930s.

From May 1930, the Lorenz Company was owned by ITT in the USA. In my opinion this was quite significant because, as a US-owned property, it could easily obtain access to their (local) market. Telefunken never became established in the avionic market, although it built, in my opinion, the most sophisticated of devices. However, for aviation equipment, it was almost completely overshadowed by the Lorenz Company.

When the hostilities over Europe started in August 1939, the Luftwaffe had already adopted all sorts of guiding aids, based upon the Lorenz BA system. After France had surrendered, they deployed a virtual armada of guiding beams over the British Isles. Firstly, they introduced the X-beams, though, as we have noticed, these were not quite successful, due to their vulnerability to jamming signals. More notable was, perhaps, the '*Knickebein*' apparatus, but this 'X-Gerät' (and its derivates) still lacked real flexibility.

The introduction of the 'Y-beams', operating over Britain, set a technical landmark, because several entirely new system elements were employed. The introduction of dash-dash keying, in conjunction with the switching of the antenna patterns in an unconventional manner, was able to camouflage the intentions of, and the recognition of, such a virtual guiding path.

We have noticed that the symbol Y- was, nearly always, related to apparatus that enabled the measuring of distance between a ground station and a moving (or stationary) platform. It was based on Koulikoff's significant invention (recently I discovered that he either must have withdrawn his patent, or that it might have been declared confidential, as no patent reference can be traced today), which has received very little recognition since.

The introduction of Sonne or Consol lasted for nearly four decades as a navigational aid. It was used during the war by both the German navy and air force. But, since more compatible aids (satellite navigation) became available, Consol was only used on relatively small ships.

Finally, we have discussed two ingenious radio beacons. The very simple talking beacon 'Hermion' for coarse azimuth bearings, and the elaborate 'Bernhard' and the later 'Bernhardine' apparatus. The system parameters of the latter were quite sophisticated, and were widely used between 1943 and 1945 by the Luftwaffe.

It is nearly certain, although I cannot prove it here, that several aspects of German technology were adopted by the Russians. Since the collapse of the Warsaw Pact in 1989/90, many artefacts, produced in the former Soviet Union, have become available on the market, and it is apparent that many of these were influenced by German concepts. I was once able to look into the cockpit of an Ilyushin Il 62 and I was astonished that so many aviation instruments were similar in appearance to those used by the Germans in earlier days. Also, I am certain that, for nearly a decade after Germany had surrendered, France adopted several navigational aids of German origin.

Acknowledgements

Firstly, I am most grateful Fritz Trenkle for his personal support given to me right up until he died in March 1996. He was the only person in Germany, and perhaps in the entire world, who systematically studied (for over four and a half decades) the technical history of commercial electronic equipment manufactured in Germany up until 1945. No serious study is possible, on this subject, without the reference of one of his publications.

Secondly, I am thankful for Heikhaus' support. He is, although retired, still involved with the Lorenz Museum collection. He lent me several historical publications from which I was able to study references at first hand.

I wish to thank Tom Going, who kindly brought several significant references to my attention.

Finally, I wish to thank my friend Richard T. Walker for his indispensable assistance.

References

[1] *50 Jahre Lorenz, 1880–1930, Festschrift der C. Lorenz Aktiengesellschaftt* – Berlin-Tempelhof

[2] *75 Jahre Lorenz 1880–1955, Festschrift der C. Lorenz Aktiengesellschaft* Stuttgart

[3] *Die deutschen Funk-Navigations-und Funk-Führungsverfahren bis 1945* – Motorbuch Verlag, Stuttgart

[4] *Die deutschen Funkführungsverfahren bis 1945*– AEG, Ulm 1987

[5] *Probleme und Stand der Blindlandung,* Paul von Handel, Vorträge gehalten in der Wissenschaftssitzung der ordentlichen Mitglieder am 27.Januar 1939. (Sitzungsperiode, 1938/1939)

[6] A.O. Bauer, 'Receiver and transmitter development in Germany 1920–1945', 100 YEARS of RADIO, IEE Conference Publication Number 411, London

[7] Die Ultrakurzwellenbake und ihre praktischen Ergebnisse als Landefunkfeuer, E. Kramar, Lorenz Berichte, NR. 1/2 Juni 1938, Vorgetragen von E. Kramar vor dem Institute of Radio Engineers, Section Washington, am 30.April 1937, p. 4–16

[8] Zum Thema: Gleitweglandung, E. Kramar, (Navigationslaboratorium) Lorenz Berichte, NR.3/4 Dezember, 1939, p. 96–100. UKW-Markierungszeichen als Funkhilfe für die Flugnavigation, R. v. Ottental (Mitteilung des Navigations-Laboratorium), p. 101–105

[9] Funk-Landegerät Fu Bl 2, Geräte-Handbuch, Nov. 1943, D. (Luft) T. 4058 (L 35) [10] R.V. Jones, *Most Secret War, British Scientific Intelligence.*

[11] Alfred Price, *Instruments of Darkness: The Struggle for Radar Supremacy*

[12] 80 kW U.K.W. Sendeanlage (Mot.), = DR 85. Ausgabe 4780. Beschreibung 2640 D date 20-3-'44 (Z 535)

[13] Experimental Wireless & The Wireless Engineer September 1929 p. 528

[14] The I.T.T. Siemens and Robert Bosch Organisations CIOS rep. File No. XXXI-38

[15] G.J. Sonnenberg, Moderne Radio-Navigatiemiddelen. Den Haag 1950

[16] Leitfaden der Funkortnung, Walter Stanner, Deutsche Radar-Verlagsgesellschaft m.b.H. 1957

[17] Peilung (Direction Finding), Paul von Handel, Das Elektron 1947 Heft 10/11

[18] 120 Watt UKW Leitstrahlsender AS 3, Beschreibung Nr. 75/710. Nov. 1942, C.Lorenz AG Berlin-Tempelhof. (LD 43)

[19] Y- Kampf ZWB 1501,(Z 321- ZR 408) (...) Archive references, of the: Foundation Centre for German Communication

NOTES

Introduction

1 We wonder about the veracity of this statement given that in Roy Conyers Nesbit's *Rudolf Hess: Myths and Reality* (Surrey: Sutton, 1999) there is a November 1940 letter from Hess to Ilse, telling her of his intention to make a flight. Moreover, later commentators have alluded to the active involvement of Ilse Hess in her husband's career. (See *The Goebbel Diaries*)

2 The authors have extensively researched the publication of this article. In 1943, the *American Mercury* was owned and edited by L.E. Spivak, whose archives are held in Washington, USA. Whilst there are detailed records of the payments made to contributing authors, in the case of the Hess article there is no such entry, simply marked 'anonymous'. Who the source was remains a mystery

3 J.R. Rees, *The Case of Rudolf Hess*, Heineman, London, 1947

4 Ilse Hess, *Prisoner of Peace*, Britons Publishing Co., London, 1954

5 James Leasor, *Rudolf Hess: The Uninvited Envoy*, George Allen & Unwin Ltd, London, 1962

6 James Douglas-Hamilton, *Motive for a Mission*, Macmillan, London, 1971

7 Derek Wood, *Attack Warning Red*, MacDonald & James, London, 1976

8 Wolf Rüdiger Hess, *My Father, Rudolf Hess*, W.H. Allen, London, 1986

9 Hansard, volume 208, column 823

10 John McBlain, *Rudolf Hess: The British Conspiracy*, Jema Publications, Moulton, 1994; John Harris and Mei Trow, *Hess: The British Conspiracy*, Andre Deutsch, London, 1999

11 Picknett, Prince and Prior, *Double Standards*, Little Brown, London, 2001

12 John Harris, *Rudolf Hess: The British illusion of Peace*, Jema Publications, Moulton, 2010

13 *My Father Rudolf Hess*, op. cit., p. 90

14 Albert Speer, *Inside the Third Reich*, Phoenix, London 1995, p. 252

15 FO1093/11

16 *The Case of Rudolf Hess*, op. cit., p. 19

17 FO1093/11, date 28.05.1941

18 *The Case of Rudolf Hess*, op. cit., p. 168

Part 1

1   13 May 1941
2   To the authors' knowledge this letter is not in the public domain. Ilse Hess also had a copy, but again her copy 'was lost in 1945 when nearly all my correspondence of those years went', *Prisoner of Peace*, op. cit., p. 27
3   The two men had lunched together on 10 May 1941
4   *The Case of Rudolf Hess*, op. cit.
5   *Ibid.* – tells of a 1937 prostatis and a general fear of cancer. Hess had also pursued alternative medicines. He brought a number of remedies with him when he landed in Scotland
6   Hess is often pictured as chairman of the 1938 International Homeopathy Conference in Berlin
7   Hess won the 'Round the Zugspitz' air race in 1934. He was a close friend of Willy Messerschmitt and his technical director, Theo Croneiss
8   Hess had been born in Alexandria, Egypt, in 1894. His father ran an import business and the family retained property in Wunsiedel, Bavaria; hence the choice of eventual burial plot
9   David Irving, *Hess the Missing Years*, Macmillan, London, 1987
10   We cite the treatment of the Haushofer family
11   Examination, 13 May 1941
12   *The Case of Rudolf Hess*, op. cit., appendix
13   Report to tribunal, 20 November 1945: 'Rudolf Hess is not insane at the present time ...'
14   *Inside the Third Reich*, op. cit.
15   *Ibid.*
16   *Hess the Missing Years*, op. cit.
17   *Halder diary*, Presidio, Novarto, 4 June 1941
18   Werner Baumbach, *Broken Swastika*, Robert Hale Ltd, London, 1976
19   *Ibid.*
20   C. Paul Vincent, *The Politics of Hunger*, Ohio University Press, Ohio, 1986
21   Corni and Gies, *Brot, Butter, Kanonen*, Wiley VCH, Weinheim, 1997, p. 19
22   Erker, *Ernahrungskrise und Nachkriegsgesellschaft*, p. 24
23   Alfred Smith, *Hitler's Reluctant War*, Book Guild, Lewes, 2001
24   *Hitler's Army Adjutant*, 1938–43
25   James Owen, *Nuremberg: Evil on Trial*, Headline, London, 2006
26   Laurence Rees, *The Nazis: A Warning from History*, BBC Television
27   Richard Breitman, *The Architect of Genocide*, Pimlico, London, 2004
28   James Douglas-Hamilton, *Motive for a Mission*, Macmillan, London, 1971
29   *Hitler's Army Adjutant*, 1938–43
30   Vernon Bogdanor, *The British Constitution*, The British Academy, Oxford, 2003

31 Commons public administration committee, *The Guardian*, 21 October 2003

32 1971

33 Hamilton had attended a dinner at the 1936 Olympics, at which Hess was present. Hamilton denied meeting Hess personally; others, including Sir Henry 'Chips' Channon, stated that the two had in fact met. Hamilton had spent much time in Europe during the 1930s, so it would not be too much of a surprise if such a meeting had taken place at some point

34 Charles I was actually imprisoned by Hamilton in Pendennis Castle, 1644

35 Hilary L. Rubenstein, *Captain Luckless: James Douglas Hamilton (1603–1649)*

36 The same could be said of the 14th Duke of Hamilton

37 W. Blackstone, *Commentaries on the Laws of England*, Clarendon Press, 1765

38 A. Douglas-Hamilton, *Lord of the Skies*, Lulu, 2011, p. 99

39 The duke holds thirteen subsidiary titles; ten Scottish, two English and one British (created after 1707).

40 The infamous 'Box: 24' of the Monkton papers

41 Richard Overy, *The Battle*, Penguin, London, 2000

42 Peter Fleming, *Invasion 1940*, Rupert Hart Davis, London, 1957

43 The Haushofer code/nickname for Rudolf Hess: *Tomodaichi* is Japanese for 'friend'

44 The Grunwalder Forest between Munich and Salzberg

45 Presumably Britain

46 Presumably Hitler, but had Hitler already made the decision to postpone the invasion?

47 A neutral location

48 General Sir Ian Hamilton

49 Presumably, the Duke of Hamilton, though possibly one of his brothers?

50 In 1940, Lisbon celebrated 400 years of independence from Spain

51 The Duke of Kent attended on behalf of Britain. Note the dismissive description of the duke

52 Gallspach is an area of Upper Austria

53 The affairs of ethnic Germans abroad

54 We believe this is important. This seems to imply that the Haushofers and Hess believe that Mrs Roberts does not reside in the United Kingdom. Who was giving this impression and why?

55 This is presumably the Lisbon address given in the previous letter

56 This, too, appears to underline the supposition that Mrs Roberts is in Lisbon

57 This now introduces a second option, that of the neutral intermediary, not Mrs Roberts, but someone who is seen to be neutral by both sides and 'who has some business over there'

58 Mrs Roberts is certainly not an 'official channel'

59 Essentially postal details

60   We are not surprised that the name of the 'neutral intermediary' is not given at this stage. We think the identity will become clearer as the story unfolds

61   Apparent evidence of Haushofer's interest in astrology

62   Bad Godesberg is on the Rhine, south of Koblenz

63   This is a record of the start of Albrecht's involvement directly with Rudolf Hess

64   Apparently an observation made by Haushofer to Hess

65   The authors are absolutely sure the answer to this question is yes. The more relevant question is how?

66   The fear of the blockade is a theme, almost an obsession. It was this that brought Germany to her knees in 1918

67   On 3 September 1940, the British and US governments concluded an agreement for fifty destroyers in exchange for the US acquisition of naval bases in the Caribbean. The British also agreed not to scuttle the fleet in the event of invasion

68   This is a reflection of the criticism of the German Foreign Office and von Ribbentrop in particular

69   In other words, no peace is possible whilst Hitler is the leader

70   This statement has often been quoted as evidence of Haushofer's naivety. On the contrary, in our view it is wholly correct

71   Ironically, so as not to be accused later of treachery. Haushofer was executed in April 1945.

72   Clearly, Hess and Hitler had been debating the issue. The official line is that Hess was acting alone

73   Douglas Douglas-Hamilton

74   Mrs Roberts

75   The memorandum already analysed

76   A summary of the reservations already expressed to Rudolf Hess, albeit in more stringent terms

77   Evidence exists to support this view

78   Evidence of the closeness of the Haushofer/Hamilton relationship

79   We think this is the first time a Haushofer/Hamilton meeting was mooted

80   This obviously assumes that Hamilton would have to ask for permission to travel to Portugal. This action would also implicate his superiors

81   A realistic assessment. If the letter route does not work then chances are neither will the neutral intermediary

82   This reiterates the 'neutral intermediary' route, which is now developing into a third party, who may not even know the Duke of Hamilton

83   A return to the 'official channels' again?

84   The Duke of Hamilton

85   There had been two military planning conferences at the Berghof, 29–31 July 1940, where the proposed invasion had been discussed amongst Hitler and his generals

86 The Blitz is usually accepted to have lasted from 7 September 1940–10 May 1941

87 See letter – Hess to Haushofer, p. 44.

88 As did Peter Allen (Martin's father) in *The Crown and the Swastika*, Hale, London, 1983

89 Commenced 25 November 1939 – Charles Entwhistle to author, 13 October 1999

90 The British Postal Museum, London

91 See Picknett, Prince and Prior, *Double Standards*, Little Brown, London 2001

92 PRO file FO1093/11

93 Coo 2188-89

94 Stammers of RAF intelligence wrote to Hamilton on 26 February 1941

95 PRO/KV235, Robertson to Air Vice Marshal Medhurst

96 James Douglas-Hamilton, *The Truth about Rudolf Hess*, Mainstream, Edinburgh, 1993

97 'D' for destruction

98 Bevir was Churchill's private secretary. Playfair was a financial expert and subsequent permanent under-secretary at the War Office

99 C.J. Burckhardt, *Meine Danziger Mission: 1937–1939*, Verlag Callwey, Munich, 1960

100 Edmund Ironside (1880–1959) would appear an odd choice for Hitler to make. In November 1938, he was appointed to the role of Governor of Gibraltar. In September 1939, he became Chief of the Imperial General Staff

101 In August 1939, Roger Makins was an up-and-coming English diplomat who eventually became Ambassador to the US in 1953

102 French diplomat 1892–1971

103 A duplicate of the intent expressed in the Hess/Haushofer letter of September 1940 and the use of a neutral intermediary

104 Who this could be will be discussed later

105 Presumably so as to safeguard the integrity of the International Red Cross

106 A clear statement of his standing at this time

107 The Royal Philatelic Society

108 *Double Standards*, op. cit.

109 James Douglas-Hamilton, *The Truth about Rudolf Hess*, Mainstream, Edinburgh, 1993. Hamilton states:'Whilst in the custody of the Home Guard, a member of the Polish Consulate from Glasgow, named Battaglia, asked the prisoner questions …'

110 Another coincidence. Mr Fairweather is Douglas Fairweather, the son of Sir Wallace Fairweather (1859–1939), who was yet another Scottish aeronautical pioneer! In 1944, he was killed in an air crash, aged 53

111 Letter to JTGH from Dr Suchcitz – The Polish Institute and Sikorski Musuem, 27 January 2006

112 Burckhardt actually details his role as High Commissioner in *Meine Danziger Mission: 1937–1939*. Battaglia is not mentioned

113 Letter to JTGH from the Sikorski Institute, 27 January 2006

114 Letter to JTGH from Jakub Forst-Battaglia, 6 July 2007

115 HO405/5008

116 28 October 1947

117 KV235, 17 May 1941: 'How on earth he got to know of Hess's arrival … I simply cannot conceive.'

118 Letter to JTGH from Wasyl Sydorenko, University of Toronto Library, 28 April 2008

119 HO405/5008

120 University of Basle, Burckhardt archive, system number 000032562

121 Marian Chodaki was the liaison official between the Senate and Government, 1936–1939

122 Sikorski Institute – Reference A11.474/2/24

123 Sikorski Institute – Reference A42/446

124 HO405/5008. Hardly surprising as Poland had again lost its independence

125 Jakub Forst-Battaglia to JTGH, 6 July 2007

126 Duff Cooper had resigned over the Munich Agreement of 1938

127 Diana Cooper had met Burckhardt previously at Venetia Montagu's house

128 Hodder & Stoughton, London 1984

129 Hamish Hamilton, London 1948

130 Died on 27 July 2006

131 The 'Passport Office System' was destroyed when Europe was overrun by the Nazis

132 The publishers

133 Ottoline Morrell was a prominent member of the Bloomsbury Group. Phillip Morrell was a Liberal politician. As a result of this association, Borenius met artists such as Roger Fry, Augustus John, Bertrand Russell, Clive Bell and Henry Lamb. Ottoline Morrell was also cousin to Elizabeth Bowes Lyon

134 Frederick Leverton Harris was a Member of Parliament and benefactor to the Fitzwilliam Museum

135 RIIA8/758

136 Anthony Cave-Brown, *C*, Collier Books, New York, 1987

137 Nigel West, *MI6: British Secret Intellingence Service Operations 1909–45*, Weidenfeld & Nicholson, London, 1983

138 'The Annunciation and Expulsion from Paradise' by Giavanni de Paolo (1435) being such an example. It is now in the National Gallery of Art, Washington, USA.

139 Haushofer, it will be remembered, had addressed the Royal Institute in London

140 *Motive for a Mission* and *The Truth about Rudolf Hess*, op. cit.

141 *Daily Telegraph*, 27 December 2004

142 Lutz was Hess' security officer and was interrogated by the Gestapo after the flight

Part 2

1   Derek Wood, *Attack Warning Red*, p. 2
2   Therefore, the correct description, for example, is a Bf 110, whereas the later aircraft is a Me 210.
3   At sea level, for five minutes maximum.
4   At sea level for one minute.
5   James Leasor, *The Uninvited Envoy*, Allen & Unwin, London, 1962, p. 11
6   Wolf Hess, *My Father Rudolf Hess*, W.H. Allen, 1986, p. 147
7   James Douglas-Hamilton, *Motive for a Mission*, op. cit., p. 154
8   Dr Hugh Thomas argues that there was no evidence of scar tissue on the 'Spandau Hess'. We would point the reader towards the 1945 medical examination of Hess by a Major Kelley. His report reads – Chest: 2 well-healed linear scars ⅛in apart are present. Thomas interprets these as evidence of a self-inflicted knife wound while in British captivity. Roy Conyers Nesbit also cites evidence to refute Thomas in the introduction to *The Truth About Rudolf Hess*
9   John Vasco and Peter D. Cornwell, *Zerstörer*, JAC Publications, Norwich
10 Heinz Mankau and Peter Petrick, *Messerschmitt Bf 110/Me210/Me410*, Schiffer, Atglen, 2003
11 *Muhlenbua und Industrie AG*, Braunschweig
12 Now in the Imperial War Museum, London and Museum of Flight, East Fortune, Scotland
13 *Rudolf Hess: Myths and Reality*, op. cit.
14 *Hess the Missing Years*, op. cit.
15 *Rudolf Hess: Myths and Reality*, op. cit.
16 Stör was tasked with delivering Bf 109s to the Japanese military
17 *The Case of Rudolf Hess*, op. cit.
18 Conyers Nesbit in *Rudolf Hess: Myths and Reality* tells of Major Graham Donald finding a fuel tank which '… only had 3–4 gallons in it …' This we now know could not have been the auxiliary oil tank
19 Thanks to Peter Devitt at the RAF Museum, Hendon
20 The camera was later returned to the Hess family
21 Email to the authors, 26 July 2012
22 *Lord of the Skies*, op. cit.
23 Group Captain 'Dickie' Richardson, *Man is not Lost*, Airlife Publishing, Shrewsbury, 1997
24 Peter Padfield, *Flight for the Führer*, Cassell & Co., London, 2001
25 R.H. Melville to the Duke of Hamilton, 22 May 1941
26 J.L. Cruickshank, 'Sheetlines No. 72', The Charles Close Society
27 Hess had contemplated a 'reverse Lindbergh' flight, Europe to the USA, in the 1930s

28 *Prisoner of Peace*, op. cit.

29 *Goebbels Diary*, 17 May 1941

30 *Hess the Missing Years*, op. cit.

31 A null area is created by a marked fall in signal strength on account of the loop aerial being in the same plane as the radio beacon

32 Arthur Bauer, email to the authors, April 2012

33 Despite extensive research, we have yet to find an Elektra chart relating to Husum. This is despite a Europe-wide search, including radio museums, U-boat museums and the Bundesarchiv

34 The Butt Report of August 1941 states that, of attacking aircraft, typically only one in three would be within 5 miles of the target

35 Helmut Kaden 1989 lecture to the Rudolf Hess Society

36 Professor Phil Judkins, citing Trenkel

37 The FuG 10EL instruction manual, p. 161

38 *Ten Days that Saved the West*, op. cit.

39 In 1995, John Costello died aged 52. He was found dead on a flight to Miami, Florida, after having eaten shellfish thirty-six hours earlier. From him we learned the important lesson never to assume evidence – go and see it

40 *The Truth about Rudolf Hess*, op. cit.

41 Felicity Ashbee died in 2008, aged 96

42 *Ten days that Saved the West*, op. cit.

43 There is a PRO file which demonstrates the fact that the Ottercops Moss radar was struggling to ascertain the altitude of incoming aircraft

44 *Ten Days that Saved the West*, op. cit., p. 6

45 Boscombe Down reports from 1941, see www.spitfireperformance.com

46 *The Truth about Rudolf Hess*, op. cit., p. 16

47 Andrews retired from the RAF in April 1945 and died in 1989. Prior to his death he lived in Cookham, Berkshire

48 *Museum Without Walls*, www.west-dunbarton.gov.uk

49 The Scottish Office report details over 1,000 deaths

50 Les Taylor, *Luftwaffe over Scotland*, Whittles Publishing, Dunbeath, 2010

51 No. 602 (City of Glasgow) was such a squadron

52 Clydesdale married in 1937, McIntyre in 1935. Clydesdale loaned McIntyre his DeHavilland Leopard Moth to travel on honeymoon

53 It should be remembered that there are stories of Clydesdale crashing a Hawker Hart at Dungavel

54 Dougal McIntyre cites his father's secondment to No. 12 Squadron RAF, in 1932 the means by which his reputation as an exceptional pilot was assured

55 *The Pilot's Book of Everest*, The Bodley Head, London, 1935

56 This failed to materialise through lack of funding

57 Company House number: 18652

58 Pre-1920, there had been two companies called Scottish Aviation Limited

59 *Prestwick in the 1940s*, Kyle & Carrick District Leisure Services, Ayr 1992

60 W.E. Nixon of De Havilland was appointed chairman of the company

61 Director of William Baird Limited, a mining company. He also lived in Prestwick

62 Dougal McIntyre mentions monthly flights from June to November 1935

63 Clydesdale and his brother flew to Berlin in 1933

64 Jonathan Falconer, *RAF Fighter Airfields of World War 2*, Ian Allan, Shepperton 1993

65 ATFERO became Ferry Command in July 1941

66 File AIR 28/40. The authors do not think that this is contentious and most authors rely upon the statement. The ability and intention of the aircraft we will discuss later. William Cuddie was killed in 1943 whilst serving with No. 46 Squadron (From the Commonwealth War Graves Commission)

67 Interview Dougal McIntyre, 3 May 2009

68 www.bbrclub.org

69 Colin Dobinson, *AA Command*, Methuen, London, 2001

70 As shown on the ROC map

71 Richard Deacon, *The British Secret Service*, Grafton, London, 1991

72 Peter Fleming, *The Flying Visit*, Jonathan Cape, London, 1940

73 For full details please see http//www.rcahms.gov.uk/hamilton

74 Alfred Douglas-Hamilton, 13th Duke, died 16 March 1940 at Ferne House, Donhead St Andrew, Wiltshire

75 The A743, Muirkirk to Strathaven road

76 Courtesy of Graham Bartlett, a Library Information Officer at the Meteorological Office, June 2008

77 'The Kennels' is a single-storey house at the top of what was the airstrip

78 *The Messerschmitt Bf 110*, Profile Publications, pre-1971

79 *Rudolph Hess Myths and Reality*, op. cit., Appendix F

80 Captain E.M. Brown, *Wings of the Luftwaffe*, Airlife, Shrewsbury, 1987

81 RAF Farnborough, the oldest military airfield in the UK, was the home of the enemy aircraft evaluation unit during the Second World War

82 The four sons of the 13th Duke of Hamilton

83 Hamilton family records

84 Letter from Mrs Baird detailing the crash at Floors Farm, *History Today*

Part 3

1 *Prisoner of Peace*, op. cit.

2 *The Case of Rudolf Hess*, op. cit.

3 Stephen McGinty, *Camp Z*, Quercus, London, 2011

4 Hess letter to wife, 9 May 1948

5 A Ludolph model OK 38H

6   Letter to Ilse Hess, 9 May 1948

7   This reported that Hess had asked for the details of a radius curve flown on an autopilot. The memo refers to the turn as regulated by the Siemens K4ü – this was 1° or 2° per second. A request was also made concerning the calibration of the Pitot tube over a distance of 410km, the same distance as the flight from A to B over the North Sea.

8   *Attack Warning Red*, op. cit.

9   Roy Conyers Nesbit and George Van Acker: '… He pushed the control column forward and went into a shallow dive from 5,000 metres, increasing speed and streaking down to a very low level …'.

10 Hugh Thomas: '… He roared across the Border country at tree top level, doing more than 300mph …'

11 *Prisoner of Peace*, op. cit.

12 *Attack Warning Red*, op. cit.

13 Email to authors from RAF Museum, 24 January 2013

14 *Hitler, Hess and Churchill* – Peter Padfield – Icon – London, 2013.

15 Letter to authors from Air Historical Branch 13th October 2013.

16 Public records office kew - Air 50/61

17 Major Graham Donald had spent time in Munich on account of his engineering business.

18 *Goebbel Diaries*, 17 May 1941

Part 4

1   We add the caveat that the landing was not actually recorded in the ORB

2   Luftwaffe reconnaissance photograph, February 1941

3   See earlier chart, 150ft at ROC West Kilbride

4   Johannes Steel, article in *Liberty* magazine, 12 July 1941

5   Wulf Schwarzwaller, *Rudolf Hess: The Deputy*, Quartet, London, 1988

6   von Hassell Diaries, 18 May 1941

7   Sir Samuel Hoare, *Ambassador on Special Mission*, Collins, London 1946

8   Keith Jeffrey, *MI6: The History of the Secret Intelligence Service*, Bloomsbury, London, 2010

9   Email to John Harris, 8 March 2011

10 Former Director of MI6

11 Book launch at Bletchley Park, 21 November 2010.

12 See *Rudolf Hess: The British Illusion of Peace*, p. 224

13 Polskie Radio, 29 April 2011

14 www.Ambail.org.uk: '… September 1941 when the first ward was opened to the public

15 North of Scotland Newspapers, 1994

16 Air 28/784 (Sumburgh) and Air 28/1570 (Wick)

17 7th Earl of Lonsdale, thank you

18 Some RAF aircrew training during the war was carried out in Canada

19 *The Times*, 23 November 1936

20 He also owned the Calypso, made famous in the 1950s and 1960s by Jacques Cousteau

21 www.thefew.info

22 A German diplomat who left the London Embassy in 1938

23 See *Double Standards*

24 Sir Henry 'Chips' Channon, *Diaries*, Phoenix, London, 1996

25 Gerhard Engel, *At the Heart of the Reich*, Greenhill, London, 2005, entry for 11 May 1941

BIBLIOGRAPHY

Air Ministry, *Atlantic Bridge* (London: HMSO, 1945)

Allen, Martin, *The Hitler/Hess Deception* (London: Harper Collins, 2003)

Baker, David, *Adolf Galland* (London: Windrow & Green, 1996)

Baumbach, Werner, *Broken Swastika* (London: Hale, 1986)

Bird, Eugene, *Rudolf Hess in Spandau* (London: Sphere, 1984)

Birkenhead, Earl of, *Halifax* (London: Hamish Hamilton, 1965)

Bloom, Ursula, *The House of Kent* (London: Robert Hale, 1969)

Bogdanor, Victor, *The British Constitution in the Twentieth Century* (Oxford: The British Academy, 2005)

Bosch, Robert GMBH, *Einspritz Anlage* (Stuttgart, 1940)

Boyle, Andrew, *The Climate of Treason* (London: Hutchinson, 1979)

Breitman, Richard, *Official Secrets* (London: Penguin, 1998)

————, *The Architect of Genocide* (London: Pimlico, 2004)

Brendon, Piers, *The Dark Valley* (London: Cape, 2000)

Brettingham, Laurie, *Beam Benders* (Earl Shilton: Midland, 1997)

Bron, Barwa, *Wojsko Polskie* (Warsaw: Interpress, 1984)

Brooke, Alan, *The War Diaries* (London: Weidenfeld & Nicholson, 2001)

Bruce Lockhart, R.H., *Memoirs of a British Agent* (London: Pan, 2002)

Burckhardt, Carl J., *Meine Danziger Mission* (Munich: Callwey, 1960)

Carter, Miranda, *Anthony Blunt* (London: Macmillan, 2001)

Cave Brown, Anthony, *'C'* (New York: Macmillan, 1987)

Channon, Henry, *The Diaries of Sir Henry Channon* (London: Phoenix, 1996)

Charmley, John, *Duff Cooper* (London: Weidenfeld & Nicholson, 1986)

Chavril, *Undercover Addresses of World War 2* (Abernethy: Chavril, 1992)

Ciano, Galeazzo, *Diaries 1937–1943* (London: Phoenix, 2002)

Collingham, Lizzie, *The Taste of War* (London: Penguin, 2012)

Colville, John, *The Churchillians* (London: Weidenfeld & Nicholson, 1981)

Colvin, Ian, *Chief of Intelligence* (London: Gollancz, 1951)

Conyers Nesbit, Roy, *Coastal Command in Action* (Stroud: Sutton, 1997)

Costello, John, *10 Days that Saved the West* (London: Bantam Press, 1991)

Cross, Colin, *Life with Lloyd George* (London: Macmillan, 1975)

Cross, Robin, *Fallen Eagle* (London: Caxton, 2000)

Davidson, Basil, *Special Operations Europe* (Newton Abbott: Readers Union, 1982)

Deacon, Richard, *British Secret Service* (London: Grafton, 1991)

Delmer, Sefton, *The Black Boomerang* (London: Secker & Warburg, 1962)

Der Reichminister der Luftfahrt, Manual Bf110 E (Berlin, 1940)

————, *Manual FUG10* (Berlin, 1941)

————, *Manual DB601N&P* (Berlin, 1940)

Dietrich, Otto, *The Hitler I Knew* (New York: Skyhorse, 2010)

Bibliography

Dobinson, Colin, *AA Command* (London: Methuen, 2001)

Dorpalen, Andreas, *The World of General Haushofer* (New York: Farrar & Rinehart, 1942)

Douglas-Hamilton, Alasdair, *Lord of the Skies* (Lulu, 2011)

Douglas-Hamilton, James, *Motive for a Mission* (London: Macmillan, 1971)

———, James, *The Truth About Rudolf Hess* (Edinburgh: Mainstream, 1993)

Engel, Gerhard, *At the Heart of the Reich* (London: Greenhill, 2005)

Entwhistle, Charles, *Undercover Addresses* (Perth: Chavril Press, 1992)

Falconer, Jonathan, *RAF Fighter Airfields of World War 2* (Surrey: Allan, 1993)

Fellowes, P.F.M., *First Over Everest* (London: Bodley Head, 1935)

Fleming, Peter, *Invasion 1940* (London: Hart-Davis, 1957)

———, Peter, *The Flying Visit* (London: Cape, 1941)

Foot, M.R.D., *MI9* (London: Book Club, 1979)

Frayn Turner, John, *The Battle of Britain* (London: BCA, 1999)

Geydye, G.E., *Fallen Bastions* (London: Left Book Club, 1939)

Goebbels, Joseph, *The Goebbels Diaries* (London: Hamish Hamilton, 1948)

Griffiths, Richard, *Fellow Travellers of the Right* (London: Constable, 1980)

Halder, Franz, *War Diary* (Novarto: Presidio, 1988)

Hamilton, Sir Ian, *The Commander* (London: Hollis & Carter, 1957)

Hammond, Reginald, *Northern Scotland* (London: Ward Lock, 1980)

Harris & Trow, *Hess: The British Conspiracy* (London: Andre Deutsch, 1993)

Harris, John, *Rudolf Hess: The British Illusion of Peace* (Moulton: JEMA, 2010)

Hart-Davis, Duff, *Peter Fleming* (London: Cape, 1975)

Haushofer, Albrecht, *Moabit Sonnets* (Toronto: Norton, 1978)

Hayward, James, *Myths and Legends of the Second World War* (Stroud: Sutton, 2004)

Heinzelmann, Martin, *Gottingen im Luftkreig* (Verlag die werkstatt, 2003)

Henderson, Diana, *The Lion and the Eagle* (Dunfermline: Cualann Press, 2001)

Hess, Ilse, *Prisoner of Peace* (Germany: Druffel Verlag, 1954)

Hess, Wolf, *My Father Rudolf Hess* (London: W.H. Allen, 1986)

Hinsley & Stripp, *Code Breakers* (Oxford: Oxford University Press, 1994)

HMSO, *Roof Over Britain* (London, 1943)

Hoare, Samuel, *Ambassador on Special Mission* (London: Collins, 1946)

Home, Lord, *The Way the Wind Blows* (London: Collins, 1976)

Hudsons Historic Houses and Gardens, *Heritage House* (Ketteringham, 2009)

Hutchinson, *British German and Italian Aircraft* (London: Hutchinson, 1941)

Imperial War Museum, *Sonderfahndungsliste GB* (reprinted London, 1989)

Irving, David, *Accident* (London: William Kimber, 1967)

———, David, *Hitlers War* (London: Papermac, 1983)

———, David, *The Virus House* (Focalpoint, 2010)

Jeffrey, Keith, *MI6* (London: Bloomsbury, 2010)

Jenkins, Roy, *Churchill* (London: Macmillan, 2001)

Jerrold, Walter, *Lord Roberts of Kandahar* (London: Partridge & Co., 1901)

Jones, R.V., *Most Secret War* (London: Coronet, 1978)

Kaspar, *Teach Yourself Air Navigation* (London: EUP, 1942)

Kershaw, Ian, *Hitler 1889–1936* (London: Allen Lane, 1998)

Kilzer, Louis, *Churchill's Deception* (New York: Simon & Schuster, 2004)

Kirkpatrick, Ivone, *The Inner Circle* (London: Macmillan, 1959)

Lamb, Richard, *Churchill as War Leader* (London: Bloomsbury, 1993)

Leasor, James, *Rudolf Hess: The Uninvited Envoy* (London: Allen & Unwin, 1962)

Leckie, Ross, *Scipio* (London: Abacus, 1999)

Lee, Celia, *Jean, Lady Hamilton* (Celia Lee, 2001)

Lee, John, *A Soldier's Life* (London: Pan, 2000)

Logue & Conradi, *King's Speech* (London: Quercus, 2010)

Luftwaffe, *BF110 g-2 Flugzeug – Handbuch* (Germany, 1943)

Mackinder, H.J., *The Rhine* (London: Chatto & Windus, 1908)

MacLean, Hector, *Fighters in Defence* (Glasgow: Squadron, 1999)

MacMillan, Margaret, *Peacemakers* (London: John Murray, 2002)

Mankau & Petrick, *Bf110/Me210/Me410* (Atglen: Schiffer, 2003)

Marks, Leo, *Between Silk and Cyanide* (London: HarperCollins, 1998)

Masterman, J.C., *The Double Cross System* (London: History Book Club, 1972)

Mazower, Mark, *Hitler's Empire* (London: Penguin, 2009)

McBlain, John, *Rudolf Hess: The British Conspiracy* (Moulton: Jema, 1994)

McCormick, Donald, *The Life of Ian Fleming* (London: Peter Owen, 1993)

McGinty, Stephen, *Camp Z* (London: Quercus, 2011)

McIntyre, Dougal, *Prestwick's Pioneer* (Bognor Regis: Woodfield, 2004)

Mondey, David, *Axis Aircraft of World War 2* (London: Chancellor, 1996)

Moorhead, Caroline, *Dunant's Dream* (London: HarperCollins, 1999)

Myerscough, W., *Air Navigation Simply Explained* (Bath: Pitmans, undated)

Nesbit & Van Acker, *The Flight of Rudolf Hess* (Stroud: Sutton, 1999)

Nowak, Jan, *Courier from Warsaw* (Detroit: Wayne State Press, 1982)

Osborn, Patrick, *Operation Pike* (Westport: Greenwood Press, 2000)

Overy, Richard, *Bomber Command* (London: HarperCollins, 1997)

———, Richard, *The Battle* (London: Penguin, 2000)

Owen, James, *Nuremberg, Evil on Trial* (London: Headline, 2006)

Padfield, Peter, *Hess, Hitler & Churchill* (London: Ikon, 2013)

———, *Hess: The Fuhrer's Disciple* (London: Cassell & Co., 2001)

Pearson, John, *The Life of Ian Fleming* (London: Cape, 1966)

Petropoulos, Johnathan, *Royals and the Reich* (Oxford, 2006)

Philby, Kim, *My Silent War* (London: Macgibbon & Kee, 1968)

Picknett, Prince & Prior, *Double Standards* (London: Little Brown, 2001)

Pleshakov, Constantine, *Stalin's Folly* (London: Weidenfeld & Nicholson, 2005)

Pogonowski, Iwo, *Poland* (New York: Hippocrene, 2000)

Polish Ministry of Information, *The German New Order* (London: Hutchinson, 1942)

Price, Alfred, *The Luftwaffe Data Book* (London: Greenhill, 1997)

Read & Fisher, *Colonel Z* (London: Hodder & Stoughton, 1984)

Read, Anthony, *The Devil's Disciples* (London: Pimlico, 2004)

Rees, John, *The Case of Rudolf Hess* (London: Heineman, 1947)

Rhodes-James, Robert, *Victor Cazalet* (London: Hamish Hamilton, 1976)

Richardson, Dickie, *Man is not Lost* (Shrewsbury: Airlife, 1997)

Roberts, Mrs Ernest Stewart, *Sherbourne, Oxford and Cambridge* (London: Martin Hopkinson, 1934)

Rohwer & Himmelchen, *The War at Sea, 1939–41* (London: Ian Allen, 1972)

Rose, Norman, *The Cliveden Set* (London: Cape, 2000)

Russell, John, *A Silver Plated Spoon* (London: Cassell, 1959)

Schmidt, Rainer, *Botengang Eines Toren?* (Dusseldorf: Econ, 1997)

Schwarzwaller, Wulf, *The Deputy* (London: Quartet, 1988)

Shacklady, Edward, *Consolidated B24 Liberator* (Bristol: Cerberus, 2002)

Shawcross, William, *Queen Elizabeth* (London: MacMillan, 2009)

Shennan, Andrew, *De Gaulle* (London: Longman, 1993)

Shirer, William, *The Rise and Fall of the Third Reich* (London: Mandarin, 1991)

Shukman, Harold, *Stalin* (Stroud: Sutton, 1999)

Smith, Alfred, *Rudolf Hess and Germany's Reluctant War* (Lewes: Book Guild, 2001)

Speer, Albert, *Inside the Third Reich* (London: Phoenix, 2001)

Srachura, Peter, *Poland in the Twentieth Century* (London: MacMillan, 1999)

Stafford, David, *Flight from Reality* (London: Pimlico, 2002)

Stanley Lewis, W., *Military Map Reading* (Exeter: Wheaton, 1941)

Stettler, M., *Kuratorium C.J. Burckhardt: Des Schriftlichen Nacklasses* (Basle: Basle University, 1978)

Taylor, A.J.P., *The Origins of the Second World War* (London: Penguin, 1991)

Thomas, Hugh, *The Murder of Rudolf Hess* (London: Hodder & Stoughton, 1979)

Thompson, Carlos, *The Assassination of Winston Churchill* (Gerrards Cross: Smythe, 1969)

Thompson, J., *The Charterhall Story* (Surrey: Air Research, 2004)

Van Ishoven, Armand, *Messerschmitt* (London: Gentry, 1975)

———, *Udet* (Berlin: Neff, 1977)

Vasco & Estanislau, *BF110 C,D and E* (London: Ian Allan, 2008)

Vasco, J. & Cornwell, P., *Zerstorer* (Norwich: J.A.C. Publications, 1995)

Von Hassell, Ulrich, *The Von Hassell Diaries* (London: Hamish Hamilton, 1948)

Von Lang, Jochen, *Bormann* (London: Random House, 1979)

Waszak, Leon, *Agreement in Principle* (New York: Peter Lang, 1996)

Weitz, John, *Hitler's Banker* (London: Warner, 1999)

———, *Hitler's Diplomat* (London: Weidenfeld & Nicholson, 1992)

Welsh, Ian, *Prestwick in the 1940s* (Ayr: Kyle Libraries, 1992)

West, Nigel, *MI6* (London: Weidenfeld & Nicolson, 1983)

Wheeler-Holohan, V., *The History of the Kings Messengers* (London: Grayson, 1935)

Whiting, Audrey, *The Kents* (London: Hutchinson, 1985)

Winterbotham, Fred, Secret and Personal (London: William Kimber, 1969)

Wood, Robert, A World in Your Ear (London: Macmillan, 1979)

Zeigler, Philip, Diana Cooper (London: Hamish Hamilton, 1981)

———, *King Edward VIII* (London: Collins, 1990)

Zwar, Desmond, *Talking to Rudolf Hess* (Stroud: The History Press, 2010)

INDEX OF PEOPLE